Simple Steps

P9-CQW-154

Other Books by Karen Miller

The Crisis Manual for Early Childhood Teachers

Things to Do with Toddlers and Twos

More Things to Do with Toddlers and Twos

The Outside Play and Learning Book

Acknowledgments

I used to describe myself as a "reporter"—someone who visits with the staff of many child care centers around the country, then shares ideas that make sense. Polly Ferraro Elam, Child Development Services Administrator at the Naval Construction Battalion Center in Port Hueneme, CA modified that title for me, naming me, instead, a "butterfly," landing in many beautiful and interesting spots and cross-pollinating ideas. I like that and the "hybrid vigor" it implies. People working with infants, toddlers, and two-year-olds in early childhood settings are a dedicated, creative, interesting lot. Many of the activities in this book were generated from such visits or from ideas shared with me through a newsletter I used to write, "Caring for the Little Ones," which is now a regular column in *Child Care Information Exchange* magazine. When I came up with an idea or activity myself, I field-tested it through this network of professionals.

My longtime professional colleagues and personal friends, Jon and Sue Jacka, were catalysts for this book. They encouraged me to create training and curriculum manuals for infant, toddler, and two-year-old child care programs. Those manuals were distilled into this volume.

Anna-Maria Crum, a gifted children's book illustrator and teacher of children's book writing and illustrating, was extremely generous with her knowledge and time, helping me hone my illustrating skills. Creating the pictures for this book gave me as much pleasure as writing it.

It's one thing to have lots of good ideas, but another to present them well. Kathy Charner, Gryphon House Inc.'s Editor-in-Chief, has a talent for making a book cohesive, attractive, and easy-to-use. Editing is a painful process for an author, but I have learned that Kathy's suggestions always improve the work. That turns it into a delightful collaboration, and I'm grateful for her patience and encouragement.

Finally, I'd like to thank the numerous relatives, friends, and neighbors who let me observe and play with their babies and benefit from their skill and wisdom as loving, involved, intuitive parents.

Simple Steps

Developmental Activities for Infants, Toddlers, and Two-Year-Olds

Karen Miller
Author and Illustrator

gryphon
house
Beltsville, Maryland

Dedication

To Bradley Kalgren, a 2½-month-old baby, who helped a whole family through their grief at the death of his wonderful grandmother, my sister, Marion Kilkka. His smiles, his interest in everything he saw, and his joy in being alive reminded us of the magic available in every moment of life.

Copyright © 1999 Karen Miller
Published by Gryphon House, Inc.
10726 Tucker Street, Beltsville, MD 20705

Visit us on the web at www.gryphonhouse.com

Text Illustrations: Karen Miller

Library of Congress Cataloging-in-Publication Data

Miller, Karen, 1942-
    Simple steps : developmental activities for infants, toddlers and two-year-olds / Karen Miller.
        p. cm.
    Includes index.
    ISBN 0-87659-204-3
    1. Play Handbooks, manuals, etc. 2. Creative activities and seat work Handbooks, manuals, etc. 3. Child development Handbooks, manuals, etc. 4. Infants--Care. 5. Toddlers--Care. I. Title.
HQ782.M55 1999   99-26411
305.231--dc21   CIP

Simple Steps

Table of Contents

Chapter 4—
Go, Go, Go!: Gross Motor
Development 85

Chapter 5—
Let Me Think About It: Cognitive
Development 109

Simple Steps

Chapter 8—
A Sense of Wonder: Nature
Activities 195

Chapter 9—
Making Your Mark on the World:
Creative Development 205

Chapter 10—
Let's Pretend: Dramatic Play
Development 221

Chapter 11—
Playing and Learning:
How to Set Up a Positive Learning
Environment 229

Chapter 12—
Teaching and Coaching:
Behavior of Infants, Toddlers, and
Two-Year-Olds in Groups 241

Chapter 13—
Meeting the Needs of Children:
Curriculum Development 253

Chapter 14—
Becoming Partners: Working With
Parents .261

Appendix 275

Table of Contents

Introduction

Watching a young child develop is one of the wonders life offers us. Everyone marvels at the miracle of birth, as a fresh, new human being who wasn't there before joins us on the planet, complete and wonderful in his or her uniqueness. With amazing speed this tiny creature captivates the admiration and services of everyone around. Every time you turn around, it seems that the child is accomplishing something new, doing something not done before.

Whether you are a child care provider, parent, grandparent, doting aunt or uncle, or admiring friend, you can enhance a child's development by offering simple activities and at the same time observe the child's own special way of interacting with the world. The purpose of this book is to give you many enjoyable activities to engage those special children in your life.

The intent of this book, with its hundreds of activities, is not to help you "teach" a child new skills or to push the child along to the next step in development. Development comes from within the child. Just as you can't *teach* a child to get taller, you can't rush a child to grasp objects, sit up, walk, speak, or think in abstract ways before the child's inner timetable makes it possible. Even if you can get a child to do something earlier than he normally would, why should you? *Earlier is not better.*

Instead, observe what the child is *already doing*. Give her many and varied opportunities to practice that skill in interesting ways to help her "solidify" the new skill. Knowing the next step on the developmental ladder—what skill comes next—is very useful. If you know the sequence of typical development, you can have the "space and stuff" in the environment to allow the child to practice the new skills that are likely to come next, as well as practice newly mastered abilities.

One of the amazing things about infants and toddlers is their "self-imposed drill." You can count on it...when a child is ready to do something, *she will do it,* over and over again. Think about the not-yet-walking infant who learns to crawl up stairs. No matter how often you pull her away, she has to go back over to the staircase and scale that mountain! It's the same with all kinds of skills—throwing things, making new sounds, learning to line things up appropriately to stick them in holes, and testing the amazing discovery that something exists even when you can't see it (peek-a-boo!).

About the Activities

Don't do too much for the child. Many of the activities encourage you to make materials available, and then step back and watch what the child does. As adults, we are so conditioned to get the "right answer" to any problem that sitting back and allowing a baby to explore materials in his own way, sometimes doing totally different things with them than you intended, can be difficult. There are no "wrong answers" for these activities. Whatever the child chooses to do, short of hurting someone or being destructive, is "just right." Try very hard not to impose your ideas. Curb your impulse to "correct" the child or show him the "proper" way. The **To Do** section of each activity offers you guidelines of how to present the activity and what to observe for.

The **Emerging Skill** section of each activity outlines the possible learning that might result. The most important reason for doing all the activities is simply because they are fun. If an activity is not fun for the child or you, don't do it. When we say "fun" that means that the child's mind is engaged, that the child feels capable and powerful. "Delight" is a key ingredient in all learning. If the child is frustrated, stop the activity and offer it at a later date. The word "practice" appears repeatedly in this section, valuing the child's need to do more of what he can already do.

Children do not learn much from isolated activities. Only through hundreds of repetitions and self-initiated variations are concepts solidified. Realize that learning is integrated. It's rare that a child learns just one thing from an activity. Physical coordination, or "motor" skills, are engaged along with language, thinking skills, and social interactions. You can never be sure exactly what a child will learn from a given activity. It depends on what the child brings to the activity— what she already knows and can do, how others reinforce the child's actions or ideas, and even the child's mood.

The Importance of Timing

Offer an activity when the child is alert, calm, and in a good mood. It makes sense that an activity will be uninteresting, frustrating, and unsuccessful if the child is tired, not feeling well, fearful, frustrated, or angry. If a child is crying because the parent just left the scene, that may not be the time to expect concentrated attention.

Don't make everything available at one time or you will find a distracted and frustrated child, unable to concentrate. Offer something new when current interest lags. Often, putting something away and bringing out something different is all that is needed to renew interest and concentration.

It is also important to know when to stop the activity. Watch the child closely. Young children, especially infants, have a limited tolerance for stimulation and new things. When the infant looks away, turns her head, drools, or seems less "together," it is time to stop. Let the child set the pace.

What is attention span? It is how long a child can give mental energy, or concentration, to one thing. It is influenced by how the child is feeling (the physical and mental state the child brings to the situation), how well the activity or material hits the target of skills the child is working on or has recently mastered, and to some degree, the novelty of the material. Sometimes an activity will occupy a child for only five minutes or so; while that is fine, even babies are capable of focusing for much longer. The author has observed a ten-month-old drop a bowl on a hard floor, observing its wobble and sound twenty-seven times in a row. Another eleven-month-old child occupied himself popping a plastic bowl in and out of a hole in a wooden box, and seeing what else would fit in the hole for forty-five minutes, until the adults had to do something else.

Resist the urge to interrupt. If a child is concentrating deeply on some activity, either one you presented or a self-invented one, let the child play it out unless something urgent requires attention. Even your own play interactions with the child can interrupt. However, when you see the child's attention lag, some interaction on your part can prolong the child's involvement. Try to do the minimum. Don't take over the scene. You might play along side with similar materials and talk to yourself, or move another object close by.

Simplicity

You may be surprised at the simplicity of many of the activities. "Who doesn't do that?" you might think. If you find you already do some of the activities, pat yourself on the back. Many activities were invented in the Stone Age by loving, responsive adults or enterprising children. But, to be honest, in our complex, technical world, sometimes adults tend to skip the simple steps. Babies have to start at step one. We all know about children who prefer playing with the box over the expensive, complex toy that came in it. These activities are full of simple materials, things that allow children to bring their own ideas to the activity.

How the Book Is Organized

The activities are grouped by domains of development—Fine Motor, Gross Motor, Cognitive, and so on—to show all the different ways a child learns. When it comes to child development, many people tend to focus mostly on when a child learns to walk, talk, and read. Yet other things are going in, and must go on, for these exciting things to happen.

Each chapter has an introduction describing the significance of that domain of development—how it relates to the whole child, factors that influence it, and the typical progression of skills.

Age Designations

Although each activity has an age designation, use your own judgment and knowledge of individual children to determine if an activity is appropriate. As you know, each child develops at her own pace. Resist comparing one child to another of the same age. Don't be bound by the age designation. If something looks like it would be interesting for a younger child, go ahead and offer it. Just observe closely and put it away if it doesn't work. Likewise, don't hesitate to offer the same activity or variations over and over again, even if the child is older than the designated age—in fact, *please do!* Young children thrive on repetition and the familiar. They will bring new levels of complexity to the activity with experience.

This book does not include activities for children under two months of age. Newborns are too busy. They are totally occupied getting used to being out in the world, establishing their body rhythms. Sleeping takes up much of their time as they store up energy for the enormous growth spurts ahead. Focus on being responsive to the baby and learning to read his "cues." Try to figure out what his gurgles and cries mean, when he is hungry or tired, and how to hold him to comfort him. This is how you establish "basic trust" with the baby—teaching the baby that someone is there to care so he can face the world with confidence. That doesn't mean you can't do things with the baby, but focus on what the baby wants and needs. Remember that every sensation—every sight, every sound, every texture—is brand new to the newborn. He has all the "stimulation" he needs just from your daily caring routines.

Why an Activity Book?

Is an activity book for infants, toddlers, and two-year-olds necessary? We have heard a lot recently about the importance of stimulation and brain growth, and that the first three years of life are critical to a child's intellectual and emotional development. There has been a rush to create "infant stimulation programs." That's not what this book is about; an "average" home and school typically have adequate stimulation for a young child. At the same time, a *lack* of stimulation can be very detrimental to a child's development. The author has spent time observing children in orphanages in Romania and has seen the devastation of lack of stimulation in these most extreme circumstances—children who had few, if any, opportunities for warm interactions with loving adults were kept in tiny cribs with no toys or opportunities to move around, all day, for two or three years. It is no surprise that many of them were delayed, often severely, in every aspect of development.

The children in this country who suffer similar consequences are born to parents who, for one reason or another, cannot respond to them in the most basic ways. These parents might be depressed, mentally ill, substance abusers, or so oppressed by poverty, dangerous neighborhoods, or their own immaturity (some teen mothers), that they are unable to focus on the baby. These babies and their parents need the supportive intervention of the wider community. They can benefit greatly by an array of appropriate activities along with loving interactions of stable adults.

Children from "typical" households can also benefit from activities such as those in this book. When you create interesting things for infants, toddlers, and two-year-olds to do, you are creating attitudes and capacities for future learning. When a child feels successful and enjoys exploring new materials, her confidence level builds and her curiosity and problem-solving skills are enhanced. This leads to greater success in school and in life.

The most important "things" in a child's environment are stable, loving, attentive adults. Without that, all the toys and activities in the world won't have much impact. That is why the chapter on emotional development comes first. The child must feel valued, admired, and powerful to take the initiative to learn.

Delightful Learning

Fun or delight is the most important reason for doing activities with children. You are building strong relationships with the child when you offer play materials and watch with interest or join in the play. Children delight in adult attention and love to play games with you alone or with a few other children. They are learning that it is fun to be with other people.

Finally, play with children for your own enjoyment. Playing is a wonderful way to "slow down" and simplify life for a few moments. It puts you in touch with your authentic self, and with what's really important. You can give yourself permission to relax and enjoy the moment—to be "fully there." When you experience a child's delight at the simplest of things, you will come back to your adult world with a new perspective.

Simple Steps

Chapter 1

The Heart of the Matter

Social-Emotional Development

Social and emotional development is about *relationships*. For a child to develop a strong sense of self and self-esteem, he must see himself in relation to others. The child learns who he is through the eyes of the loving adults around him. Of all the things adults involved with a child must do well, tending to the child's healthy emotional development is the most important. All the toys and well-designed activities in the world cannot compensate for a lack of loving interactions that foster a sense of security and well-being in young children. Helping children develop emotional and social skills enables them to enjoy the company of others and to feel good about themselves and who they are within a group. As you can see, social development is inseparable from emotional development.

If a child's needs are responded to quickly and gently, he learns that he is valued. On the other hand, if a child gets no response from a parent or caregiver, or a negative response, he stops trying to communicate. He learns to feel that he doesn't matter. When a child doesn't feel safe and doesn't have basic trust in the individuals around him, he must always be "on guard." That takes all of his mental energy, and he is not free to explore, experiment, communicate, and develop. When this child feels valued just for *being* and feels safe and secure in the loving protection of a few familiar individuals, he can thrive and develop cognitive, physical, and social skills.

The child's first "social" experience is with his parent or parents. The brand new baby makes eye contact with his mother and stares intensely into her face, beginning a strong bond of love. Many first-time mothers and fathers remember feeling surprised at the powerful emotional pull of this behavior. Gradually, the baby's social circle expands to include others, members of the family, and trusted caregivers. For this reason, it is good to try to copy the parent's "style" with the baby as much as possible. Look at how the parent holds the child. Ask the parent how the child is comforted.

The earliest social interactions come when the baby is awake and comfortable. You'll see eye contact, widened eyes, and waving arms, and you'll hear coos and gurgles. At about six weeks of age comes that wonderful social smile when a friendly face appears. Who can resist a baby's glorious smile? Our natural reaction is precisely the right one—we make fools of ourselves cooing and gurgling back in a high voice, bobbing our heads, and making silly facial expressions. What we are doing is imitating the baby's gestures and making contact on the baby's level. We "connect" and the social interaction is prolonged. When we respond in this way we are telling the baby, "I value you. You are important." Don't feel that the daily routine—the diapering, feeding, record keeping, and other chores—get in the way of social interactions. They are the one-on-one times you have with children and can be "fuel" that babies need for developing relationships throughout life.

One caution: be sure you are following the baby's lead and having fun when the *baby* is in the mood, not when you happen to feel like it. If a baby doesn't respond or looks away or otherwise "turns off," respect that and come back to play at other moments in the day. Invite, but don't coerce. When we cajole and tickle and "force" the baby to respond, we are putting our needs ahead of the baby's. Maybe the baby just needs calming or cuddling at that time instead of social play.

Learn a baby's preferred mode of having fun. It can vary from baby to baby. Watch how the parents interact with the baby and ask them how the baby likes to play. Lap games like gently bumping foreheads or rubbing noses elicit eye contact and giggles. Repeatedly walking a toy toward a baby and having it nibble a toe with accompanying sound effects can be fun. Even fingerplays that are used with older children are fun to do with the baby. You see the baby engage as he anticipates the repeated action.

When a young baby feels distress, his only option is to cry. With luck, somebody will notice and respond. As the first year progresses, the baby acquires a wider range of options. This not-yet-talking baby can communicate through gestures, tone of voice, and movement. An eight-month-old child will point and grunt to "ask" for an interesting object or a bottle. Arms up means, "Pick me up." A turned head and scowl and a push of a chubby hand say, "No more peas!" Read these gestures, which, of course, will be slightly different for each baby, and respond appropriately. You become an interpreter of signs. Describe out loud what you think they mean. "Oh, I see you want me to pick you up. Yes, I will pick you up. Up we go!" Even when you can't respond that instant, you can acknowledge what the child is saying in an empathetic way. Believe it or not, the child will understand and trust you, even though she may not like it. "Yes, Jennifer, I know you are hungry. It is hard to wait. I will bring you your bottle in a minute, as soon as it is ready." All this gives the baby a sense of power and security.

Stranger Anxiety

Usually, a phase of "stranger anxiety" starts at about seven or eight months of age, although you may see signs of it developing earlier. It lasts several months or longer. Actually, it is a sign of healthy development. It shows that a child has learned who is "his," indicating a strong attachment. After a certain amount of experience, parallel with the cognitive development of "object permanence," infants develop anxiety with new people and situations. Object permanence is when children can keep a mental image of something even when it is not present. When confronted with someone new, they say to themselves, "This is strange. I don't know what to expect. This is not my Mommy. My Mommy is not here." In some cases the child's anxiety is extreme. Other children have only a "mild case" as they work it out in their heads. It's often an issue of temperament.

Be the "anchor" or the "safe haven" for children in your care. You will see that as they bond to you, they will develop an "invisible rubber band" that attaches them to you. They will feel safe to develop their independence as long as they can keep an eye on you. They may venture out a little, exploring, and then come back and touch you occasionally. When a stranger comes in they may move closer to you.

Sometimes a child becomes upset when a caregiver leaves the room. If you can, bring the child along occasionally on errands in the building. But you can always "tell" the child that you are leaving and that you will be back in a few minutes. Be sure to say good-bye at the end of the day if you leave before some of the children; don't just disappear.

Interacting With Other Children

Infants enjoy interacting with other children. When you sit down on the floor to play with children, either hold the smallest infant in your lap, facing the other children, or place the child near you, close to the action. The little one will enjoy seeing the faces and hearing the voices of the other children. If there is a toddler or older child in the group, help the older child notice how the baby responds to him. "Look, he is smiling at you. That means he likes you."
One delightful advantage of group care for infants, toddlers, and two-year-olds is that we see actual friendships develop among the children. They recognize each other and show delight at this recognition. Sometimes even a special friendship develops. When one child is missing, the other child may look for him or act worried. His face brightens when the other child appears. The baby may bring something over to the "friend" and hand it to him.

A common behavior of young toddlers is to hand an object to a person they want social contact with. This might be another child, but often it is a visiting adult. Through this action, the non-verbal child is saying, "I want you to pay attention to me. I want to play with you." If a child hands you an object, see if you can get him to take it back and hand it over again. Repeated several times, these actions become a game.

Most social lessons are learned by example. When a child sees people responding with empathy and kindness to the distress of others, he learns empathy and kindness. When new people are greeted warmly, the child learns openness and friendliness. The child watches every interaction you have with him and with the other children and adults. Every action is a social activity! Social interaction is easier and increases as children gain more skill with language, so do all you can to support language development. One thing you can do is model social interaction phrases. Even give the child phrases to parrot. Tell Josie, "I have this now." Ask Carrie, "May I have a turn?" Also help children hear the requests of others. "Sandy, Pammy said she wants a turn. Let her know when you are done."

Testing Limits

You will see some interesting, if at times exasperating, behavior toward the end of the first year and into the toddler year when the child tests limits. Although "no" is among the first group of words that a child understands, that does not mean he will listen to this word. You will even see a young toddler chant "No, no, no" as he goes ahead and does the prohibited action. Testing the limits is also a "cause and effect" activity for a child. He starts to feel his power as he learns that he can get a reaction. He enjoys making it happen again and again. You become a convenient and very interesting toy to manipulate. Try to keep it light, as you let the child "win" some of the time.

Stubbornness

Toddlers are often very set in their ways. They might only drink out of a certain glass, or go to bed only when all the stuffed animals are arranged in a certain way. Each child has his own agenda. A child this age is also sometimes "oppositional" or rebellious. "No" becomes the favorite word.

Try to figure out how to make the child think that doing something is all his idea. For instance, one young mother anticipated a trip to visit relatives in a foreign country, accompanied by her active two-year-old boy. Knowing that they would often be in crowds and she would have her hands full of luggage, she thought a leash attached to her little one would be a good idea. She prepared him for this by taking him for frequent walks in the neighborhood and noticing all the "happy" dogs who were walking alongside their owners. She told him, "They feel happy because they know they are safe." Then she wondered out loud if she could find a leash for him, but said it was probably not possible. One was finally located—a bright red one. The child was promised that if he was "good" she would "let" him wear the leash when they went for a walk. The plan succeeded. By the time the trip took place, her little son was happy to wear a small harness attached to a leash and walk calmly and proudly at her side.

Choices

It is also wise to give a toddler a few choices whenever possible. "Do you want your cereal in a small bowl or a big bowl?" "Shall we play inside or outside now?" "Do you want to use trucks or shovels and pails in the sand box?" (If you have a preference, state it as the second choice; the child is more likely to say what he heard last.) All of this gives the child a sense that he has some power and control in his life. Although there are times when nothing seems to please the child, or you cannot provide the choice he wants, empathize and reflect the child's feelings while you move forward. "I know you wish you could stay at the park longer, but we have to go now." Even though the child may protest, he will feel acknowledged and respected.

Toddler Friends

This is one of the "big" things that happens in the toddler stage. The child's world is broadening. In addition to being the central focus of a family, this necessarily egocentric little individual is learning how to become "one among others," a valued part of a group of equals. Toddlers *want* to have friends. They enjoy other children. Often, however, they are very bumbling in their efforts and benefit greatly from the gentle and understanding guidance of adults.

Child-Invented Games

Toddlers often invent their own games. Usually these games involve straight imitation. One child will begin doing something interesting, like running and falling down, or falling backward off of a log on the grass, and others will come over and start doing the same thing. You see eye contact and hear giggles. By all means, join in yourself. Make a note of these games. Who initiates them? Will a follower become a leader at other times?

Sharing and Taking Turns

Remember that young children do not know what the word "share" means. You must demonstrate the process. Talk about sharing in context. Create natural situations where sharing happens and comment positively. Instead of *telling* toddlers to share, we must *show them* how to share. Begin by commenting on sharing behaviors in order to build an awareness of them. You may bring in several new picture books and announce, "I think I will share these books with you." Or, put a bowl of pegs between two children who each have their own pegboard and say, "I'll let you two share these pegs." Sit down next to a child who is coloring and ask, "Will you share these crayons with me?" Then comment, "Now we can both have fun together. Thank you for *sharing* the crayons." Continue to do this with various items of interest and watch what happens. Toddlers are imitators! Continue to verbalize what is taking place: "Travis! You shared your crackers!" Also verbalize the feelings of the children who receive: "That made Tara feel happy when you shared with her."

Be careful that you don't teach children that sharing equals losing what they have. If two children are fighting over a toy and the teacher says, "You have to share," then takes the toy away from the possessor and gives it to the other, the child is learning that sharing is not a pleasant and desirable experience. The toddler's unspoken question, reflecting his natural egocentrism, is "What's in it for me?" Develop many pro-social activities that are more fun to do with someone else than alone, then comment how playing together is more fun.

Sharing and taking turns are closely related, but not the same. Sharing involves using the same materials at the same time. Taking turns involves alternating who uses an object or material. Taking turns is more difficult because it means delaying gratification and waiting. Like sharing, taking turns is something that has to be negotiated and young toddlers do not have the verbal skills to do this. However, an adult can do much to smooth the way.

■ Teach the children how to ask for a turn. You will have to give them the words to imitate at first. Say, "Tiffany, I want to have a turn on the horse when you are finished, okay?"

■ Help the asker be heard. Repeat the child's request clearly to the possessor of the toy. "Stacy would like a turn on the horse. Will you give her this horse in a few minutes when you are finished with your turn?"

■ Let the child who is the rider give up the horse on her own terms. It sometimes happens surprisingly quickly. If you force it, on the other hand, you are more likely to encounter resistance or even a tantrum.

■ Have alternative activities for both children. "Here, Stacy. While you are waiting to ride the horse, you can get the hay ready in the horse's stable."

- When the rider gives up the toy, express appreciation. "You made Stacy happy when you let her have a turn on the horse. Would you like to feed the horse some hay now?"
- Older children can learn to use kitchen timers or count laps, but these concepts are beyond toddlers and two-year-olds. They might enjoy using music as a cue, however. You can make a game of it. Play a short song on a cassette player and tell the children that when the song ends it is time to switch places.

The three key things to remember are:
- Help the waiting child ask and be understood.
- Have something equally interesting for the waiting child to do.
- Praise the child for handing over the coveted item and see to it that he has something interesting to do next.

Laughter and Humor

The child also learns humor by example. Adults often laugh even harder when a baby joins in the laughter of a joke. They like to be part of the gang! Laughter is fun, and humor is a fine tool in relating to adults as well as children. The atmosphere of warmth and lightness will help develop social and emotional skills in children.

The sample activities listed below are designed to make it fun for young children to interact with others. Add your own ideas and variations, especially those that are more fun to do near or with someone else than alone.

Who's Here?

 3 MONTHS +

Be sure to point out the baby's reaction to the parent, reinforcing the parent's primary importance for the child.

Materials

To Do

- When the parent arrives to pick up the child, ask the parent to call out the child's name and talk to the child before the child actually sees her.

Observations

- Does the child focus on the sound and pay attention?
- Is there a change in his movement or posture?
- Does he vocalize?
- Does he brighten up in anticipation?

Watch the Light Show!

Materials

camera (optional)

To Do

■ Try to catch on film (or notice out loud with the parent) the child's reaction and facial expression when the parent shows up at pick-up time.

■ Say, "Wow! Did you see that? He was fine a few minutes ago, but look at the joy on his face now! You are really special to him."

Observations

■ Watch the child's expression, body posture, and movement upon seeing the parent at the end of the day.

■ Also look for the same things with the parent. Remember that your most important function is to strengthen the bond between the parent and the child.

Emerging Skill

You are reinforcing the parent-child bond.

Gotcha!

Never tickle a child. This is forcing laughter when the child has no control.

Materials

toy with a face, such as a small stuffed animal or puppet

To Do

■ Seat the child in an infant seat, or if he sits independently, simply seat him in front of you on the floor.

■ Have the toy call the child's name and move slowly toward the child making a funny, growling noise.

■ When the toy reaches the child's foot say, "Gotcha!"

Observations

■ After a few times, does the child anticipate the contact?

■ Does the child giggle, kick, and coo?

Simple Steps

More Ideas

■ Walk your fingers up a child's arm and gently tap his chin or nose, perhaps saying, "toot, toot, toot" when you tap. Invite the child to tap your nose and also "toot" then.

Emerging Skill

These anticipation games are an enjoyable social interaction.

Personal Clapping Game

6 MONTHS +

To Do

■ Sit the child on your lap and do the motions together.
■ As a variation to the "classical" "Pat-A-Cake" game, create your own rhyme and motions, and include the child's name. For example:

> *Clap your hands now, 1,2,3.*
> *Tap your head now, just like me.*
> *Roll your hands now, just you see,*
> *Kick your feet like (child's name) and me.*

Observations

■ After you have done this game with the child numerous times, does he catch on and do the motions by himself?
■ Does he enjoy the physical contact and individual attention?

More Ideas

■ Let a large rag doll do this with an older infant.

Emerging Skill

The child enjoys simple social interactions with an adult.

Social Rituals

6 MONTHS +

Materials

To Do

■ Whenever anyone enters the room, say "Look, *Sara* is here! Hi, *Sara*!"
■ Wave. Help children wave the greeting too.
■ When someone is preparing to leave, say, "Bye-bye, *Max*," and help children wave good-bye.

Observations

- When does a child start to do this spontaneously?

More Ideas

- Make a game out of this by going in and out of a door yourself, again and again, while chanting the greetings.
- Make a doll or stuffed animal appear and disappear behind a partition or in and out of a large box while saying the greeting and waving with the children.

Emerging Skill

Children practice waving "bye-bye" and using social greetings. The children might also learn the names of other people in this way, which makes people feel welcome and like they are important members of the group.

Class Photo Book

Materials

sturdy photo album with plastic over-lay pages
camera

To Make

- Take a close-up photo of each child in the group.
- Put one photo on each page.
- Include staff members and other familiar adults in the program, such as the director and the cook, or spouse, siblings, and pets in a child care home.

To Do

- Enjoy paging through the photo album with one or two children on your lap.
- Let them pat the pictures and turn the pages.
- Encourage them to point to the people in the room as they see them in the photos.

Observations

- Does the child seem to make the connection between the photo of a person and the real person?
- Does he look toward or point to the person represented in the photo?

Simple Steps

More Ideas

■ Put several photos on a single page and then ask the child, "Where's *Jennifer*?" and see if the child can point to the correct photo.
■ Include family members that children see frequently. "Where's Sarah's daddy?"

Emerging Skill

Children learn names of familiar people and feel like an important member of the group.

Who's Here Magnets

12 MONTHS +

Materials

photo of each child, laminated with clear contact paper
box or basket for storage
self-stick magnetic strips
cookie sheet or other metal surface

To Make

■ Stick a piece of magnetic strip on the back of each photo.
■ Hang the background cookie sheet at child height.

To Do

■ As a greeting activity, let each child find his own photo in the basket or storage box and "sign in" by sticking the photo on the cookie sheet.
■ You can also talk about the photos that are already up there—who has already arrived.

More Ideas

- Do this as a small group activity early in the day. Hold up each photo in turn. Ask, "Who is this?" "Is Jamie here today?" Then let the child put his own picture on the board. Talk about who is not there.
- A puppet could help with this activity.

Emerging Skills

Children will learn each other's names and that they are valued members of the group.

Take-Home Photo Album

12 MONTHS +

This activity will make your environment seem less strange to the child. The book also gives parents a specific way to speak positively about the experience that lies ahead for the child. In addition, the book could also be an excellent public relations tool as parents show friends and grandparents.

Materials

camera
small photo album

To Make

- Take pictures of toys, people (adults and children), and places (such as the playroom, the outside yard, the entrance) that new children are likely to see when they visit your program.
- Arrange these in a photo album with labels and send it home with the parents and new child after their orientation visit.

To Do

- Encourage parents to read the new book with their child.

More Ideas

- Perhaps the parents would like to make a similar book about their home and send it along to your program with the child.

Transitional Photos

12 MONTHS +

This activity can really help the child feel secure and comfortable in a new environment. Even children who have been with you a long time will enjoy occasionally "touching bases" with the parent or family photo. This also builds respect between the parent and the caregiver and makes the child feel secure and loved by all parties.

Materials

photograph of the parent or whole family
smiling photograph of your face (have numerous copies made)
laminating paper or clear contact paper

Simple Steps

To Make

- Laminate the photos on both sides.

To Do

- Let the child carry around the photo of the parent, or place these photos in a particular spot where the child can retrieve his any time.
- Send home with the child a picture of your home or center.
- Encourage the parent to put it in some visible spot like low on the refrigerator or near the child's bed.
- Encourage the parent to talk about you and your program frequently.

Observations

- Does the child look at the parents' pictures every now and then?
- Does this help the child when he is missing his parents?

More Ideas

- Children often quickly learn to recognize all the parents. You might play a "matching game" with the photos. Put all of the photos in a shoebox. Hold up one at a time and ask, "Whose daddy is this?" "Whose mommy is this?" Give the photo to the child to hold, then restate, "These mommies and daddies are all busy working now, and I'm taking good care of you and playing with you until they come back."
- Develop a "favorite folks ring" with several pictures of people in the child's life, such as grandparents, neighbors, pets, etc. Punch holes and place them on a large key ring.

Poor Becky!

12 MONTHS +

Materials

To Do

- When any child is in distress, perhaps from a hurt from a fall, or crying because a parent has left, involve other children in comforting, if possible.
- Verbalize the situation. "Oh, poor Becky. She is crying because she misses her mommy. What can we do to make her feel better? I will rock you, Becky. Look, Todd is bringing you a teddy bear. That makes Becky feel better, Todd."

Observations

- Does a child show empathy when another child is distressed?
- Does the child join in crying?
- Does the child attempt to comfort the crying child? In what way?

More Ideas

- Do this in "pretend play" either acting out the role yourself, or having a doll or stuffed animal cry. Help the child think of how to comfort the doll.

Emerging Skill

The child is developing empathy, and you are encouraging kindness.

Push the Trucks

16 MONTHS +

Materials

two or three trucks or other toy vehicles

To Do

- Seat several children in a circle. Include another adult to help, if possible, especially if the game is unfamiliar.
- Push a truck to one of the children in the circle.
- Help him push it to another child. Often, a young child will simply hang on to the truck when it reaches him. If he refuses to give it up, continue the game with a second truck.
- When a child does push the truck to another child, see that he gets it back again soon, so that the benefit of giving it up becomes apparent and the child learns the pleasure of give and take.

Observations

- How quickly does an older infant discover the point of this game?
- Can you get children to do this without an adult in the circle?

More Ideas

- Use other rolling toys.

Emerging Skill

Children are naturally possessive at this age. This activity gives them practice cooperating, and teaches them they will get something back after they have given it up.

Simple Steps

Sharing Bin

Materials

dish tub or other large container
small toys of similar type (such as plastic cars) stored in the container

To Do

- When you see two children seated near each other, put the tub of toys between them and say, "Here...I'll let you two *share* the toys that are in here."
- When there are plenty of toys, they usually will take them out and share them without a problem.

Observations

- Do they each take the toys out and play with them?
- Does one child, or both, try to "hoard" all the toys?

More Ideas

- Use this technique with older children. For example, put playdough toys between two children playing with playdough. Put a tub of large pegs between two children with peg boards. Put a tub of crayons between children who are scribbling. Always include the word, *share*.

Emerging Skill

Children gain successful experiences sharing and see some positive sides of the concept.

Social-Emotional Development

Tape-Recorded Love Stories

This is a wonderful way to invite meaningful parent involvement in your program. It communicates respect for the parent and helps to strengthen the parent/child relationship. There are also some language development benefits as the child hears familiar phrases over and over and associates them with pictures in a book.

Materials

cassette tape recorder/player   blank cassettes

To Make

- Invite parents to read one of the books you have in your room to their child while you record it.
- Ring a little bell, or make some other noise when it is time to turn the pages.
- If the parent prefers, let him tell a favorite story or sing a little song.

To Do

- When the parent is away, invite the child to listen to his parent's story while turning the pages of the book himself. This can be very comforting to the child.

Observations

- Does the child seek out the parent's tape and enjoy listening to it?

More Ideas

- Play the tapes to the whole group and ask, "Whose daddy is this?" "Whose grandma is this?" This is an auditory discrimination exercise that also acknowledges each child's family.
- Record a story, a song, or some fingerplays on a cassette and send it home with the child (first confirm that the family has a cassette player at home). This is a nice school-to-home bridge for the child, and can also help parents learn the words of new songs and fingerplays you are teaching children.

Chair Line-Up

Stay close by in case chairs are placed in an unstable position or your help is otherwise needed.

Materials

child-sized chairs that children can lift and move

To Do

- This is actually a universal child-invented game. Toddlers naturally seem to like to line up chairs.
- Whenever there is a lull, suggest this activity. Let the children line up all the chairs in the room.

Simple Steps

- Then let them sit on the chairs, make vehicle noises, and pretend to drive somewhere.

Observations

- Do they ever do this spontaneously, without your direction?
- Do they develop pretend situations? How long does the play continue?

More Ideas

- See if they can line the chairs up two-by-two.
- Perhaps you can lead them in some guided dramatic play. "Where are we going?" "Let's drive to the grocery store."
- Give everyone a paper plate to use as a steering wheel.
- Cushions, pillows, and other items could also be lined up.
- Invite dolls and stuffed animals to come along for the ride.
- Try throwing a blanket over the chairs to create a cave.
- By all means, join in the play!

Emerging Skill

Not only are children involved in social play and getting ideas from each other, they are also engaged in some simple dramatic play. They are learning to use objects (chairs) as symbols (vehicles), which is a cognitive activity as well. They are interacting with each other from within their roles, which is a form of "socio-dramatic" play.

Share the Paper

 18 MONTHS+

Materials

large sheet of freezer wrap, shiny side up
masking tape
finger paint

To Do

- Tape the large piece of paper to the table.
- Ask the children to stand around it as they paint.

- Say, "I'll let you all *share* this great big piece of paper when you paint. And I'll put the paint right here in the middle so you can *share* the paint too. You can *share* and work together so that we can have a great big picture!"

Observations

- Do their paintings ever overlap?
- Do they protect their own space, or see the whole page as theirs?

More Ideas

- When they are through, label the picture, "This paper was shared by Jason, Brian, Kendall, and Scott." Parents can also comment on the fun of sharing.
- Instead of taping the paper down, you can simply use large clamps like those designed to close open bags of chips to fasten the paper to the tabletop.

Emerging Skill

Children have a successful experience sharing something and come to see sharing as an enjoyable thing to do.

Share the Music

20 MONTHS +

Materials

lively recorded music

To Do

- Help all the children find a partner and hold hands.
- Then announce, "We're going to *share* some music now and have fun dancing together."

More Ideas

- Another way to share music is to jump up and down together while it plays.

Emerging Skill

While children rock back and forth together they are learning that it is fun to be with other children and do things together.

Simple Steps

Flannel Board Photo Dolls

Materials

full-body photo of each child
transparent contact paper
glue
felt or flannel
flannel board

To Make

- Cut out the photo of the child around the body outlines.
- Encase this in the clear contact paper.
- Glue felt or flannel to the back.
- Make one for the adults in the room too.

To Do

- These will have many different uses. The children can identify themselves and their friends.
- You can put up "the helpers" who will help set the table.
- You can also use these to recreate and act out an event like a nature walk.

Observations

- Do the children like to play with the Photo Dolls independently?

Emerging Skill

This activity is a self-esteem booster. Children will also be able to "abstract" some of their actions using these symbols of themselves—a cognitive skill.

Share the Box

24 MONTHS +

Materials

large appliance box
scissors
yellow and black paint
paintbrushes

To Do

- Let the children help you paint a large appliance box yellow.
- Be sure to notice how they are all *sharing* the paint when they do.
- When it is dry, cut out window holes and paint on the details in black.
- Then announce that they can all *share* the box to go for a ride together.

Social-Emotional Development

Observations

■ Do they recognize that this is supposed to represent a school bus? Have they seen school buses?

Emerging Skill

As well as gaining a positive experience sharing space, the children are getting some valuable experience with dramatic play. Ask questions about who the driver is, where they are going, etc.

Old Wallets

24 MONTHS +

Materials

old wallets donated by parents or found at garage sales
photos of the children and their families

To Make

■ Place the children's photos along with some family photos in the picture sleeves.

To Do

■ Say nothing, just place these in the dress-up corner.

Observations

■ Do the children discover and open these spontaneously?

Emerging Skill

Children are usually delighted when they find their images in the wallets. Their smiles and enthusiasm can be very affirming. This activity also teaches the children an understanding of family diversity. Opening and closing the wallets gives them some fine motor practice as well.

Simple Steps

Chapter 2

Let's Talk

Language Development & Early Literacy

Watching the development of language in young children is truly inspiring! From day one, an infant begins trying to figure out this code that sets humans apart from other beings. Learning to talk is one of the marvels of human development. Anyone who has tried to learn a foreign language knows how difficult it is. And yet, here is this tiny person amazing us daily with the things that come out of her mouth.

Understanding language and talking are two different processes. Both require that a child hears well enough to distinguish meaningful sounds. Understanding is a sensory perception process sometimes called "receptive language." A child will understand many words before she starts to use them in speech. Speaking is a motor process—getting the muscles of the tongue and mouth to function together just right to produce the desired sound. This is often referred to as "expressive language."

Studies show that a newborn is able to distinguish her mother's voice. A baby will stop random movements when she hears an interesting sound, as though she is allowing herself to concentrate better. Soon the baby responds by making eye contact or moving her mouth when a parent or caregiver talks to her face to face.

General Sequence of Language Skill Development

Crying and random sounds

Crying is the baby's first form of expressive language. It's all part of the communication process. When you respond in a caring way, the baby will discover that making noises come out of her mouth is one way to make things happen and get some relief from distress. Soon the baby develops different cries for hunger, pain, rage, and boredom and a familiar caregiver learns to tell which is which. It's not long before the infant learns to cry in order to get attention and make an adult appear.

When a baby is content you'll hear all kinds of random coos and gurgles. Now you can really have fun getting into a real conversation with the baby, trading coos. Imitate the sounds you hear the child making and take turns. This is one of the first skills in learning to communicate—to be quiet while someone else talks, and then to say something while the other person listens. This is an exciting social activity for the child, but you'll also hear her practice these sounds on her own. As time goes on, more and more sounds emerge.

Listening skills

A baby under eight months of age will turn her head to locate the speaker visually and will often stop crying when someone speaks in a comforting way. You'll see the child respond to tone of voice. For example, she may be frightened by angry intonations or smile at a happy voice.

Babbling and jargon

This repeating of syllables is such fun to listen to. First, at two or three months, babies start with just two or three repetitions of a sound such as "ma, ma, ma." As time goes on the child may mix several different sounds. Later, an infant demonstrates that she has learned one of the most basic elements of communication—intonation, the melody of language. The child will make simple vowel sounds and play with pitch and rhythm. Laughter and squeals are part of this. Especially when she is playing alone, you'll hear the jabber of a string of nonsense syllables that sound like actual speech. The child's voice will go up and down as though she is asking questions or making demands. That is called "jargon speech."

Between four and eight months, the child also enjoys a "cooing conversation," taking turns with an adoring adult. She also learns to use speech sounds to get attention, show enthusiasm, or reject something.

Understanding words

As the child approaches one year of age, she begins to understand the meanings of a few words, such as "bottle" and "bye-bye." She can understand simple commands such as "come here," "sit down," and "don't touch" when used emphatically. The child will also respond to her own name, and can turn and point to familiar people and a few familiar objects.

Saying single words

Toward the end of the first year a baby may start to come out with single words. She's discovered that objects and actions have specific sounds attached to them. Not only does the child realize that a certain combination of sounds represents something, but she learns how to move her lips, tongue, and mouth to produce sounds that others can interpret. Needless to say, this takes months of practice! That's what was going on with all the jabbering! The child may also try to echo words others say. "Dada", "Mama," "Hi," "Bye," and "No!" accompanied by gestures are among the common first words. So is "Uh-oh!"

Telegraphic speech

Telegraphic speech occurs when the child puts together two or three words, sounding like the old telegraph messages (usually not before two). "Want juice!"

Grammar

A most interesting phenomenon is the acquisition of grammar—learning the rules of language. A two-year-old child will figure out a rule of grammar just from listening. For instance, she will learn to add the "s" sound to create a plural: "My shoes are wet." She may apply the grammar rule to new situations inappropriately: "My feets are wet." Another example involves the use of "ed" to create past tense: "I danced all night." The child transfers that rule to other situations: "I throwed the ball." Although the child is making "mistakes" in these phrases the mistakes actually show thinking skills. In many ways, toddler grammar is more logical than the "correct" grammar they come to use later on. Eventually, depending on the language models the child has, the child-invented grammar is replaced by the standard usage.

Parents' and Caregivers' Role

Talk to the baby. Doing so helps shape the brain for language. Talk about what is going on right now. Surround the child with an "envelope of language." Even with non-verbal infants, talk about what the child is seeing or doing at the moment. Be a "broadcaster." Just like a play-by-play announcer would do, describe what the child is doing, looking at, and feeling.

All activities—planned, spontaneous, formal, informal—are "language activities." Infants don't need to be taught language. They learn language naturally by hearing it used in context, and they learn to talk by being talked to and listened to. When a child starts to utter words and phrases, get down on her level and listen patiently as she tries to express herself. Instead of correcting mistakes in pronunciation or grammar, simply repeat the word or phrase correctly in your own sentence as a natural part of the conversation. "Yes, I see. Your *feet are* wet." Expand on what the child is talking about because that is obviously interesting to her at the moment. "Did you step in the puddle when we were outside?" Hearing language used meaningfully in the routines of the day is the most powerful "language lesson."

It's important to know that language coming from a television, even from so-called educational programs, has no value for an infant. Those sounds are meaningless because the flickering shape on the screen is abstract and the speech is too fast. Most parents and caregivers automatically gear their speech to the child, speaking slowly and clearly, with the child's full attention.

Also remember that communication involves more than words. Understanding a baby's attempts at communication means interpreting not only the sounds she makes, but also her facial expressions, gestures, intonations, and situations. Your responsive care and kind words send a clear message that you are interested in what she is trying to communicate, that language does serve a purpose.

When Should You Be Concerned About a Child's Language Development?

You may be apprehensive about a young child's mispronunciations, but these are the years when the child is just learning to manipulate the sounds so there is usually no cause for concern. The following "red flags" may advise a visit to a speech and hearing professional for an evaluation:

- The child is not using any words by two years of age.
- The child's speech cannot be understood by three years of age, with many consonant sounds omitted.
- The child is not using phrases of more than two or three words by the age of three.
- The child's speech and sounds are very harsh or nasal.
- The child has a history of recurrent ear infections, which could result in a hearing loss or language delay.

Early Literacy

A discussion of language development automatically evolves into an examination of "literacy"—reading, in other words. We live in a society that relies heavily on the written word. Learning to interpret symbols to read and write are critical for success. In a broader sense, literacy refers to communication—the ability to give and receive information.

Parents and caregivers can develop "literacy skills" (pre-reading skills) in infants, toddlers, and two-year-olds by:

- Supporting over-all language development.
- Giving children lots to talk about and opportunities to express themselves.
- Telling them little stories.
- Exposing them to pictures (which are also symbols).
- Reading to them from age-appropriate picture books.
- Allowing them to handle books.
- Communicating the attitude that reading books is fun.
- Providing experiences that foster learning and increase knowledge about the world.

What About Teaching the ABC's?

Learning to sing the "ABC Song" has very little to do with learning how to read. Children really have very little need to know the sequence of the alphabet until they learn "dictionary skills" in elementary school. Many children's alphabet books and television shows endeavor to teach children to recognize letters, and children impress adults by being able to point to a letter and name it. Again this is only a very small step in learning to read. While it won't hurt children to learn letters, more important skills should be focused on at this age, like increasing vocabulary and learning to speak in sentences.

Using Books With Infants and Toddlers

Learning to love books is an important part of "literacy." This can start in the infant stage. When you involve a child in looking at a bright picture book while warmly snuggled on your lap, the child absorbs the idea that reading is a *very pleasurable* thing to do. Many studies have shown that one very influential factor in helping children learn to read when they are in elementary school is having been read to during their early childhood. When parents and caregivers read to children often and with enthusiasm, children come to see reading as pleasurable and interesting. They learn, for instance, that books have a beginning, middle, and end, and that stories progress. They learn that the marks on

the page have something to do with the pictures. On a more subtle level, children also learn the "expectation" that they too will learn to read because this is something that people do.

Young toddlers enjoy the hinge action of sturdy board books. You might see a toddler turning a page back and forth, over and over again. She is creating her own "peek-a-boo" experience, watching a picture appear and disappear over and over again. Sturdy cardboard pages also help the child learn to use the thumb and forefinger to turn the pages, the skill for mastering paper pages later.

Have a variety of different types of books available. Put some away and take different ones out occasionally to keep interest high. Looking at books can be relaxing and comforting. Through this exploration children begin to make sense of how books work.

Even young children *can* be taught to respect books and turn the pages carefully. Demonstrate how to turn the page and let each child imitate you. Praise them. Have them show you how to put the book back on the shelf and praise again. If a book develops a tear, let the children watch while you repair it with tape, and repeat a demonstration of how to turn the pages gently. Of course, books will be damaged, that is inevitable with heavy-handed toddlers. You will want to keep some books out of reach and bring them out at special times. Children should have other books they can handle. Wallpaper sample books (out-of-date copies donated by suppliers) are great. Toddlers can practice turning the sturdy pages and enjoy the pretty patterns.

Easy Homemade Books

A number of the activities in this and other chapters suggest using homemade books. They allow you to "customize" books for your child. Use pictures you cut from magazines, photographs, or drawings. Here are some simple ways to make books that are durable enough for young children to handle.

■ Photo albums with "magnetic" clear plastic pages make ideal, durable books. You can also slip pictures into small photo albums with plastic sleeves.

- Sew sandwich-size, zip-closure plastic bags together along the bottom edge, either by hand or machine. If you cut thin cardboard (such as that used for file folders or poster board) to fit inside the bags, you can use both sides. You can easily change the pictures in this book to keep it interesting.

- Mount pictures on construction paper trimmed to fit inside a small loose-leaf notebook. Mark where the rings will be and punch holes. Stick reinforcers around the holes. Cover the front and back of each page with clear self-adhesive paper and repunch the holes. Insert these pages in the loose-leaf notebook.

- Fold several sheets of construction paper in half. Glue pictures on each half and on the backs. Cover these sheets with clear, self-adhesive paper. Stack these covered sheets and sew with a sewing machine down the fold line.

Tips on Reading Books to Toddlers

- Your playful interactions with children and books support language development and foster a love of reading.

- Anticipate with pleasure. "In a minute, when we finish putting these things away, we'll be able to read a book together."

- Set the stage. Get cozy. Snuggle into some pillows or a big, soft chair.

- "Talk" the book rather than read it at first. Comment on the picture on the page.

- Show your own interest. How you read can keep a toddler listening and support a sense of wonder and fascination.

- Don't rush. Leave time to look at the pictures. Respond to comments.

- Describe the process of reading as you do it. For example, look at the cover. Say, "What do you think this book is about? Let's open it and see. Oh...look at this picture. What's that? What's she doing? Here is what these words say." Then point to the words as you read them. "Let's turn the page and see what happens next."

- When the child is familiar with the book, let her tell you what will happen on the next page.

- End the book by saying something like: "And that's the end of the story. That was a nice story, wasn't it? I like this book. Do you want to read it again?"

A "Demo" Tape

This activity allows you to be more aware of the child's progress and delight in new developments.

Materials

cassette tape recorder • blank cassette

To Do

- When you hear the baby cooing, babbling, and gurgling, grab a tape recorder and record her sounds.
- Afterward, state the date of the recording.
- Add new sounds made by the baby periodically as a record of her language development.

Observations

- Be aware of what types of sounds the child is making. When is the child most likely to engage in this free, random experimentation with sound?
- Does the type of sound vary when the child is in a social situation with other people?

More Ideas

- Use a video tape instead of, or in addition to, an audio tape so you can note the physical progress as well. Add to the same cassette over time.
- Simply create a written "language file" for the child. Describe each new development as you notice it, starting with the random sounds the child makes, which syllables the child repeats in babbling, and then moving on to more complex sounds, first words, and vocal interactions.

Follow the Leader Sounds

This is also a social activity.

Materials

To Do

- When the child is paying attention to you, even if it's while you're changing her diaper, start chanting a sound you have heard her utter before. "Da-da-da...."
- Pause for a moment and give the child an expectant look.

Observations

- Does the child take up the chant?
- Does she "get the drift" of the game?
- See how long you can carry on the back and forth sound "conversation."

Simple Steps

More Ideas

■ Wait until the child comes out with a sound spontaneously and then chant her sound back to her. Does she then pick up on the game and chant it back?

Emerging Skill

This activity also encourages the child to practice language skills and use sounds to interact with someone else.

Where's Teddy?

6 MONTHS +

This is also a social game.

Materials

stuffed animal, pet, or familiar person

To Do

■ When there are several very familiar people, pets, or toys with names in the room, ask the child, "Where's Teddy (or whoever)?"
■ Clap and show approval if the child indicates correctly.

Observations

■ See if the child looks toward or points to the correct individual or thing.

More Ideas

■ Do this at various times when different familiar individuals are present.
■ As the child gets older and develops more language skills, make your questions more complex and include a wider range of objects. "What's that noise coming from?" "Where's the garbage truck?"

Emerging Skill

The child demonstrates understanding and strengthens social ties as she recognizes the names of familiar people and a few familiar objects.

Talk Through a Tube

The child has a legitimate way to make a lot of noise and use her voice in a powerful way.

Materials

large, empty gift wrap tube

To Do

- Talk to the child through the tube.
- Experiment and make your voice sound different ways—high, low, squeeky, etc.
- See if the child will imitate you when you hand the tube to her. Say, "Oh...you sound funny!"

Observations

- Is this fun for the child?
- Does she do it spontaneously again later?

More Ideas

- An especially fun variation is to do this with a long length of (unused) dryer duct. You can even make it go around corners.
- Children love to holler with a large bucket over their heads. (Supervise closely; be sure they are sitting down and don't attempt to walk with the bucket on their heads.)

Where's Your Nose?

This type of activity also has to do with the child's self-image. Describe the body parts with admiration. "And what a cute little nose it is!"

Materials

To Do

- Ask a child to point to various body parts: "Where's your nose?" "Where's your foot?"

Simple Steps

- If a child is unable to do this, be sure to talk about various body parts with her as you dress her, etc. For example, "Give me your foot. I'm going to put your shoe on your foot now."

Observations

- Does the child know what you want her to do?
- Is she able to point to all the body parts you name?
- Which does she know and which not?

More Ideas

- Let a puppet or stuffed animal kiss the body part you name.
- Ask the child to point to toys and other objects you name to assess her receptive vocabulary.

Emerging Skill

The child learns vocabulary about her body and feels interesting and valued.

Talk to Grandma on the Phone
10 MONTHS +

This is also a good thing to do when the child has trouble separating from a parent or someone else. It acknowledges that you know she misses that person. Pretend play like this also helps the child use symbols (the toy phone).

Materials

toy telephone

To Do

- Help the child "pretend" to call "Grandma" (or other persons important to the child) on the phone.
- Or, you could make the phone ring and answer it and say, "Grandma! Oh yes, Sarah is right here. It's for you, Sarah...talk to Grandma."

Observations

- Does the child know what to do?
- Is she pretending, or does she wait for a voice on the phone?
- Does she talk "jargon" on the phone, jabbering syllables?

More Ideas

Use two toy phones, and you supply the conversation for "Grandma."

Emerging Skill

The child can use "jargon" talk (strings of syllables with intonation that sounds like real speech). This becomes more complex over time, involving more sounds. And the child is getting practice in valuable pretend play.

Help Me Pack

 12 MONTHS +

Materials

small shopping bag or suitcase   familiar objects

To Do

- Start putting objects in the bag and indicate to the child or children that you want help.
- Name one familiar object after another and see if the child will get it for you and put it in the bag.

Observations

- Does the child seem to get the idea of the game?
- Does she understand the individual words, or pick up any random object?

More Ideas

- Let the child "unpack" a bag full of familiar objects. Name each object as it is removed.
- Use a puppet to pack the bag. Children are often eager to cooperate with a puppet. If the child doesn't succeed, the puppet can find the object and name it.
- Try this activity at clean-up time, naming items to be put into a laundry basket, or on a toy shelf.

Emerging Skill

The child will associate words with objects and solidify new receptive vocabulary words. It is also a social activity, doing something together with you.

Fun With Picture Cards

Materials

pictures of familiar objects cut from magazines • index cards or thin cardboard • clear self-adhesive paper • sturdy container such as a food storage box

To Make

- Cut out pictures and laminate them onto cardboard cards, with clear self-adhesive paper.

To Do

- Put the box of picture cards on the floor or a low shelf, accessible to the child.
- She will enjoy taking them out of the box, either one at a time or dumping them.
- The child might bring a card over to you.
- Talk about the pictures the child shows you. "That's a teddy bear, isn't it?" "That's a car."

Observations

- Does the child name the picture?
- What else does she do with the pictures?

More Ideas

- Have several sets of cards for different categories of things—toys, animals, vehicles, babies, etc.
- Make a picture-to-object matching game. See if the child can bring the picture card to the matching real object in the room.
- Do this with individual photos of all the children and adults involved in your program that the child might have contact with. Parents too!
- Affix the pictures to metal juice can lids instead of cards. They make a great noise when dumped.

Emerging Skill

This might just be a dump-and-fill exercise for a younger toddler. It might turn into a vocabulary stretcher as the child learns labels and descriptive words for familiar objects. It can be a social exercise if an adult enjoys looking at the cards with the child.

Language Development and Early Literacy

Animal Sounds

This can be an enjoyable social activity when several children are involved.

Materials

pictures of familiar animals or animal book

To Do

- Look at the animal pictures with the child.
- Point to and name the animal, then make the animal sound.

Observations

- Does the child imitate the animal sounds after you make them?
- Later, will the child point to the picture and make the animal sound without your model?

More Ideas

- Use stuffed animals or small plastic animals instead of pictures.
- The child might like to imitate the animals' movements as well.

Emerging Skill

The child enjoys imitating sounds and generally has fun with language.

My Own Word Book

12 MONTHS +

Materials

photo album with magnetic plastic pages, or other homemade book (see pages 40-41) • magazine pictures, photos or drawings

To Make

- As the child comes out with new words, add a picture of each in her own personal word book. It's a fun way to keep track of a growing vocabulary.

To Do

- Seat the child on your lap and enjoy looking at the pictures together.
- Do not correct the child's pronunciation. Simply repeat the word in a sentence yourself. "Yes, that's right...that is orange juice."

Observations

- See if the child spontaneously points to the picture and names it.

Simple Steps

More Ideas

■ You might also add a few pictures of very familiar objects that the child has not said yet. You can test "receptive vocabulary" by saying, "Where's the kitty?" and seeing if the child points to it.

■ Make a book like this of people familiar to the child.

Emerging Skill

Children this age enjoy pointing at things and naming them. It give them practice with productive vocabulary.

What's in the Box?

12 MONTHS +

Make sure objects are safe, or supervise closely and put the objects away or out of reach when you are finished.

Materials

an attractive box, preferably with a hinged lid
different objects to go inside the box

To Do

■ Put a different object inside the box each day.

■ Sit down on the floor and let the children gather around you. The presence of the box is a good way to draw their attention.

■ Open the box, take out the object, and talk about the object with the child.

Observations

■ Does she know what the objects are?

■ Can an older child tell you what each is for?

More Ideas

■ Each object will present variations of vocabulary.

■ Some objects might lead to an activity. Others might be left out for the child to play with.

■ A special person, like a grandparent, might loan you something for the box that the child associates with that person.

■ Invite a different child to take the box home each day and bring it back the next day with something special in it.

Emerging Skill

This gives you something concrete to talk about with the child, increasing their vocabulary of objects and descriptive words. It also engages curiosity.

Photo Experience Box

Materials

camera and film
photo album

To Do

- ■ Bring your camera along when you do a simple activity with the children, such as taking a walk around the neighborhood or making a salad.
- ■ Take a picture of each thing that you do, for instance getting coats on, leaving the front walk, looking at the neighbor's dog, looking down into a puddle, having a snack at the park, saying hello to the letter carrier, and returning.
- ■ When the pictures are developed, show them to the children and talk about them. "Who's that? What were we doing there?"
- ■ Help the children put the photos in sequence in a homemade book (see pages 40-41).
- ■ Enjoy looking at the pictures and "reading" your book together many times.

Observations

- ■ Do they associate the photos with the experience?
- ■ Can they recognize events?
- ■ Are they able to sequence the pictures?

More Ideas

- ■ You could create many of these—they will all be a hit with the children.
- ■ Parents could do this for virtually every routine, such as going to bed, grocery shopping, or getting ready to go out in the morning.
- ■ Instead of a book, create a storyboard. Take a series of photographs and mount them on a large piece of poster board in order, leaving space to print a brief caption describing the activity. Cover with clear contact paper and hang on the wall at the children's eye level.

Emerging Skill

The vocabulary you use to describe the pictures will be meaningful because the child actually experienced it. It's a good way to represent action words (verbs). The photos are *symbols*—representations of things that they actually did. They will experience sequencing as they help you put the photos in the correct order. And they'll gain a feeling of self-worth and belonging to see themselves represented. It's a great pre-reading exercise.

Simple Steps

Materials

two pieces of sturdy cardboard, each about 8″ by 10″ (20 cm x 25 cm)
colored contact paper to cover
duct tape, or other wide, flexible tape
two strips of self-adhesive velcro, about 8″ (20 cm) long
pictures from a magazine glued to a piece of tag board and laminated with
clear contact paper

To Make

- Cover each piece of cardboard with the colored contact paper on both sides.
- Make a hinge with the duct tape, leaving a little space between the two cover pieces.
- Put a strip of the velcro at the top and bottom of the back cover of the flap book.
- The corresponding pieces of velcro go on the back of the picture card.
- You can create any number of these picture cards and change the picture in your flap book as often as you wish.

To Do

- Just place the flap book where the children can get at it.
- They will enjoy opening and closing the flap book, and seeing the "surprise" picture inside. Older toddlers may name the picture.

Observations

- See how many times they open and close the flap.

More Ideas

- It would be fun to use photos of other children and special friends on the picture cards.
- A series of these could be hung on the back of a shelf or room divider.

Emerging Skill

The child can handle and "experience" a book, and get used to the "mechanics" of books. The major appeal of peek-a-boo is practicing the cognitive skill of object permanence. (Books are really a large peek-a-boo system.)

Language Development and Early Literacy

18 MONTHS +

Materials

poster board
glue
old catalogs, pictures from boxes toys came in, or magazine pictures of toys you
have
clear contact paper

To Make

- Cut out pictures of many toys and other objects in your environment that the children are familiar with.
- Glue these to the poster board in random order.
- Cover it all with clear contact paper and attach the poster to the wall at the child's eye level.

To Do

- Bring one of the objects over to the poster and ask a child to find the picture of it on the poster.
- Continue with other objects as long as the child has interest.
- Talk about the objects and compare the real thing to the picture.

Observations

- Do children ever do this spontaneously?
- Do they name the objects pictured?

More Ideas

- Do it in the other direction. Go over to the poster with your child and point to an object on the poster. See if she can find that object in the room and bring it over to you. The child has to maintain a mental image of the object as she searches for it.

Emerging Skill

Visual discrimination involves singling out certain shapes from others and noticing similarities and differences—basic skills for reading. This exercise also lets children compare real objects to their symbolic representations, and it can be a good receptive language exercise as well.

Simple Steps

Busy Little Hands

Fine Motor Development

What is more beautiful than a baby's hands? The graceful little fingers open out to touch the world. These information-gathering tools get busy very quickly as the child starts to explore his surroundings. By the time the child has entered the second year of life, these precious little hands have developed into pudgy tools and he begins the famous "into everything" stage of development, exploring all the relationships of space, shape, size, and mechanics—putting the universe into logical order.

Although there are many toys on the market designed to give infants, toddlers, and two-year-olds interesting things to do with their hands, often simple objects are best. Household items with interesting textures that make interesting sounds or movements when they are dropped or pushed, or that might fit inside each other, make perfectly wonderful play objects. Just make sure objects are clean, unbreakable, and larger than the child's fist so the child cannot choke on them.

Fine motor development is about the child's growing ability to use the small muscles of his hands in a coordinated way. We cannot "teach" children to acquire fine motor skills; we can, however, provide the opportunity—they just have to figure it out for themselves.

General Sequence of Fine Motor Skill Development

Grasping objects

In the first weeks of a child's life, the body is flexed and tense. Hands are usually in tight fists. If you touch something to the open palm of a newborn's hands, such as your finger, the tiny fingers will clamp around it in a tight grip. For this reason, some people like to put a rattle in the hand of a newborn, but that is not a good idea. Arm movements are uncontrolled and jerky, and the baby might hit himself in the face with the rattle. Furthermore, the child is not really aware of the rattle so the exercise is useless.

Batting at objects

First the child will stare intently at an object. Arms might wave excitedly in a jerky, random fashion. Gradually, the child learns to control these waving appendages enough to hit the target if a toy is within reach.

Using fingers to explore

The child has discovered that one gets interesting sensations when fingers make contact with surfaces. You see little fingers exploring surfaces like sheets, satin bindings, terrycloth, and grass even before the child can pick things up.

Playing with hands and feet

What fun to watch an infant's discovery of his hands! He has seen his hands waving around for a while, but gradually he learns that he is causing them to move. Waving movements can be difficult to control, but as he watches them move, he is practicing eye-hand coordination. Not long after the child discovers his hands he starts to move his fingers in interesting ways and watch them, also bringing them to his mouth. When his hands bump into each other, he might by accident grab the other hand, and later figure out how to do this on purpose. Then the child discovers those other things waving around—feet! The whole body rocks as he pulls on his feet, and tries to suck on his toes!

Simple Steps

Grasping objects purposefully

The child must practice for some time to learn how to open his hand before he makes contact with an object and close his hand at the right time to hang onto the object. Now you should put away delicate crib mobiles.

Releasing objects

The child learns to grasp before he learns to release. This takes practice too. Providing a bucket or other container for the child to drop objects into is one fun way to give the child practice, but he will practice without this motivation. In fact, dropping objects becomes a compulsion!

Putting objects in the mouth

Even before birth babies have the instinct to bring their hands to their mouth and suck. Once they can grasp objects, they bring them right to the mouth, as a way of gaining more sensory information.

Moving objects from one hand to another

Once a child can grasp and release an object, he seems to like moving it from one hand to the other and back again.

Banging objects on the floor

In endless explorations of cause and effect, the child likes to see what kind of sound every object makes.

Throwing objects

Throwing is harder than one might think. The child must discover the exact moment to open his hand while moving his arm to make the object sail through the air. How exciting! This must be tried again and again.

Picking up small objects with thumb and forefinger

Gradually the child learns to use just the thumb and forefinger. This is the time to do a special safety check of the environment, because the child will be driven to pick up every stray staple, paper clip, dust ball, and thumb tack that may have fallen to the floor.

Picking up small objects with a raking motion

Presented with an array of small objects such as dry cereal, the child will first use the same motion he uses to grasp larger objects, all the fingers together.

Feeding self with fingers

The baby will enjoy picking up small pieces of soft food such as cubed cooked carrots, peas, and raisins and getting them into his own mouth. Watch out! He may offer some to you as well!

Placing an object in a container

The little scientist experiments with cognitive concepts of size and shape, on an endless quest to combine things. It may start with just dropping one object into a cup. The hands must cooperate in grasping and releasing the object at the right time and getting the angle just right to make it happen.

Dumping things out of containers

Many a caregiver and parent has experienced frustration as a one-year-old systematically dumps every container around him. This action is one of the true compulsions of young toddlers. What's going on here? Power. While the child is discovering what happens when he rotates his wrist while holding on to something, he is also learning, "I can make things happen." The child is exploring cause and effect. Things make noise when they hit the floor and move, roll, and bounce in interesting ways. Why not engineer some legitimate dumping practice?

Poking things in holes

Ah, yes, the transition to toddlerhood! Much of the fine motor activity that toddlers do spontaneously seems to be focused on improving the aim of their forefinger. They love to poke their fingers in holes, and to put other objects in holes. Think of interesting holes you could make for the child to explore. Make sure electrical outlets are covered!

Feeding self with a spoon and using a cup

These skills involve learning to rotate the wrist. Have you watched a determined one-year-old child put food on his spoon and then dump it as the spoon rotates on the way to his mouth? With much practice, he eventually learns to rotate his wrist as his arm changes angle on the way up. Likewise, tipping a glass at just the right angle for liquid to get into the mouth and not down the front of one's clothing takes practice.

Nesting objects that fit together

What a great discovery: things fit together, and when they do they look different. The child will experiment with a wide variety of things. Toys that fit together become popular.

Stacking

During "nesting" experiments, the child discovers that when an object doesn't fit inside, it may rest on top, and sometimes it falls off. "Why?" the child wonders, and so experiments some more. When two or three boxes, blocks, or containers sit on top of each other, they look different. And of course, the best part is being powerful and knocking them down, making a grand noise and causing interesting movements to watch.

Holding a crayon

The child needs to learn how to grasp the crayon, but then must discover that making contact with the paper, applying a certain amount of pressure, and moving the hand while maintaining the pressure creates a mark. Amazing! Quite a complex maneuver!

Turning the pages of a book

The child will have watched adults do this many times, so part of this action might be social imitation. First the child will just try pushing the page over, using the whole hand. Grasping a page with thumb and forefinger and moving an arm in the proper arc to turn the page requires quite a bit of control. Flaps and levers of all kinds fascinate the child.

Rotating wrist

The child is also learning to rotate his wrist to position objects. Children about a year old like screwing on jar lids and playing with simple shape boxes and puzzles.

Dumping: A Toddler's Joy

Dumping 101—provide two plastic cups and one large bead (too large to choke on). Let the child "pour" the bead from one cup to another.

Bottle Dumping—cut the tops off of large, preferably transparent, plastic bottles with handles (such as those that laundry detergent comes in). Provide things too large to choke on that the child can put into the bottles and shake out again. Possibilities: pop beads, clothespins, large thread spools, hair curlers, table blocks.

Dump and Haul—tie a cord through the hole in the end of a rubber dish tub. Let the child dump small toys into the tub and drag it across the room holding the cord. Then the child can dump the contents back into the original storage tub.

Basket Drop—find a basket or other container with a handle. (Toddlers love things with handles.) Put two large containers such as laundry baskets on opposite sides of the room. Fill one with small objects. Let the child fill one basket, carry it across the room, and dump it into the waiting container, then return for more. When all of the toys have been thus transported, the child can carry them all back again!

Fill and Spill Bucket Over the Sand Box—suspend a plastic bucket from a tree or other overhang so that it hangs about twelve inches (thirty centimeters) above the sand. Children will enjoy using scoops and shovels to put sand into the bucket and dump it out again.

Dump Truck—find a large plastic dump truck for children to use indoors with small toys or outside in the sand area.

Pouring—dumping can be refined into pouring. Give children many opportunities to practice with sand and water and containers of different sizes and shapes.

Napkin Tent

2 MONTHS +

Do not use flimsy crepe, organdy, or silky textured scarves. When these fall on a young infant's face, they can block the child's nostrils.

Materials

large cloth dinner napkin

To Do

- Place a young baby on his back on a clean blanket on the floor.
- Place the napkin so that it sticks up like a tent, off to one side of the baby, but within reach. (Most babies face their head to the right most of the time, so you might place the napkin on that side.)
- The baby may notice the scarf, turn toward it, and reach for it.
- If the palm of the baby's hand touches the object, his fist may close on it instinctively. The material is easy to grasp and the child can pull it over his face without danger and explore this new object.

Observations

- Observe what the child does when he notices the napkin or when he manages to grasp it.
- Does he try to do it again the next time you offer it?

More Ideas

- Collect different colors and patterns of napkins.

Simple Steps

Emerging Skill

The child is practicing the instinctive skill of grasping something when the palm of the hand touches it. This can be quite exciting to a young baby because he is actually making something happen. Cognitive learning takes place when the child begins to notice this cause and effect. Gross motor skills are also involved as the child twists to one side and reaches out. Intentionally letting go is a skill that comes later. Watch for it to begin.

Satin Streamers

 2 MONTHS +

Materials

canning jar ring, plastic bracelet, other small hoop, or plastic coffee can lid with the inside part cut away • satin ribbons 8" (20 cm) long, several different colors

To Make

■ Tie ribbons securely to the hoop.

To Do

■ With the baby sitting supported in your lap or in an infant seat, dangle the ribbons in front of him where he can reach them, dragging them lightly across the palm of his hand.

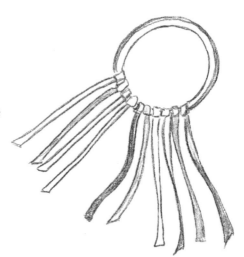

Observations

■ Does he grasp the ribbons?
■ Does he seem to enjoy the sensation?
■ How long can you keep his interest before he turns away?

Safety

■ Make sure the ribbons are not long enough to wrap around a child's neck, especially if you leave this hanging for the baby to explore when you are not right there.

More Ideas

■ Try this with other interesting, dangling materials and textures.

Emerging Skill

The child is practicing grasping an object when it is placed in the hand. This pleasing sensory experience lets the child become aware of the sense of touch.

Fine Motor Development

Materials

interesting, unbreakable objects too large to choke on
sewing elastic—¼" (½ cm) or more wide
the back of a shelf or a divider or other *extremely stable* vertical surface

To Make

■ Tie a length of the elastic about eighteen inches (forty-five centimeters) long to each object.
■ Securely attach these to the vertical surface, such as threading it through the holes in the pegboard back of a shelf bolted to the floor.
■ Have the toy dangling about six to eight inches (fifteen to twenty centimeters) above floor level, or where a baby in an infant seat or lying on the floor can easily reach it.

To Do

■ Sit with the child on your lap, or place the child in an infant seat or on the floor in a position where he can easily see and reach the hanging objects.

Observations

■ Does the baby notice the objects?
■ Does he try to reach for the objects?
■ Is he successful in making contact?
■ Does the child's hand remain closed or is he opening the hand before making contact and attempting to grasp?

Safety

■ Make sure that the vertical surface to which the objects are attached is very stable so a child could not pull something over on himself if he happens to grasp and pull. Make sure the child could not possibly get the elastic wound around his neck.

Simple Steps

More Ideas

- This activity has as many variations as there are interesting objects to hang.
- Use a short piece of PVC pipe about one inch (three centimeters) in diameter and about one foot (thirty centimeters) long. Hang the objects from the pipe. A piece of rope could be threaded through the pipe and then attached to a firm overhead brace or tree limb outside. Suspend the pipe so the objects dangle where the child can reach them.

Emerging Skill

The child can practice batting at objects. If the object makes a noise when it is moved, cause and effect is enhanced.

Texture Quilt

2 MONTHS +

Materials

6 or 8 large patches of textured washable materials
backing and polyester quilt batting
trims such as rickrack, plastic zippers, fringe, and lace
needle and thread

To Make

- Sew the patches with other trim together.
- Assemble backing, batting, and top and sew together, binding edges.

To Do

- Place the child on the quilt, tummy down. (Only do this with babies who can comfortably hold their head up when placed on their stomach.)

Observations

- Does the child notice the textures and feel them with his fingers?
- What else does he do?

Safety

- Do not sew on such things as buttons or jingle bells that might eventually work loose and could cause choking. Materials used should be washable.

Fine Motor Development

More Ideas

- Try many variations of textures. You could make several such quilts.
- Sew pockets on some of the pieces that small toys can fit inside of.

Emerging Skill

This allows the child to use fingers in exploration and, as a "sensory" activity, gives the child experiences with the sense of touch. It could also be considered a gross motor activity if the child practices rolling, reaching, wiggling, and scooting.

Funny Booties 4 MONTHS +

Materials

colorful socks, a little larger than baby's feet

To Do

- Put the socks on the child's legs and place the child on his back on the floor.
- Of course, you don't need to do anything special at all—many babies automatically play with their feet when they are lying on their back at this stage. This adds a little fun for both of you.

Observations

- Does the child notice the new socks?
- Does he try to pull them off?

Safety

- Make sure the socks are clean and haven't been mouthed by another baby.

More Ideas

- Use a variety of colors and textures of socks. Also try sewing little stuffed animals to the toes of the socks.

Emerging Skill

The child uses hands to grasp these interesting things and gets a sense of his whole body and how it works together when he plays with hands and feet.

Rattle Collection 6 MONTHS +

Materials

variety of commercial rattles or homemade shake toys (see page 113)
rubber dish tub or other sturdy box

Simple Steps

To Do

- Place the box of rattles next to the child on the floor.
- You might attract interest by saying, "Look, (child's name), here are lots of things that make a noise."
- Pick up one of the objects and give it a little shake.
- Then put it back and see what happens.

Observations

- What does he do with the rattles?
- Does he pick them up?
- Does he grasp them with his whole hand? With two hands?
- Does he put them in his mouth, bang them on the floor?
- How long do these hold his attention?

Safety

- Make sure all rattles are in good repair and none of the contents can spill out.

More Ideas

- See how many different kinds of rattles you can find. You might make several different collections of four or five rattles to present at different times to keep interest high.
- You could hang the rattles from a suspended bar using sewing elastic to make a "rattle interest center."

Emerging Skill

The child practices grasping objects. A rattle is also a "cognitive" toy, giving the child experience with cause and effect.

Grab Bag Collection 8 MONTHS +

Materials

large cloth bag or sturdy plastic shopping bag
lots of different objects with interesting shapes such as plastic measuring spoons linked with a ring, a large key ring with plastic objects attached, a large plastic kitchen spoon with holes in it, small plastic bowl, a small doll

To Do

- Place two or three different objects inside the bag and place it in front of the child on the floor.
- Show the child what is inside.
- Sit back and see what happens.

Observations

- Does the child reach in and remove the objects?
- Is the child able to grasp the objects easily?
- Does he turn the objects over, and move them from hand to hand?
- Does he try holding on to them in different places and in different ways?
- What does he do with the objects?

Safety

- Make sure all objects are too large for the child to choke on.

More Ideas

- There are as many variations to this as there are interesting objects. Put different objects in the bag each day and present them to the child.

Emerging Skill

The child practices grasping objects of different shapes and sizes. Cognitive learning occurs as the child explores relationships of size, shape, and space.

Handle Collection 8 MONTHS +

Materials

all kinds of unbreakable objects with handles: plastic cups, small plastic totes, small purses, plastic jugs, pitchers
large container for objects

To Do

- Present the child with the container full of objects and let him play with them randomly.

Observations

- Does the child use the handles to grasp the objects?

Emerging Skill

The child practices grasping objects. Handles are interesting to young children. They will use them to drag and "haul" containers.

Rag Bag 8 MONTHS +

Materials

cloth bag or pillowcase
elastic
needle and thread (or sewing machine)
assorted clean rags

Simple Steps

To Make

- Sew a hem around the open end of the bag.
- Thread elastic through the hem and attach ends so that the opening is about three inches (eight centimeters) wide when the material is gathered (large enough for a baby to see inside and get his hand through).
- Stuff the rags inside the bag.

To Do

- Present this to the baby.

Observations

- Does the baby reach inside and try to pull the rags out?
- Does he get all the rags out?
- Does he ever try to put them back in?

Safety

- An elastic opening rather than a draw string is recommended to reduce the risk of strangulation. Don't let the child put the bag over his head.

More Ideas

- Draw or embroider faces on the rags.
- Substitute small stuffed animals for the rags.

Emerging Skills

While the child is having fun grasping and pulling objects, cognitive learning involving object permanence is taking place. Feeling the different textures of the rags is also a sensory experience.

Drop It!

8 MONTHS +

Materials

large container such as a plastic bucket or dish pan
variety of small objects for the child to pick up and drop in, such as blocks, clothespins, and small stuffed animals

To Do

- Place the child on the floor or on your lap, if the child does not yet sit independently.
- Put the objects within reach and the container on the other side, also within reach.
- When the child is watching, pick up one object and drop it into the container.
- Then sit back and do nothing.

Observations

- Does the child imitate your action and also pick up an object and drop it in the container?
- Does he have any difficulty releasing the object?
- Does he continue with more objects?
- Does he pick up the objects in the container and take them back out?
- Does the child spontaneously pick up and drop objects when simply "exploring" on the floor?

Safety

- Make sure all objects are too large to choke on.

More Ideas

- Work on collecting a wide variety of interesting objects for children to handle.
- Simply place the child on the floor where a number of interesting objects are accessible to the child and see if he is motivated to pick up and release them.

Emerging Skill

The child is learning to release objects. The child will also enjoy hearing the "plunk" the object makes when it falls into the container—a sensory and a cognitive activity.

A Round of Applause!

8 MONTHS +

Materials

To Do

- Sit down on the floor in front of the sitting child. Clap your hands together.

Observations

- Does the child imitate you and also clap his hands?
- Does he hold palms open and succeed in having hands meet at the midline (in front of the body at the center)?

Simple Steps

More Ideas

■ Clap and say "Yea!" whenever the child accomplishes something. Soon he will probably give himself a round of applause.

■ Clapping together is a tiny "group activity" that older infants sometimes enjoy doing .

Emerging Skill

While the child practices making hands meet at midline, he also engages in a natural social game.

Hitting Two Objects 8 MONTHS +

Materials

small objects a child can grasp that make interesting sounds when hit together, such as two hollow metal tins with lids that candy comes in or two small plastic bottles with things inside

To Do

■ Place the objects in front of the child.

■ Pick up two and hit them together.

■ Then put them down within reach of the child.

Observations

■ Does the child imitate your action, hitting the objects together?

■ Does the child do this spontaneously with other objects?

Safety

■ Make sure any objects that you give the child to pick up are unbreakable, and, if they are metal, that the edges are not sharp.

More Ideas

■ Collect a wide variety of objects for the child to try this with.

■ Include a few things that do not make much noise, like small stuffed animals.

Emerging Skill

The child practices aiming hands to meet—another cause and effect, cognitive activity.

Materials

shoebox, or other container with lid

various small toys, such as a small doll, or stuffed animals that will fit inside the box

To Do

■ Simply place the empty shoebox and the toys near the child on the floor.

Observations

■ Does the child open the box?

■ Does he spontaneously put some of the toys in the box?

■ What does he do when the toy doesn't fit?

■ Does he put the lid on the box?

More Ideas

■ Collect different sizes of containers with lids so the child can experiment with what fits where.

Emerging Skill

The child has to position objects correctly to fit. This is also a cognitive activity as the child explores concepts of size and space and makes things disappear under the lid and appear again when he takes the lid off.

Dish Tub Fill and Spill

12 MONTHS +

Materials

dish tub
empty milk jug, top removed
clothespins

Simple Steps

To Do

■ Let the child poke the clothespins into the milk jug and then dump them out again into the dish tub.

Observations

■ Does the child do this spontaneously, if the materials are present?
■ Does he put all the clothespins in the milk jug before dumping them out again?
■ What else does he do with the containers?

More Ideas

■ Collect all kinds of interesting containers children can use for filling and dumping out.

Emerging Skill

The child learns how to rotate wrists to dump objects out of containers. Cognitive learning about cause and effect and shapes and spaces is also possible.

Stick-It-On and Peel-It-Off Picture   12 MONTHS +

Materials

contact paper (pattern doesn't matter)
magazine pictures
scissors
construction paper or poster board
clear contact paper

To Make

■ Place contact paper on the wall at the child's level, *sticky side out*.
■ Cut out magazine pictures, mount on construction paper or poster board for stiffness, and encase front and back with clear contact paper (or laminate in a laminating machine).

To Do

■ Let the child press the laminated pictures onto the sticky paper. Then let the child peel them off again.

Observations

■ Is the child able to peel off the picture?
■ Does he use his thumb and forefinger to get it loose?

More Ideas

■ Use photos of other children in the group or family members.
■ Use fabric swatches and other things that will stick.
■ When you observe a child peeling off pictures that you have put up at their level for decoration, you can redirect the child to this activity.

Emerging Skill

This gives children practice using their thumb and forefinger to manipulate things. The child is learning language as he learns the name of what is on the picture. If you use photos of other children in the class, or family members, this becomes a social activity. This is also a sensory activity as the child learns about "sticky."

Screw the Top On

12 MONTHS +

Materials

plastic wide-mouthed jar with screw top—small enough for the child to grasp, but too large to choke on

To Do

■ Let the child try to screw the top on the jar and off again.

Observations

■ How does he hold the lid?
■ Can he figure out how to take the lid off?

Safety

■ Make sure the jar lid is too large to choke on.

More Ideas

■ Put one or two interesting objects (too large to choke on) inside the jar for the child to dump out and put back in.
■ Have several different sizes of jars and lids so the child has to match the right lid to the right opening.

Emerging Skill

The child practices rotating the wrist.

Materials

manufactured one-piece wooden inlay puzzle or homemade puzzle made with stiff cardboard, plastic cookie cutter, scissors, glue, and paint

To Make

- Plastic cookie cutters make good one piece puzzles.
- Just trace around the cookie cutter on the cardboard. Cut out the shape. Glue this piece of cardboard to another piece of cardboard.
- Cut a cookie cutter shape out of the stiff cardboard.
- Paint it a different color from the background cardboard.

To Do

- Simply place the puzzle in front of the child and allow the child to experiment.

Observations

- Does the child remove the puzzle piece and attempt to put it back in?
- When the child holds the puzzle piece, does he rotate his wrist in an attempt to line up the piece with the hole?

More Ideas

- Start with a circle, which will fit no matter how the piece is positioned. Later offer different shapes.

Emerging Skill

The child practices rotating the wrist. This is also a cognitive activity as the child learns about positive and negative shapes, relating the puzzle piece to the hole.

Collections of Holes 12 MONTHS +

Materials

things with holes such as strawberry baskets, plastic spoons with drainage holes, plastic baskets, large mesh net bags

To Do

- Simply have these types of things available to the child in the play area.

Fine Motor Development

Observations

- Does the child discover the holes?
- Does the child put his fingers in the holes or try to put other things through them?

More Ideas

- You could have a special box full of "hole stuff."
- Provide some thin plastic tubing or plastic drinking straws for the child to push through the holes.

Emerging Skill

The child gets practice using his forefinger independently and is discovering relationships of size and space (a cognitive skill).

Poking Things in Holes

 12 MONTHS +

Materials

empty coffee can with plastic lid, metal lid discarded
sharp knife or cutting tool (teacher only)
old-fashioned clothespins

To Make

- Cut a round hole in the lid of the coffee can, just larger than the diameter of the clothespins.

To Do

- Let the child poke the clothespins through the hole in the lid.
- Then the child can peel the lid off, dump the clothespins back out again, put the lid back on (perhaps with your help), and repeat the process.

Observations

- Does the child figure out how to line the clothespin up properly to fit through the hole? If not, can he do it after a demonstration?

Safety

- Make sure any sharp edges on the coffee can are filed off.

More Ideas

- Collect all sorts of cylindrical objects that might fit through that hole, such as pieces of plastic straws, hair rollers, and wooden dowels.

Simple Steps

- Use this type of container to store crayons. Children will love putting them away.
- Create several different lids, each with a different shape hole. Offer it with differently shaped objects for the child to push through.

Emerging Skill

Children use fine motor skills as they line the object up with the hole and push it through, as well as when they peel the lid off.

Paper Cup Nesting Toys

Materials

large stack of paper cups

To Do

- Simply let children play with these, seeing how they come apart and go back together.
- Note what the child does with these.
- If there is no spontaneous activity, you might show them once how they come apart and fit back together, to attract their interest.

Observations

- Does the child shake the cups apart?
- Does he attempt to put them back together again?

Safety

- Do not use Styrofoam cups because the children could bite off small pieces and swallow, choke on, or inhale them.

More Ideas

- Use a stack of soft plastic tumblers (such as Tupperware) for a more permanent version.
- Square or rectangular refrigerator storage containers present a more difficult version. The child must line up the corners.

Emerging Skill

The child is learning to align shapes properly to fit together. This is also a cognitive activity as the child explores shapes and spaces.

Fine Motor Development

Nesting Bowls

Materials

set of graduated plastic mixing bowls

To Do

- Simply put these near the child.

Observations

- Does the child separate the bowls and try to put them together again?
- What happens when the child tries to fit a larger bowl into a smaller one?

More Ideas

- A more difficult version is to use square containers of graduated sizes.

Emerging Skill

The child practices nesting objects together and sees the relationship of sizes. This is also a cognitive activity as the child explores relationships of size and space.

Build a Tower

Materials

4 or 5 wooden blocks of the same size and shape

To Do

- Sit down with the child.
- While the child watches, stack the blocks on top of each other.
- Let the child knock them down.
- Then sit back and see if the child tries to make a stack.

Observations

- How many blocks is the child able to stack?
- Does he seem to make an attempt to line them up?

Safety

- Stay near, in case the child decides that throwing them is more interesting. If that happens, redirect to things that are okay to throw.

More Ideas

- Find other things that are interesting to stack such as plastic shoeboxes, square plastic food storage containers with lids on, or empty food cartons.

Simple Steps

Emerging Skill

The child learns a little about balance and gravity as he moves his arms to carefully place the blocks.

Through the Tube

Materials

paper towel or toilet tissue tubes
scarf
small toys that will fit through tube such as little cars
piece of wooden dowel about 10″ (25 cm) long or a rhythm stick

To Do

- Give the child this collection of objects to play with independently.
- He will probably think of this on his own. If not, show him how to make things go through the tube.
- Use the dowel or rhythm stick to push the scarf through so it sticks out the other end of the tube and then pull it the rest of the way.

Observations

- How long does this keep the child's attention?
- Does the child find other things to stick through the tube?
- Does the child do other things with the materials instead?

More Ideas

- Use PVC pipe for a more permanent variation.
- Provide different lengths of tube.

Emerging Skill

Children use hand muscles in different ways as they make things go through the tube.

Material

plastic bottles of all types, such as large plastic water cooler bottles, plastic pop bottles, gallon milk jugs, and shampoo bottles

things to put inside bottles, such as yarn pieces, cotton balls, plastic straws, clothespins, pipe cleaners, hair rollers

To Do

- Give children the empty bottles and materials to put inside (one bottle and one material at a time).
- Don't offer everything at once. Put out a variety of different materials on different days.
- Let them take their time figuring out what will fit through the hole in the top and watching it drop through.
- They will also enjoy shaking the bottle and dumping the contents back out again.

Observations

- Does the child seem to understand the concepts of finding something the right size to fit through the hole, and lining it up?
- What does the child do when the object won't fit?

Safety

- Since small bottle caps are often the right size to choke on, leave them out of this activity completely. Be sure children do not put soft items such as yarn or cotton balls in their mouths.

More Ideas

- Let children practice filling bottles with water at the sink and dumping them out again.
- This might be a good "taking turns" activity with two children or a small group. Give guidance and comment on how much fun it is to take turns like this.
- Children can screw on the tops of large-mouthed plastic jars used for this activity.

Emerging Skill

This activity challenges children's developing fine motor skills. Lining up a long plastic straw with the small hole in the top of a bottle to make it drop through is challenging.

Simple Steps

Materials

newspaper
trash bag

To Do

- Give each child a piece of newspaper to tear up.
- Then simply demonstrate as you say, "Let's tear this newspaper into little, little pieces."
- Describe what you are seeing and hearing: "Suzanna is tearing a big piece off of hers. Roxanne is tearing hers too. Wow...listen to that noise. All this tearing. Look at all the little pieces we are making."
- You could sit down on the floor with them and just enjoy throwing the newspaper up in the air.
- Then make a game out of getting every little piece into the trash bag.
- Be sure to wash hands (and faces) when you are all done!

Observations

- Is the tearing easy for them?
- Do they participate in the picking up?

More Ideas

- Crumpling up pieces of newspaper into balls and throwing them can be just as much fun.

Emerging Skill

This can be a good way to expend extra energy or release tensions. Tearing and crumpling also provides a little fine motor/hand muscle exercise. This can be a good redirection activity when you see children tearing something they should not, like a book. It's pro-social because it's more fun to do with others than alone.

Fine Motor Development

Toothbrush Holders

Materials

plastic toothbrush holders (for travel) that come in several different colors

To Do

■ Let the children pull the containers apart and fit them back together again.

Observations

■ Does the child try to fit the pieces of the same color?
■ Does the child realize that the end of one half is slightly smaller than the open end of the other half and that a small one must be fit into the larger one? If not, does the child catch on once you demonstrate and explain?

More Ideas

■ Collect things (too large to choke on) that children could put inside the containers, such as clothespins, plastic drinking straws, or other long, slender objects.

Emerging Skill

Fitting the pieces together and placing objects inside give children fine motor practice. As they match colors they are also getting classifying experience (a cognitive skill).

Water Transfer

Materials

two-compartment plastic bucket
food coloring
sponge
water

To Do

■ Let the child help you put water in one compartment of the divided bucket and add a couple drops of the food coloring of his choice.
■ Then show the child how to squeeze the sponge to deposit the water on the other side.
■ Let the child continue to transfer the water.

Simple Steps

Observations

■ Does the child understand the sequence of putting the sponge under water, squeezing it, and then lifting it out of the water and squeezing it on the other side?

■ Or does the child just enjoy squeezing randomly and watching the drips?

Safety

■ Stay close to supervise so the child doesn't suck on the sponge or bite off pieces.

More Ideas

■ Give the child a variety of containers to fill.

■ Find several different kinds of sponges for the child to try at the same time.

■ Let the child use a turkey baster to do this.

Emerging Skill

As he enjoys playing with soothing water, the child can gain some hand strength in the process.

Flaps Galore!

 18 MONTHS+

Materials

2 pieces of poster board
scissors
pencil
glue
interesting materi-
   als and textures
   to glue under
   flaps

To Make

■ Cut all different shapes of three-sided "flaps" in the top piece of poster board, such as those in the illustration.

■ Position this cardboard with the flaps over the other piece of poster board.

■ Use the pencil to trace the shape of the openings onto the bottom piece of cardboard.

■ Then glue the interesting textures in these tracings on the bottom piece.

■ Place the poster board with the flaps on top and glue or tape the two pieces together.

To Do

- Hang this on the wall at the children's level and let them explore it in passing.

Observations

- Does the child open and close certain flaps over and over again?

More Ideas

- Possible things to glue under the flaps: plexiglass mirror, shiny paper, stickers and stars, feathers, photos of children.
- Eliminate the bottom piece of cardboard and the textures and simply tape the cardboard with the flaps on the window at the children's eye level. They can open the "doors" to look outside. Tape some colored cellophane behind some of the doors!

Emerging Skill

- Young children, especially toddlers, love flaps—anything with a hinge action that opens and shuts. It's a way for children to experience "object permanence"—making things appear and disappear. This is a visually stimulating toy. They will also use thumb and forefinger to open the flaps.

Baby Food Jar Lid Clicker

18 MONTHS +

Materials

baby food jar lids that have a raised "pressure dome"

To Do

- Place the jar lid, rim side down, on a hard floor surface.
- Show the child how to press on the middle and release to create a "clicking" sound.

Observations

- Is the child able to do this?
- Does the child use one finger or more?
- Does the child later repeat the action without prompting from you?

Emerging Skill

The child uses fingers to explore cause and effect.

Eyedropper Play

Materials

plattic eyedropper

plastic eyedropper
several small containers such as a small bottle with a narrow opening, a tiny
bucket, a small pitcher, a dish with a few depressions in it
small piece of sponge
water with food coloring in it
small tray to hold everything

To Do

- Let the child help you put water in the small container and color it with food coloring of his choice.
- Now let the child use the eyedropper to transfer water to the various small containers.

Emerging Skill

The child gains pincer muscle practice squeezing the eyedropper with thumb and forefinger.

Wrap It Up

Materials

lots of recycled wrapping paper, tissue paper, or newspaper
tape
toys in the room

To Make

- While the children are napping or for a surprise first thing in the morning, wrap a few of the toys in the paper.
- Put them back in their familiar places.

To Do

- Let them have the fun of unwrapping and "discovering" familiar toys.

Observations

- Do the children notice the wrapped toys or do you have to point them out?
- Is it difficult for them to remove the wrappings?

More Ideas

- Can the child guess what the toy is before he unwraps it?
- Let the child help you wrap the toys.

Fine Motor Development

Emerging Skill

This gives toddlers and two-year-olds fine motor practice as they tear the paper and uncover their toys. It may also renew interest in some toys.

Pouring From Pitchers

22 MONTHS +

Materials

two small unbreakable pitchers, preferably clear plastic
food coloring
small sponge
water

To Do

■ Let the child help you fill one of the pitchers half full with water.
■ Add food coloring of the child's choice.
■ Let the child practice pouring the water from one pitcher into the other and back again. If there are spills, the child can wipe them up with the sponge.

Observations

■ How successful is the child in getting all the water into the second pitcher?
■ Does success increase with practice?
■ Does the child seem to notice spills?

More Ideas

■ Give the child other small containers, such as plastic cups, to pour the water into.

Emerging Skill

The child is gaining fine motor practice using hands to pour without spilling. The "self-help" skills gained also boost a child's self-esteem.

Golf Tees and Margarine Tubs

22 MONTHS +

Materials

plastic food tub with a soft plastic lid
golf tees of various colors
permanent markers in colors to match the golf tees
hole punch
tray or plate to contain the golf tees while the child is playing

Simple Steps

To Make

- Punch a hole for each color golf tee in the lid of the tub.
- Using the permanent markers, color a ring around each hole to correspond with the colors of the golf tees you make available.
- The tees can be stored inside the tub.

To Do

- The child will enjoy peeling off the lid, dumping the tees onto the tray, replacing the lid and then putting the tees in the holes, "birthday candle style."

Observations

- Does the child match the colors of the tees to the rings around the holes?

Safety

- Make this activity available only when you are able to supervise, since some children may want to stick the golf tees in their nose or ears or poke someone else.

More Ideas

- Try this with larger, "easy grip" plastic pegs.
- Punch holes in different patterns on different lids.

Emerging Skill

This activity provides some interesting fine motor practice, both in peeling off the lid and in placing the golf tees in the holes. The child may also absorb some color concepts. Sorting and matching activities are cognitive/pre-math activities.

Tongs and Muffin Tins

 24 MONTHS +

Materials

muffin tins
spring-loaded kitchen tongs
small objects
container for the objects

To Do

- Let the child use the tongs to pick up each object and place it in a separate compartment of the muffin tin.

Observations

- Can the child figure out how to use the tongs after you demonstrate?

Safety

- Make sure the objects are not small enough to choke on.

More Ideas

- Select a wide variety of small objects such as pieces of sponge, cotton balls, spray can tops, little animals, bristle blocks.
- Offer the other type of "scissor action" tongs.

Emerging Skill

When the child places one object in one compartment, he is practicing one-to-one correspondence—a math learning concept. He is also gaining fine motor practice.

Clamp It On 24 MONTHS +

Materials

plastic clamp-type clothespins
cardboard or plastic container, open on top

To Do

- Children enjoy squeezing the clothespins and clamping them along the sides of the container.
- When not clamped to the sides, the clothespins can be stored in the container. This is more difficult than simply putting the old-fashioned type clothespins around the edge of a container, since it requires more hand muscle strength.

Observations

- Does the child know how to make the clothespins work, and have the strength to pinch the tops together?

More Ideas

- Provide different shapes of containers for them to clamp the clothespins around.
- Older children might make a pattern with different colors of plastic clothespins.
- You might also find different types of clamps such as large, colored office clips. Of course, you need to find clamps that have rather weak tension so the children can manipulate them.

Emerging Skill

Children like making mechanical things work. As well as gaining hand muscle practice, they are also using a simple tool.

Go, Go, Go!

Gross Motor Development

Gross motor development, the development of the large muscles of the body (arms and legs and trunk), is the most visible aspect of development. It might also be rated the most exciting, but the rest of the child is developing right along with the bones and muscles.

What a child needs is physical freedom on a clean floor in a safe, *interesting* environment. When the child is ready to crawl, sit, stand, or walk, she will do those things. There is no rushing it. A child cannot roll over, sit, or walk before the muscles, nerves, and bones can support the skill. Furthermore, the child must practice, on her own, over and over again, finding her own balance and making her muscles do the necessary things to achieve the new skill. You do not need to "motivate" a typically developing child because the drive to master emerging skills is strong.

Two major tasks are relative to *fostering* gross motor development: first, be aware of the developmental sequence of motor skills and, second, give the child the opportunity to practice each skill once she starts doing it on her own. By knowing the sequence of typical development, you can see to it that there is "space and stuff" in the environment to allow the child to practice the new skills that are likely to come next, as well as to practice the newly mastered abilities.

Gross Motor Development

The greatest concern is that the child not be *prevented* from acquiring new skills when she is developmentally ready because the parent or caregiver keeps her physically confined. *Too many babies are kept practically all day in cribs, infant seats, slings, baby carriers, bounce chairs, walkers, high chairs, and swings.* All of these devices greatly restrict the physical movement of a child. Sometimes adults use these because they think babies would be bored if they were just on the floor. Nothing could be further from the truth. Infants enjoy learning to use their bodies.

For young infants who are not yet moving around the room:

Provide a place for them to be on the floor where they can stretch, twist, and move. Spread out a clean sheet with edges tucked under an area rug or a clean blanket for the baby to lie on. Put interesting objects such as bright pieces of fabric, empty plastic bottles, and brightly colored objects and toys nearby, but not too close, to entice the child's interest and movement toward the object.

For mobile infants:

Provide things that move in an interesting manner that the child can pursue, such as balls of all sizes, plastic bowling pins or empty plastic soft drink bottles, nesting bowls, toys that make a noise when they move. Create interesting surfaces for children to negotiate. Ramps and inclines, small platforms (an old table leaf with corners rounded or padded is fun), a set of steps (gate off all but the first two or three steps of a flight of stairs), cushions, and expandable fabric tunnels are possibilities. Simple cardboard boxes to crawl in and out of provide much fun. Create variety in the environment by rearranging the elements—how you combine the platform and the ramp, which balls you make available with which boxes, and the objects you make available.

General Sequence of Gross Motor Skill Development

Tense, jerky movements

Newborns are tense. Their legs and arms are usually drawn up tight and fists are tightly closed. When you place a child under three months on her back, her arm and leg movements are jerky.

Head wobble

At two months the child can move her head from side to side when on her back, but cannot hold her head up when held in a vertical position. Adults need to support the child's head when she is lifted and held.

Head control

When she is a few months old, the child can hold her head up for a few seconds when placed on her stomach. The head will bob up and down as she tries to gain control and see more of the world around her. Gradually, with arms propped under her, she will hold more and more of her sternum up, lifting her shoulders off the floor. She might even start to reach for things a few inches in front of her.

Kicking

Kicking and thrusting legs when on her back is a favorite activity. Even though a baby cannot hold her head up when placed on her stomach, she can propel herself when angry just by kicking and digging feet into the mattress of the crib.

Twisting and stretching

When placed on her back, a three- or four-month-old baby will start twisting her torso, and stretching her legs from one side to the other. The child gains more control of the limbs and can start to make more intentional and less jerky moves.

Hanging onto feet

About the time the child gains the fine motor control to open and close her hands in the right sequence to grab things and aim at objects to grasp, she discovers her feet when lying on her back and hangs onto them. Watch the baby's delight at this whole body sensation.

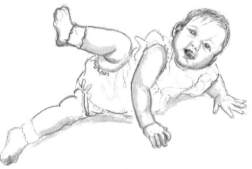

Rolling over

An infant around the age of six months is often quite startled when she suddenly rolls over while stretching a leg to one side and reaching for an interesting object. Usually, but not always, she rolls from back to stomach first. Now the child can hold her head up and look around, amazed. Soon, when placed on her back, she will purposely roll herself over to her stomach. Once on her stomach, more twisting and turning occurs. One leg goes off to the side and straightens and her body tips to the side. The child is learning to gain control of this leverage, and before long, she rolls back onto her back. Now watch the fun! Placed on her back on a clean floor with interesting objects around, the child will experiment endlessly with body mechanics, moving this way and that.

Scootching

A decidedly unscientific term, because it is very imprecise, scootching happens between about six to eight months of age, ushering the child into the "mobile infant" category. Babies "scootch" in all different ways, inventing their own fashion of propelling themselves from one area to another. Some babies even roll from one end of the room to the other. Many babies like to do the "army crawl," where they use elbows and knees to haul their bodies along, stomach on the ground.

Crawling

Most babies learn to crawl with abdomen off the floor between eight and eleven months. At first, some have difficulty getting into forward gear and actually crawl backward, to their frustration. Some children crawl with stiff back legs. Most manage a cross-lateral movement of arms and legs. Some can attain amazing speed!

Sitting independently

Once the child is crawling around, sitting happens very quickly. The child may be on all fours, reach for something, turn, reach for something else and suddenly she's upright with both hands free. What an exciting development! Curiosity usually has a new burst now because the child can see farther away and has both of those busy hands available to grab, hold, and manipulate things. It's amazing how children learn to reposition themselves in a sitting position, switching their legs around, twisting and turning, all the time maintaining their own balance.

Simple Steps

Pulling to standing

Stabilize the furniture! Children have a very strong drive to become vertical at the end of the first year. The child will crawl over to a piece of furniture like a couch, kneel, and reach both hands up to the top. Then, with great persistence, she will learn how to position her legs under herself to be able to straighten them and stand up. The child will usually look around with amazement when this is first accomplished to see if you noticed.

Cruising

Once the child can pull to stand up, side steps start and the child moves along, holding onto anything available like chairs, walls, even the family dog. The child doesn't know that a tablecloth is not stable, so make sure anything that hangs down gets tucked away.

Down and up

Once she can stand while holding on, the child will see something she wants on the floor, squat down to pick it up, and stand up again.

Standing alone

After much experience walking while holding on, the child will let go of the support and find herself standing out in space, with nothing but her own balance to keep her vertical. Often the child isn't really conscious of doing this and lasts only a second or two on her feet. That first step isn't far away!

Toddling

A child gains the developmental status of "toddler" when she can stand on two feet and "toddle" without holding on. This is a wide-stance, choppy gait. You may notice the toddler will hold something in each hand while walking independently, as though she is still holding onto something. Eventually the toddle turns into a walk. The child learns to bend knees and elbows and swing arms.

Squatting

She can also go from an independent standing position to a squatting position and back up again.

Running

The child soon learns to run, before she learns to stop! Gradually the skills of turning, slowing down, and stopping are incorporated into the child's moving behaviors.

Climbing

Even before the child is standing alone, and often before she develops an awareness of danger, she learns to thrust that chubby leg up and over something. Crawling up and down stairs, climbing on a small climber, and climbing on furniture are all compulsive movements at the end of the first year. Create safe opportunities, supervise well, and help only as needed.

A toddler is a bundle of energy, constantly "on the go" until she drops. Activities involving the large muscles of legs, arms, and torso are what dominate a toddler's interest. She is "driven" to run, jump, climb, push, and thrust. A wise adult plans the environment and routines of the day to allow for as much varied physical activity as possible. Work with these emerging skills.

Toddlers have an internal motivation to practice their new skills over and over again. These new human beings don't yet have the judgment to realize when they might get hurt. So your challenge is to give children many opportunities to move in as many ways as possible, without hurting themselves. Falls and bumps are inevitable, but good planning and a watchful eye will go a long way to minimize the damage.

Floor Mirror

2 MONTHS +

This is also a social activity—infants are interested in faces.

Materials

unbreakable mirror

To Do

- Place the mirror on the floor in a horizontal position.
- Spread a clean blanket on the floor in front of the mirror and place the child on it, on her stomach, head facing the mirror.

Observations

- When the child lifts her head, does she notice the face in the mirror? Is it interesting to her?
- Does she lift her head repeatedly to see the face?
- Does she reach out to try to touch the face?

Safety

- Make sure the mirror is unbreakable and cannot tip over onto the child. Supervise very closely.

Emerging Skill

The child gains practice lifting her head and using torso and arm muscles.

Dangling Beach Toy 4 MONTHS +

Materials

inflated beach toy such as beach ball or plastic animal
string

To Make

- Tie the string to the inflated toy and hang it from the ceiling so that the toy dangles about six inches (fifteen centimeters) above the floor in the Play Area.

To Do

- Place the child near the hanging toy.

Observations

- Does the child notice that the toy swings when she bumps it?
- Does she give it more pushes?
- Is she surprised when it comes back and bumps into her?

Safety

- Make sure the ball is securely attached to the ceiling or other part of the room.

More Ideas

- Hang stuffed animals to push back and forth.
- Hang object outside from a tree limb or building overhang.

Emerging Skill

The child uses large muscles to explore cause and effect. If she pushes something back and forth with another person, this becomes a social activity.

Fun Things to Kick

4 MONTHS +

Materials

objects that make interesting noises when kicked, such as
- manufactured crib gym
- safe small toys suspended from wooden or plastic rod
- hanging beach toys, as described on page 91

To Do

■ Place the child on her back on the floor. Suspend the crib gym or toys within reach of her feet. Jiggle them a little.

Observations

■ Does the child kick out at the dangling objects?
■ Is she interested in watching them move?
■ Does she repeat kicks?

More Ideas

■ Hang different things from time to time.

Emerging Skill

This activity encourages babies to kick at surfaces placed at their feet.

Under-Inflated Beach Toys

6 MONTHS +

The child feels powerful when she is able to pick up something that is very large.

Materials

large plastic inflatable beach toy such as a beach ball, swim ring, or inflated animal

To Do

■ Blow up these toys so that they are still soft. This makes them easier for small hands to grasp.
■ Place the child on the floor with these toys.

Observations

■ What does the child do with these large, bright objects?
■ Does she crawl over them?
■ Does she pick them up with two hands or with one hand?

Simple Steps

■ Does she roll on her back and drag them on top of herself?

Safety

■ Do not use balloons, which can pop and cause choking if the child puts the rubber in her mouth.

More Ideas

■ Fully inflate the beach toys from time to time. They will act differently as the child plays with them.

Emerging Skill

The child will practice various motor skills as she picks up these large, light objects.

Let's Make That Move 6 MONTHS +

The child is learning all about cause and effect, a cognitive discovery.

Materials

safe objects that move in interesting ways when bumped or pushed, such as plastic bowling pins from a game, plastic eggs, metal juice can tops, jar lids, plastic bowls, roly-poly toys, balls

To Do

■ Place the child on the floor where she can move freely and scatter these objects around the child.

Observations

■ Is the child interested in these things?
■ Does she attempt to make them move?
■ How does the child get from one place to another?

Safety

■ Make sure all objects are too large to choke on and have no sharp edges.

More Ideas

■ Put different objects out from day to day to keep interest high.

Emerging Skill

These interesting objects motivate the child to move across the floor and practice ways of getting from one place to another.

The child is gaining experience with cognitive concepts of space and size.

Materials

moveable furniture
large boxes
blanket or sheet

To Make

■ Arrange the furniture, boxes, and blanket to create interesting spaces for the child to crawl in and out of.

To Do

■ Simply place the child on the floor and let her go.

Observations

■ Does the child notice the new arrangement?
■ Does she move in and explore these new spaces?
■ How does she get there? What does she do?

Safety

■ Make sure nothing could hurt the child if it falls over. Anchor heavy pieces of furniture securely. Stay close in case the child gets stuck or frightened.

More Ideas

■ If the child gets stuck, instead of just rescuing the child, move in close and help the child figure out how to get out by herself.

Simple Steps

Emerging Skill

The child can practice all types of motor skills moving in and around these spaces.

Dish Tub Seats

8 MONTHS +

Cognitive learning occurs as the child learns about spaces and places.

Materials

rubber or plastic dish tub

To Do

■ An empty dish tub is inviting to a child who can crawl and sit unaided.
■ Just put it in the environment and see what the child does with it.

Observations

■ Does the child climb into the dish tub and sit in it?
■ Does she ever turn it over and sit on it?

More Ideas

■ Provide several dish tubs and see if the child makes a train of them. Suggest giving stuffed animals a ride.

Emerging Skill

The child may feel secure sitting in the tub and hanging onto the sides. It defines a space.

Box Tunnels

8 MONTHS +

The child gains physical experience with "inside," "outside," and "through," which are concepts of space.

Materials

several large, empty cardboard cartons
masking tape

To Make

■ Remove the ends of the boxes and tape them end to end to create a long tunnel.

To Do

■ Simply place the child on the floor near the tunnel.
■ You could also place a doll or small toy inside the tunnel.

Observations

- Does the child move near the tunnel and investigate it?
- Does she go inside?
- How does she move?
- Try peaking in at the child from the other end.

More Ideas

- Line boxes with different textures.
- Connect boxes to go around corners and up and down small inclines.
- Bring the box tunnels outside.

Emerging Skill

The child will practice a variety of gross motor skills, especially crawling and creeping.

Stocking Balls

8 MONTHS +

Materials

old stockings or pantyhose
fabric dye (optional)
scissors
polyester fiberfill stuffing

To Make

- Dye the pantyhose different colors before making balls, if desired.
- Tie a knot at the bottom of one leg.
- Put in a large handful of stuffing and pack it down to where the knot is.
- Tie another knot above it.
- Cut the stocking below the lower knot and above the upper knot. Continue making several more in the same way. These can be machine washed and tumble dried.

To Do

- Present these to the child to throw.

Observations

- Does the child chase the same ball to throw again or choose other balls nearby?
- Does the child seem surprised by where the ball ends up?

More Ideas

- Put a large number of these stocking balls in a laundry basket or large box in the middle of the room. Invite several of your older infants to throw these together, perhaps aiming for a corner or another large container. When all the balls have been thrown at the "target" spot, throw them back to the original container again.
- You can also make balls by stuffing socks or balling up two socks together.

Emerging Skill

The child practices throwing. This becomes a social activity if many children are throwing at the same time.

Shoebox Train

 10 MONTHS +

Materials

several cardboard shoeboxes
string

To Make

- Punch a hole in the ends of the shoeboxes and tie them together, end to end, to make a little train. Leave a string about ten inches (25 centimeters) long at the end of the last box for the child to pull on.

To Do

- Let the child fill the boxes with small toys and drag the train across the floor.

Observations

- Does the child drag the train spontaneously, without coaching from you?
- How far does she drag it?
- Does she fill and empty the compartments?

More Ideas

- Also offer the lids to the boxes so the child can cover up what is in the compartments.
- Chant "choo, choo" as the child drags the train.
- A more permanent version could be made with plastic shoeboxes.

Emerging Skill

The child will walk along to pull the train and will see how pulling something can make it come closer.

Collection of Balls 10 MONTHS +

Materials

balls of all kinds such as small, medium, and large rubber balls; a beach ball; a football; tennis balls; cloth balls
large container such as a laundry basket

To Do

- You might have one or two of the balls around at all times, but sometimes bring out the whole collection and let the children play with them. The more, the better!

Simple Steps

Observations

- Watch what she does with the balls. Does she push, bump, roll, kick, and throw them?
- Does she crawl after the same ball or go to another?

More Ideas

- Combine balls with boxes to put the balls into and take them out of.
- Interact with the children. Push the balls back or "parallel play" using the balls yourself beside the children as they play.

Emerging Skill

While she practices various gross motor skills, the child is learning that the angle and force of her own actions affect the balls in different ways.

How About a Push? 12 MONTHS +

Materials

large grocery cartons, or dish tubs
dolls and stuffed animals

To Do

- Let the child put the dolls and stuffed animals in the boxes and push them around the room.

Observations

- Does the child do this spontaneously, or does it take a suggestion from you?
- Does the child prefer to play with the boxes in different ways, like climbing in herself?

More Ideas

- Paint "headlights," "wheels," and "doors" on the boxes to suggest cars.

Emerging Skill

The child feels powerful as she makes something move, and must practice balance and walking. As she takes on roles and pretends, she is engaging in dramatic play.

Materials

floor space

To Do

- Lie down on the floor with a child and assume the same position as the child.
- Then let the child do different movements and poses, and try to imitate them.

Observations

- Does the child notice that you are imitating her?
- Does she seem to be getting pleasure from this fact?

More Ideas

- Let the child do something with an object like a ball or toy and you try to make exactly the same thing happen. Involve other children in this game of imitation to make it a social experience.

Emerging Skill

This is tremendously empowering to young children, especially children with motor challenges. They are the boss. They are making something happen. Their self-esteem is boosted. They also learn a little about taking turns. After they do something, they have to wait for you to do it. Then it is their turn again.

Simple Steps

Materials

"feet on floor" riding toys
furniture dividers or large cardboard boxes
masking tape

To Make

■ Tape together the cardboard boxes or line up the furniture dividers to make two long "walls" for the child to ride between.

To Do

■ See if this long "road" space is enticing to the child and if she automatically rides the vehicle down it.
■ Perhaps make a large circle instead of a straight road.
■ Leave some "doors" so the child doesn't feel trapped inside and can come and go.

Observations

■ Does the child pay attention to this arrangement and use it spontaneously, or does she need the suggestion from you?

More Ideas

■ Arrange this outside as well as inside.
■ Put tape or chalk markings on the floor or sidewalk.

Emerging Skill

The child may use riding toys more and begin to develop a sense of direction.

Hoop-Ti-Do!   16 MONTHS +

Materials

plastic hoops in various colors

To Do

■ This is a good material to bring out when you sense that you need to introduce something new, or when free play time seems to be deteriorating.
■ Watch what children do with the hoops and describe their actions.
■ They might stand inside one, pick it up, hold it and turn around, put it on the floor and jump in and out of it, etc.

Gross Motor Development

Observations

■ What do children do with the hoops if you just put them out, saying nothing?

More Ideas

■ Put the hoop around both yourself and a child. "Now we're *both* inside the hoop."

■ Let the children hold onto the outside of the hoop and sing "Ring Around the Rosie" as they go around together.

■ Tie the hoops together, let the children stand inside a hoop, holding the hoop, and make a train that can go chugging around the room or playground.

Emerging Skill

While children are exploring spaces, they learn a little about inside, outside, round, and circle. They get ideas from each other, gaining some social experience as well as vocabulary reinforcement.

Animal Slippers

16 MONTHS +

Materials

large, fuzzy slippers with animal heads on the toes, or make some using old stuffed animals and slippers

To Do

■ Toddlers love to slip their feet, shoes and all, inside these soft slippers and walk around the room.

Observations

■ What does the child do differently with the slippers on?

More Ideas

■ Find some music that reflects the animals on the slippers (such as "Old MacDonald Had a Farm" or "Five Little Ducks") and encourage the children to dance, rocking side to side.

Emerging Skill

Toddlers love experimenting with different ways to move. The slippers cause them to take big steps and create just a slight challenge for their balance. They also have a way of "transforming" the child, giving a little practice in role playing.

Haul It 18 MONTHS +

Materials

collection of containers with handles such as lunch boxes, baskets, shopping bags, purses, old briefcases, rubber tote boxes, plastic pails

To Do

■ Toddlers love to "haul" things! Let them put all kinds of toys and other objects in these containers and carry them around. You will find that adding some interesting new containers to your environment will give new life to old toys.

More Ideas

■ You might put a large box or laundry basket at one end of the room. Let the children use the containers with handles to carry things to the box and dump them in. Then they could push or pull the large box or basket back across the room.

Emerging Skill

Children gain "physical knowledge" about objects as they carry them and feel their weight and size. They learn a little about what can fit into what (a cognitive skill). They might learn some vocabulary about inside and out, and they use large muscles to carry the objects.

Materials

objects that cause no harm if thrown, such as plastic dish scrubbers, small stuffed animals, cloth covered foam blocks, and other soft toys
large box or container

To Do

■ When you see the child spontaneously throwing things, instead of reprimanding her, say, "Oh, that's not for throwing, but here is a whole box of things that are okay to throw."
■ Give the box to the child.
■ Toss some of the objects back to the child.

Observations

■ Is the child interested in throwing the new objects?
■ Does the child seem to experiment with the process?

Safety

■ Make sure none of the objects could hurt another child if they got hit. Try to position the child so throws are not likely to interfere with other children.

More Ideas

■ Hang up some aluminum foil, a cookie sheet, or a pizza pan that might make an interesting "gong" sound if a thrown object hits it.

Emerging Skill

The child practices throwing objects, watching what happens when she moves her hand in a certain way, releasing an object at a certain time. With your involvement, this becomes a social activity.

A Hanging Bar 20 MONTHS +

Materials

wooden closet rod or a chinning bar and the hardware to install it.
cushioning material, such as old couch cushions, an old mattress, or thick pillows

To Make

- Find a space where this can be installed without disrupting traffic, such as at the back of a narrow space or in a closet with the door removed. Or, perhaps you can figure out a way to install a chinning bar in a doorway, but make sure it can be removed easily. Place the bar at a height so that children must reach up and fully extend their arms to grasp it when they are standing on cushions. Place cushions underneath.

To Do

- Let children reach up and grasp the bar and then hang from it. *Important:* see safety note.

Observations

- What do they do with their feet?
- Do they use their abdominal muscles and raise their legs?
- Do they like to do this with a partner? Do they get ideas from each other?

Safety

- Let the children chose this activity and manage it on their own. You should not have to lift them up to reach the bar. They should have control of the process. Never put a child on a rod to hang where she cannot reach the floor safely if she chooses to let go.

Emerging Skill

This activity gives children a rare opportunity to stretch their bodies and use torso muscles. It is an excellent strength-building activity. Children enjoy hanging on the rod and some even pull up their knees.

Gross Motor Development

Materials

variety of empty food boxes and containers • large ball

To Do

■ Show the child how to stack the boxes as a target for the ball.
■ Then invite the child to roll the ball to knock over the target boxes.
■ Do not draw a starting or "foul" line or create any other rules.
■ Let the child decide where to stand.
■ You could act as "pin setter," but the child might enjoy setting the target up again and deciding how to group the containers as much as knocking them over. Don't get into score-keeping or any type of competition between children.

Observations

■ What variations does the child come up with on her own?
■ Does the child ever set this up spontaneously?

More Ideas

■ Give the child a variety of balls to choose from or let the child try rolling other objects instead of a ball, such as a toy car.
■ Children could enjoy playing this side by side, each with things to knock over rather than "taking turns."

Emerging Skill

The child will gain all sorts of "physical knowledge" about objects as she rearranges things in space and experiments with the force and direction of the ball. This can be a good "redirection" activity if a child is "crashing cars" in inappropriate places.

Simple Steps

Great Big Blocks

Materials

large fabric or vinyl-covered foam blocks

To Do

- Toddlers love handling these blocks. They might line them up and ride on them, and later they might try to stack them.
- You probably won't have to give any direction.
- Later you can be the "building assistant" by handing the child blocks, etc.
- Ask the child what her plans are rather than just taking over.

Observations

- What does the child do with these without any suggestions from you? Does she line them up end to end? Does she stack them and knock them down? Does she lift and carry them?

More Ideas

- Find boxes of all different sizes. Let the children help you wad up newspaper and stuff it inside of the boxes until the boxes are completely full. Tape the lids or flaps down on the box. Cover with self-adhesive paper (optional) for decoration and added durability.

Emerging Skill

These large "blocks" are relatively light. The toddler feels powerful as she lifts them and stacks them, and she will enjoy knocking them down again.

Jumping on a Mattress

Materials

old box spring mattress
contour sheet to cover, and keep clean

To Do

- Place the mattress on the floor away from other furniture.
- Let the children jump up and down on it.
- You could sit nearby and chant, "Jump, jump, jump."

Observations

- Does the child already know how to do this?
- Does she watch other children before trying it?
- How is her balance?
- What is her facial expression?

Safety

■ Limit the number of children on the mattress at one time to no more than two, and stay close to intervene if it gets too wild, or if you think children might bump into each other.

More Ideas

■ Older two-year-olds could try holding hands and jumping at the same time.

Emerging Skill

This is fun exercise for leg muscles and challenges children's balance skills.

Simple Steps

Chapter 5

Let Me Think About It

Cognitive Development

Cognitive development involves activities that promote thinking skills, enabling children to figure out how the world works and how things are organized. Infants, toddlers, and two-year-olds are like "little scientists" engaged in endless experimentation as they learn to use tools, make things happen, and find out about the physical properties of things around them. All this leads to their ability to solve problems and later engage in more abstract thinking.

Sensory Exploration

When very young infants are awake and alert, they enjoy looking at contrasting patterns and brightly colored objects. They are learning to use their senses to find out about the world. They also learn to turn toward the source of a sound. They engage in sensory exploration when they put their hands in their mouths and suck on them. When children are allowed to lie on a clean floor with interesting objects near by, they will move toward something that attracts their attention, touch it, and examine it in different ways. When children can sit up and crawl, they can spot things at a greater distance. They move across space to reach the desired object, learning to negotiate different angles and get around obstacles in the process.

Cognitive Development

In the first year and a half of life, children have a powerful urge to find out everything about the objects in their environment. "Object Hunger" is a very fitting term often applied to this stage because children actively put everything in their mouths. They also have a mental hunger to explore objects. Children gain *physical knowledge* about their world as they touch, turn over, gum, pound, push, and throw objects.

Cause and Effect

Have you seen the gleam in a baby's eye when he discovers that he can make things happen? *Causality* is a very exciting discovery and children experiment with it endlessly. Probably the earliest experience with cause and effect is when a baby discovers that if he cries, someone will appear. This discovery has enormous emotional significance. The child finds out he has power and can trust special people to meet his needs.

When children learn that they can make things happen, they bang objects on the floor to hear interesting sounds. They push something and it moves in an interesting way. "Can I make that happen again?" they ask themselves, and repeat an action over and over again, adding slight variations.

As toddlerhood approaches, children start to do things intentionally. You see repetition. You see goal-oriented behavior. Children explore their power in the world as they switch light switches, flush toilets, honk car horns, and otherwise make things beep and squeak and bounce and roll. Their endless experiments with cause and effect relate to the later development of problem-solving skills.

Using Tools

In infancy and toddlerhood children learn to use tools of all types. An important "tool" is an adult. Infants quickly learn to use adults to get their needs met, whether it is to get fed or to bring a toy within reach. As time goes on, they also learn some basic "mechanics," such as how to use levers to switch things on and off, strings to pull things, small hammers to pound, and ramps to slide objects. Shhh! Physicist at work!

Object Permanence

In the second half of his first year, a child learns object permanence—the fact that objects and people continue to exist even when they cannot be seen. At first, if you hide an interesting toy that a six- or seven-month-old has been looking at, he will simply look away and seem to forget it was there. Later on you will notice him staring briefly at the spot where the object disappeared. Then comes the moment around eight months or so, when the child uncovers the hidden object, indicating that he was able to retain its mental image. Endless variations of peek-a-boo ensue as the child makes objects disappear and reappear. Then the child becomes fascinated with containers that open and close. He loves crawling behind barriers and back out again, opening and shutting cabinet doors, sticking things in holes, and dropping things over the side of a table or highchair tray.

Size, Shape, Space

In their random explorations of objects and their environment, children find out about the relationships of shapes and spaces. Some things fit inside other things. Combining objects to see what fits where is an early interest. Infants and toddlers get stuck a lot as they crawl under and around things, using their bodies for spatial experiments. These experiences form the necessary foundations for later understanding of mathematical concepts of space, size, and quantity.

Using Symbols

Children start to notice that certain things represent other things. A toy telephone represents that "thing" he has seen his daddy use. A little car with a steering wheel represents that "thing" he gets in each morning. Pictures and photographs have a relationship to things and people he has seen in his environment. A certain combination of sounds (a word) stands for some object or action.

Math Concepts

When children have had a lot of experience playing with symbols like toys and looking at pictures of things they know, they are better able to use more abstract symbols like letters and numbers later on. Exposing toddlers and two-year-olds to number symbols won't hurt them, but using number words and concepts in children's real experiences will be more meaningful. "I'm giving everyone *two* crackers." "This glass holds *more* juice than that one." Toddlers and two-year-olds don't have a clear understanding of quantity. They rely on their senses rather than logic. You've probably seen a two-year-old protest that his friend has "more" crackers than he does because the friend's cracker has split into two or three pieces and takes up more space on the plate. Likewise a child will be convinced that there is more juice in a tall, skinny glass than a short, wide one. Only lots of direct experience pouring liquids back and forth and playing with substances like sand and playdough will bring them to a real understanding. Counting books are not particularly useful with children under three. Instead, allow children to hear you think out loud and use counting in everyday life. "Let's see. How many of us are here today? One, two, three, four, five, six. If Sherry arrives, that will be seven. That means we will need seven sandwiches so everyone has one." Helping set the table is a math exercise.

Concept of Time

Children's perception of time is a very different reality from our own. To say "Mommy will be back soon" when a parent will not return for several hours is no comfort to a crying toddler. Gradually hearing the words used in context, toddlers and two-year-olds learn what soon, later, yesterday, today, and tomorrow mean. Use these time words in your daily routine to make them more meaningful. "Soon we will be finished with lunch and then we can snuggle down for a nice nap." "We'll go outside later, after snack." To practice using these words in a meaningful context, try doing a three-day project, like painting rocks one day, washing the paint off the second day, and painting them a different color the third day.

Three Important Cognitive Skills

Imitation

We see the youngest babies imitate the sounds and expressions of a parent or caregiver in that lovely cooing dialog. Later other gestures are imitated—clapping hands when they accomplish something grand like sitting up, pretending to talk on a toy telephone, pointing their fingers at a sound, wiggling to lively music. "I can do that too" seems to be the unspoken message. The development of language—speech—is the ultimate imitation and is a cognitive development that leads to more abstract thinking.

Curiosity

Curiosity is an *attitude* about being in the world, rather than a "skill." Young children are programmed to be curious, to want to find out about all the things they encounter in their daily lives. The wonder of it all! Many parents and caregivers of infants have said that watching the curiosity of babies reminds them of what a wonderful, varied world we live in. Model curiosity yourself. Show children your own interest in things that are new and different.

Classifying

As the child gains thousands of experiences handling objects, he starts to classify and sort things, noticing particular attributes. This all relates to later learning of mathematics and reading and the ability to engage in problem solving. But *first* the child must handle lots of different materials.

Very little of the learning described above can take place if a child is confined to an infant seat, crib, swing, sling, walker, bounce chair, highchair, or other device. An important tool in any child's development is a rich, safe environment that a child can explore to exercise his curiosity. The next time you become exasperated with children crawling everywhere, dumping tubs of toys, getting into low cupboards, stop for a moment and celebrate their drive to explore. They are normal, curious, developing human beings. Instead of thinking about how to confine children, challenge yourself to give them even more interesting objects and situations to explore with their whole minds and bodies.

Remember that you don't "teach" cognitive skills. These skills develop while the child has hundreds of casual experiences that allow him to draw conclusions and practice variations.

See-Through Shake Toys

5 MONTHS +

Materials

small plastic soft drink bottles with
   screw tops
hot glue gun or super glue
interesting objects to put inside such
   as buttons, colored sand, beads,
   small pompoms

To Make

- ■ Soak off labels in soapy water. (Rub mineral oil on glue residue to help remove it.)
- ■ Put one or more interesting materials inside.
- ■ Glue top on bottle securely.

To Do

- ■ Place one or more of these near the child.

Observations

- ■ Does he pick them up?
- ■ Does he notice the objects move and make noise inside the bottles?
- ■ Does he shake the bottles to repeat the effect?

Safety

- ■ Check frequently to make sure the tops are glued on securely.

More Ideas

- ■ Use all types of safe containers, such as plastic bottles of varying shapes, tin coffee and tea boxes, empty spice boxes.

Cognitive Development

■ Collect many containers and put them in a large box. Let the child reach in and choose the ones he wants to play with.

Emerging Skill

The child explores cause and effect. This is also a sensory activity.

Vision Bottles

5 MONTHS +

Materials

transparent sturdy plastic bottles with screw tops
water
food coloring
mineral oil
materials to put inside, such as small pieces of yarn, beads, plastic glitter, marbles
hot glue gun or super glue

To Make

■ Put a liquid, or combination of liquids, inside the bottle to fill completely.
■ Add some of the interesting materials, as desired.
■ Glue the top on securely.

To Do

■ Place one or more of these bottles where the child can get to them.

Observations

■ Does the child pick up, bump, or roll the bottle?
■ Does he notice the motion inside and try to make it happen again?

Safety

■ Make sure the top remains glued on securely and the bottle does not leak.

More Ideas

■ Fill the bottle about half full with colored water and add dish detergent. Glue the top on. The child will enjoy shaking it to make bubbles inside.

Emerging Skill

The child explores cause and effect creating interesting movements in the bottle. This is also a sensory experience as the child focuses on interesting visual effects, and a fine motor activity, giving the child something to grasp and move in different ways.

Simple Steps

Noisy Dumping

Materials

numerous metal juice can lids
basket or other container

To Do

- Simply place the basket filled with juice can lids (the more the better) where the child is playing, preferably on a hard floor.
- Later, you could also help the child put the juice can lids back in the basket so he can repeat this loud action.

Observations

- Does the child dump the basket?
- Is he delighted at the loud noise?
- Does he go after the rolling lids and put them back in the basket?
- Does he try to repeat it?

More Ideas

- Substitute other safe, noisy objects.

Emerging Skill

The child explores cause and effect. He also gains fine motor practice and gross motor practice if he crawls after the lids.

Hide the Teddy

Materials

teddy bear or other large stuffed animal

To Do

- Partially hide the teddy bear, leaving a large part sticking out.
- Ask, "Where's Teddy?"
- See if the child can find it.
- Then, with great drama say, "Oh! There's Teddy! You found him!"

Observations

- Is the child able to follow your cues to play the game?
- Can the child find the bear with only a bit of the bear visible?

More Ideas

- Hide different objects.
- Hide the bear under a blanket or scarf so its shape is plainly visible.

Cognitive Development

Emerging Skill

When part of an object is visible, the child will look for the whole object and relate the part to the whole. This is also a language activity and a social activity.

What's Under the Flap?

8 MONTHS +

Materials

pictures of babies, pets, or other familiar objects cut from magazines

clear contact paper

duct tape

fabric pieces to go over pictures

fiberboard

drill

sandpaper

To Make

■ Have the fiberboard or other light board material cut to the desired size and shape.

■ Drill two holes in the top corners of the board so you can hang it.

■ Sand and round edges.

■ Cut the contact paper one inch (three centimeters) larger in size than the pictures.

■ Use to adhere the pictures to the board.

■ Cut the fabric so it is the same size as the pictures. Use the duct tape to attach the fabric flaps along the tops of the pictures.

■ Hang this on the wall or on the back of a shelf at children's eye level.

To Do

■ Let the child enjoy lifting the fabric flaps to see the pictures underneath.

Observations

■ Does the child discover this on his own or do you need to show him once?

■ Does he repeat the action over and over again?

More Ideas

■ Put an unbreakable mirror under one of the flaps.

■ Put photos of other children or of family members under the flaps.

Simple Steps

Emerging Skill

The child learns about object permanence. If you name the pictures the child uncovers, he is learning language as well.

Peek-a-Boo

8 MONTHS +

Materials

blanket or towel (optional)

To Do

■ Play classic peek-a-boo. Use a blanket, towel, or just your hands to cover and uncover your face, chanting "Peek-a-boo!"

Observations

■ Watch the child's reaction. Is there confusion? Delight?
■ Does the child squeal or try to say "peek-a-boo?"
■ Does the child imitate your gestures?

More Ideas

■ Pop up and down from behind a piece of furniture.
■ Follow the child's lead if the child initiates the game.
■ Give the child the blanket or towel to cover himself.

Emerging Skill

The child sees a favorite person appear and disappear, learning that someone or something still exists when not visible. When the child hides himself, he is taking control, feeling personal power. This is also a social game.

Scarf Peek-a-Boo

8 MONTHS +

Materials

sheer fabric

To Do

■ Let the child cover his face with the sheer fabric and uncover it to say "peek-a-boo."
■ Infants like this because they can still see through it.

Observations

■ Watch what the child does with the scarf.
■ Does he need a demonstration from you?

Safety

- Be careful that the fabric is not so sheer that it could block the child's eyes or nostrils when he inhales.

More Ideas

- Hang a sheer "curtain" from a low, sturdy rod that the child can stand behind.
- Find scarves of different colors so the child can make his world change colors.

Emerging Skill

This activity gives children more chances to experiment with object permanence. It's also a social activity.

Compartments

Materials

egg carton or plastic ice cube tray
small toys that can fit inside compartments such as table blocks, plastic eggs, little people, and animals

To Make

- Put a toy in each compartment and place it near the child.

To Do

- Let the child simply explore the toy.

Observations

- Does the child remove the toys and then put them back again?
- Does he try to put other things in the compartment?
- Does the child pay attention to the compartments at all?

Safety

- Make sure toys are safe and too large to choke on.

More Ideas

- Attach a string to the ice cube tray to make a simple pull toy.

Simple Steps

Emerging Skill

The child fits objects inside each other, becoming conscious of size relationships. This is also a math game of one-to-one correspondence.

Chip Can Scarves

Materials

empty potato chip can, or
    other similar container
as many light scarves as you
    can stuff into the box
needle and thread
scissors

To Make

- Sew the scarves together, end to end.
- Cut a hole, about the size of a dime, in the plastic lid of the can.
- Stuff the scarves into the can.
- Stick the end of the scarf chain through the hole in the lid, and put the lid on the can.

To Do

- No instructions necessary! A young toddler will love pulling the scarves out of the can.

Observations

- How many times will the child repeat the activity after you stuff the scarves back in again while he watches?
- See if you can interest him in stuffing them back in.

More Ideas

- An empty diaper wipes container works well for this.
- Stuff unattached scarves into an empty tissue box. Children will love pulling them out one by one.

Emerging Skill

Finding things hidden inside a box is a favorite activity, reinforcing children's recent learning that things still exist even when they can't see them (object permanence). They also gain fine motor practice grasping the scarves.

Cognitive Development

Materials

ball
chair, bookshelf, or other piece of furniture the child cannot see through

To Do

- Roll the ball back and forth with the child to get the child's interest in the game.
- Then, with the child watching, roll the ball behind a chair or other visual barrier.

Observations

- Does the child anticipate that the ball will come out at the other side of the barrier, or does he look for it where it disappeared?
- Does this eventually change with experience?

Safety

- Make sure any barrier is stable and could not fall over on the child.

More Ideas

- Use other toys that roll such as little cars. You could create a "screen" or use a flannel board to roll the car behind.

Emerging Skill

The child learns to imagine the continued motion of a hidden object. It is also a social game.

Hinged Boxes That Open and Close

10 MONTHS +

Materials

boxes with hinged lids, such as lunch boxes or cigar boxes
small toys (too large to choke on)

To Do

- Put one or more small toys in the box and close the lid.
- Give it to the child.

Observations

- Does the child open the lid without prompting from you?
- Does he take the toy out and put it back in again and close the lid again?
- Does he repeat this action?

Simple Steps

More Ideas

■ Use boxes with loose lids, like shoeboxes.

Emerging Skill

The child learns about object permanence and size, shape, and space.

A Place for the Animals

Materials

compartmentalized shoe bag
(door hanger type)
small stuffed animals and dolls
to fit in compartments
rubber dish tub, basket, or other
large container

To Make

■ Hang the shoe bag where a "cruising" child can get at it and reach all the compartments.

■ Put the dish tub with all the small stuffed animals in front of the shoe bag.

To Do

■ Say nothing. Simply place the child in the area where the materials are.

■ If the child does not respond after a period of time, let the child see you "playing" with the stuffed animals, and then putting them in the pockets of the shoe bag.

Observations

■ Does the child notice the shoe bag and the tub of animals?

■ Does he eventually put the animals in the pockets without any prompting from you?

■ If not, after viewing you do this, does he then imitate what you have done?

■ Does it seem interesting to him?

■ Does he repeat the action?

■ Does he find other things to put in the pockets?

Safety

■ Use washable stuffed animals and wash and dry them from time to time, especially when you see that children have put them in their mouths.

Cognitive Development

More Ideas

- Other small toys could be substituted for the stuffed animals.
- Find other things with pockets for the child to fill and empty.

Emerging Skill

The child experiences relationships of size and space as well as the math concept of one-to-one correspondence.

Napkin Rings

10 MONTHS +

Materials

variety of safe napkin rings (enough to fill a shoebox if possible)
accessories such as short, thick pieces of rope; short, thick dowels; and colorful scarves

To Do

- This is a "toy" that children use in many different ways as they develop.
- Young children enjoy grasping these interesting objects, turning them over and over and mouthing them. When dropped, the rings roll in interesting ways.
- They are fun to look through.
- Children also enjoy hanging them on all sorts of things that stick up or out, like the ends of chairs or low coat hooks. Toddlers enjoy stringing them onto colorful scarves, rope, dowels, pieces of plastic tubing, etc.
- Although this activity should be chosen and directed by the child, you might occasionally describe what the child is doing, giving words to the concepts he is exploring. "You are sticking the black scarf through the red ring."

Observations

- Observe what the child does with the different materials over time.

Safety

- Make sure rings are too large to choke on and have no parts that could come off.

More Ideas

- Find similar items such as plastic bracelets, metal and rubber canning rings, tissue tubes, key rings, and shower curtain rings. All could be added from time to time for variety.

Emerging Skill

Children are learning the properties of round things—that they can roll away. They explore the idea of inside and outside and spatial relationships as they push objects and scarves through the rings. They also gain a little fine motor practice.

Simple Steps

It's in the Bag

Materials

cloth bag
familiar toys

To Do

■ Put a familiar toy inside the cloth bag so the shape of the toy is visible. Place this near the child.

Observations

■ Is the child's curiosity aroused?
■ Does he look inside the bag and take out the toy?

More Ideas

■ You could bring the bag with the toy over to the child and encourage the child to feel the toy through the bag. Ask, "Do you feel the truck inside the bag?" Then back off and see if the child tries to get the truck out.

Emerging Skill

The child learns to look for hidden objects and relates the shape to the thing.

Turntable Merry-Go-Round

Materials

kitchen turntable or lazy susan
containers such as film canisters,
spray can tops, jar lids
super glue or hot glue gun
small people toys and/or animals

To Make

■ Glue the film canisters, spray can tops, or other containers open side up, on the turntable.

To Do

■ Toddlers love spinning the turntable around and around. They also enjoy putting the little people and animals in the containers to "give them a ride."

Observations

■ Does the child think of other things to give a ride?

Safety

■ Make sure objects are too large to choke on.

More Ideas

■ Make variations with different configurations of containers. For instance, one turntable could have many film canisters glued all around the perimeter. Another one could have all jar lids. Vary the objects you give them to put in the containers.

Emerging Skill

Children learn about cause and effect and about the nature of a circle as objects go around. They may pick up some ideas about what fits into what. Imaginative play is also involved.

Reverse Pull

12 MONTHS +

Materials

peg board back of a shelf
long shoelaces or plastic-coated string
thread spools or large colored beads
paint and paintbrush (optional)

To Make

■ Paint spools different colors, two each.
■ Thread the shoelaces through the pegboard so both ends hang out.
■ Tie spools or beads of matching colors to each end. Do this with several colors.

To Do

■ The child will discover that when he pulls down on one spool, another spool will go up.

Observations

■ Does the child seem to notice that the same color bead goes up?
■ Does the child then grab the bead that went up and pull it down?

Safety

■ Make sure the shelf or peg board panel is well anchored so the child cannot pull it over on himself.

Simple Steps

More Ideas

■ Find other matching items to tie to the ends of the strings, such as two small stuffed animals.

Emerging Skill

Children see that one action causes another to happen, in this case a reverse of direction. It might make them aware of *same* and *different* as well.

Tubes Inside of Tubes

Materials

tubes of various diameters. Possibilities: toilet paper tubes, paper towel tubes, heavier paper roll cores, mailing tubes, PVC pipe of various diameters cut into lengths of about 12" (30 cm), and plastic drinking straws
container to put everything in

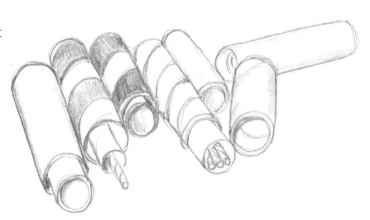

To Do

■ At first, say nothing and just see what the child does with the collection of tubes.
■ See if children spontaneously experiment putting the various tubes inside of each other.
■ Later, if the child demonstrates and talks about what he is doing, sit down and show your interest.
■ Notice with the child that the smaller tubes fit inside the larger cylinders.

More Ideas

■ Let the child have fun sticking things through the tubes. Small cars might go through some. A piece of clothesline might be pushed through. Can the child figure out how to stuff a scarf through a cylinder?

Emerging Skill

■ This is a cognitive activity in which children discover relationships of size and space. They'll also have fun looking through the tubes.

Cognitive Development

Materials

construction paper
animal pictures
clear contact paper or laminating paper
unbreakable baking pans with raised rims
sand

To Make

■ Cut the construction paper to fit exactly into the baking pan.
■ Place animal pictures on the paper and cover, front and back, with the clear, contact paper.

To Do

■ Put the picture in the baking pan and cover it with a layer of sand.
■ Let the child push the sand aside to expose the animal pictures.

Observations

■ Does the child identify the animal, or make an animal sound to match the animal?
■ Does the child enjoy spreading the sand back over the picture to cover it up, and then uncover it again?

More Ideas

■ Use shaving cream instead of sand. Supervise closely.
■ Have a collection of different picture pages to put in the tray on different days.

Emerging Skill

The child is creating his own peek-a-boo game, practicing object permanence by covering and uncovering the pictures. If you name the pictures, you are also developing the child's vocabulary.

Graduated Nesting 14 MONTHS +

Materials

plastic bowls of graduated sizes that nest together

To Do

■ Simply present these nested bowls to the child and see what he does.
■ Do not show him how to nest them or try to correct mistakes.
■ This idea is best learned by discovery.

Simple Steps

Observations

- Does he take the bowls apart and try to put them back together again?
- Does he make mistakes? If so, is he discouraged or does he keep trying?

Safety

- Use only unbreakable materials.

More Ideas

- Instead of presenting them to the child in a nested state, present them separately. See if the child discovers that they nest together.
- Use boxes that can nest and also be stacked.

Emerging Skill

The child becomes aware of properties of size and space as he fits objects inside each other. Fine motor practice occurs as well.

Jar Lids Nesting Toy

14 MONTHS +

Materials

clean jar lids of various sizes that will fit inside each other

To Do

- Let the child experiment and play with these, nesting them and stacking them.

More Ideas

- You could spray paint them (away from the children) so they are all a uniform color.
- Store them in a margarine tub with a lid.

Emerging Skill

The child becomes aware of the relationship of sizes, and what fits where.

Materials

coffee can or large margarine tub with plastic lid
Exacto knife or sharp cutting tool
small toys

To Make

■ Use the cutting tool to cut a round hole about one and a half inches (four centimeters) in diameter in the center of the plastic lid, then put the lid back on the container.

To Do

■ Present the empty container with lid to the child.
■ Place the small toys near by.
■ Say nothing about what to do with the toys.

Observations

■ What does the child do with the materials?
■ Does he feel the hole? Put his hand in it?
■ Does he spontaneously stick the toys through the hole?
■ Does he try to peel off the lid to get the toys back out?

Safety

■ Make sure the can has no sharp edges and that the toys are too large to choke on.

More Ideas

■ Cut an "X" in the lid instead of a round hole.

Emerging skill

The child fits objects inside each other. The child practices fine motor skills as he lines up the toy to fit through the hole and peels off the lid.

Easy Shape Boxes

14 MONTHS +

Materials

two coffee cans with lids
baby food jar lids
old-fashioned wooden clothespins
sharp knife

Simple Steps

To Make

■ If necessary file any sharp edges on the cans.

■ Cut a slot hole in the lid of one can for the baby food jar lids, and a small round hole in the other lid for clothespins.

To Do

■ First let the child play with the cans and their contents separately, simply enjoying sticking the objects through the lid.

■ Later, put both cans, the baby food jar lids, and clothespins in front of the child. Have the lids on the cans.

Observations

■ See if the child knows which object to stick where.

More Ideas

■ Find other objects with distinctive shapes.

■ Cut both hole shapes in the same lid.

Emerging Skill

When cans and lids are played with separately, this is a fine motor activity. If you use them together, this becomes a cognitive activity as the child discovers which object goes into which hole.

Slot Box
14 MONTHS +

Materials

shoebox with lid
metal baby food jar lids
sharp knife

To Make

■ Cut a slot in the lid of the shoebox just the right width and length to fit the lids through.

To Do

■ Probably no introduction is needed. If the child does not know what to do with this activity, show him how to make the lids go through the slot to drop into the box.

■ The child will enjoy sticking all the lids through and then dumping them back out again.

More Ideas

■ Use juice can lids instead of jar lids.

■ Make "mailboxes" and let the children put junk mail and cards through the slot.

Store toys with many pieces, such as toddler plastic blocks, in a box with a lid that has a hole in it. Children will enjoy putting the pieces back in the box.

Emerging Skill

The child will have to line up the lids correctly to fit through the slot, examining the shape of both the lids and the slot.

Jar Lid Puzzles

16 MONTHS +

Materials

fiberboard or other thin board, or stiff cardboard—2 pieces the same size (about 12″ or 30 cm square)

skill saw and sandpaper or Exacto knife if using cardboard

jar lids

pencil

wood glue

To Make

- Place the jar lid in the middle of one of the pieces of board.
- Trace around it with a pencil.
- Using the saw or Exacto knife, cut out that circle so that the jar lid will fit comfortably inside the circle. Sand any rough edges.
- Glue the two pieces of board together.
- When dry, place the jar lid inside the circle.

To Do

- Let the child lift out the jar lid and put it back in the circle again.

Observations

- Does the child sometimes invert the lid when he puts it in?

More Ideas

- Glue matching pictures inside the jar lid and inside the circle on the board to make a simple matching game.
- Use two or three different sizes of jar lids and cut corresponding holes in the board, so the child must be aware of size as well.

Emerging Skill

The child relates the positive and negative spaces, and practices fine motor skills.

Simple Steps

Peek-a-Boo Card

Materials

cardboard   old greeting cards   clear contact paper or laminating paper
scissors   glue

To Make

- Fold the cardboard in half.
- Cut out the main image of the greeting card and glue it on the inside of the cardboard.
- Cut little "doors" in the cover, positioned over the picture to reveal part of the image.
- Laminate everything with clear contact paper for durability.

To Do

- Let the child lift the flaps to reveal the picture underneath.
- Talk about the parts of the picture as the child lifts the flaps.
- Later the child might even be able to find a particular flap for you. "Where's the foot?" This indicates that the child's spatial memory is developing.
- Then let the child open the folded card to reveal the whole picture.

More Ideas

- Use magazine pictures.
- Put a photo of different children in the class in each folded piece of cardboard.
- Recycle used file folders for this.

Emerging Skill

This gives children a part-whole awareness related to later skills in math and reading.

Baby Basketball

Materials

small hoop of some sort, about 12" (30 cm) in diameter. You might make one out of heavy wire or flexible plumbing tubing.
fabric to cover hoop and hang down around it
needle and thread
box of balls to fit through the hoop.
rope, heavy string, or yarn to suspend the hoop from the ceiling

Cognitive Development

To Make

- Make a hem in the fabric to fit over the hoop and sew up the tube of fabric hanging down from the hoop.
- Leave it open at the bottom.
- Suspend this from the ceiling so the hoop hangs about two feet (sixty centimeters) above the floor.
- Place the box of balls next to it.

To Do

- You probably will not have to demonstrate what to do. Sooner or later the child will try to push the ball through the hoop.

Observations

- Does the child do this spontaneously, or do you have to demonstrate?
- Does the child then enjoy doing it repeatedly?

More Ideas

- The child will probably invent variations of his own, trying to fit other objects through the hoop.
- You could make several hoops of different diameters and let the child figure out what fits through what.

Emerging Skill

This is really a peek-a-boo (object permanence) activity. The child enjoys seeing something disappear and come out the other end of the fabric tube. He also explores the concepts of size, as he figures out what fits through what.

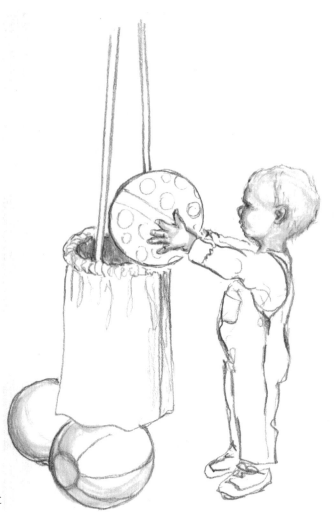

Food Shapes

18 MONTHS +

Materials

food that can show shapes such as toast or finger gelatin (made with half the amount of liquid so children can pick up shapes), homemade pretzels, or cookies
cookie cutters

To Make

■ Use cookie cutters to create shapes in these foods.

To Do

■ Let the child enjoy exploring the shapes in the foods, picking them up, turning them over, and changing the shapes by taking out bites.

■ Talk about it with the child.

Observations

■ Does the child continue this type of exploration at other times?

■ Can the child recognize and name shapes correctly?

More Ideas

■ Consciously notice, with the child, the shapes inherent in all the foods he eats—apple sliced horizontally, carrots sliced into circles, cracker squares, etc.

Emerging Skill

The child is gaining "physical knowledge" of shapes using all the senses.

Tubes at an Angle 20 MONTHS +

Materials

several different diameters of gift wrap paper tubes or PVC pipe
balls and small toys that will fit through the tubes, gathered in a box
duct tape

To Make

■ Tape the tubes at different angles to your fence, climber, or some other object outside, so that the children can reach the upper end. (You can drill holes in PVC pipe and use wire to attach it to the fence for a more permanent toy.)

To Do

■ Show the child how to put the toys or balls in the top of the tube and watch them come out the bottom.

Observations

■ Does the child discover this on his own, without instruction from you?

■ Does the child figure out which toys fit through which tubes?

Safety

■ Make sure objects you offer are too large to choke on.

More Ideas

- While the child watches, change the angles of the tubes and let him notice how this affects the rolling of the balls.
- Tape a number of tubes together, changing angles at joints.

Emerging Skill

The child might learn that things roll downhill. This is also a peek-a-boo game because things disappear and reappear.

Match the Lids

24 MONTHS +

Materials

two copies of the same magazine
clear contact paper
scissors
glue
baby food jar lids, or other lids of identical size

To Make

- Cut the same pictures out of each magazine—things children are familiar with like cars, babies, and dogs.
- Glue these inside the lids and press pieces of the clear contact paper over them to make them last longer.

To Do

- Put one set of these in front of the child.
- Hold up one at a time from the second set and say to the child, "Can you find the picture that's the same as this?"
- Describe each picture as you do this.

Observations

- Does the child understand what you want him to do?
- Does he talk about the pictures?

More Ideas

- Mix up both sets, give them to the child, and challenge him to put the ones that are the same together (older two-year-olds do this best).
- When a verbal child is very familiar with the pictures, give him one set and just describe the picture you are holding without letting him see it. Can he find the matching picture, just listening to your words?

Emerging Skill

The child explores the concept of *same* and *different* and gains descriptive vocabulary.

Simple Sorting

Materials

collection of two different kinds of toys, such as toy vehicles and small animals
two containers

To Do

- Put all the toys in front of the child.
- Say, "These are all mixed up. Can you put the animals in this box and the cars in this other one for me?"

Observations

- Does the child do this spontaneously without suggestion from you?
- Does he understand what you want him to do?
- Does it seem enjoyable to the child?

More Ideas

- The child can watch you make a picture label for each box.
- This could be used as a clean-up time game, or a small group activity, with the children helping a puppet.
- As time goes on, give them items that are more similar to sort, such as crayons and pencils or cows and horses.

Emerging Skill

Children are learning the concept of *same* and *different* and how to notice attributes of objects.

Classified Objects

24 MONTHS +

Materials

wide variety of objects that represent certain properties such as
    Soft: small plush toy, powder puff, little pillow, cotton balls, sponge
    Hard: hard plastic toy, tin box, large jar lid, metal spoon, wooden block
    Round: ball, turntable, large jar lid, juice can lids, plastic bottles
large containers such as plastic baskets or rubber dish tubs

To Do

- Put all of the objects for each category in a separate container.
- Give the child one category of objects at a time to play with.
- Even though it may be too early for some children to express the vocabulary concepts, talk about the characteristics of the objects as the child plays.
- Later, when the child is very familiar with all the objects, offer two boxes (two categories) at the same time.

Cognitive Development

- When it is time to clean up, have the child hand you the objects as you describe them, and put them back in the separate containers.

Observations
- Can the child eventually anticipate which container each object gets put away in?

Safety
- Make sure all objects are safe, and supervise things like cotton balls and sponges closely so that the child doesn't chew on them.

More Ideas
- You could collect: things that bounce, bumpy things, smooth things, big things, small things.

Emerging Skill
- The child explores properties of objects and is exposed to the vocabulary for them. Sensory learning is happening as well as fine motor practice.

Category Books

 24 MONTHS +

Materials
12 sandwich-size zip-closure bags
needle and thread
thin cardboard cut to fit exactly inside bags
construction paper trimmed to fit inside the bags
magazines and other usable pictures
glue stick
scissors

To Make
- Ahead of time, sew sets of four zip-closure bags together along their bottom edges to create "books."
- Slip the cardboard inside of each bag.

To Do
- Tell the child you'd like to make three books—one about dogs, one about babies, and one about cars.
- Ask the child to help you find pictures in magazines of dogs, babies, or cars to cut out and put in the books.
- Sit with the child and flip through pages.
- When the child identifies a picture, cut it out. Create a separate pile for each type of picture. Let the child help you decide which pile to place each picture in. You will need eight examples for each category, one for each side of the cardboard page.
- Let the child help you put glue on the back of each cut-out picture, mount it on the construction paper, and then slip it into the pages of the correct book.

Observations

- Is the child able to find examples in the magazines?
- Can he tell you what pile to put it in?
- Does he talk about the pictures?

More Ideas

- Create many different categories over time. Develop topics children are interested in or see around them—shoes, food, toys, holiday pictures, families, cleaning supplies, hats.
- You could use just one zip-closure bag book, and simply switch the pictures in the pages from week to week.
- Any other type of homemade book works for this. The zip-closure books simply give you a little more flexibility.

Emerging Skill

Children create their own categories and books, "sorting out" the world.

Fancy Mitts

 24 MONTHS +

Materials

collection of pairs of mittens

To Do

- Put a pile of these mittens on the floor.
- Just let the children explore. They will do all sorts of things with them. They might stick their hands inside, exploring inside and outside. They might pull them over their shoes. Two-year-olds might find matching pairs and pull them on.

More Ideas

- Make a more organized game for older children. Put one mitten on one hand of each child and with all the children seated in a small group or circle, hold up one of the matching mittens at a time. Let the children decide whose mitten it matches. Then let the child pull that mitten onto his other hand.
- Use fancy socks or dress-up play shoes instead of mittens.

Emerging Skill

Children explore the inside and outside of something. Mittens can present various textures, colors, and patterns. Some simple sorting might take place.

Materials

camera
clear contact paper

To Make

- Take a photo of various objects in your room, for example: child's chair, table, toilet, sink, door, goldfish, doll, ball, favorite book, toy truck, blocks.
- Encase the photos in clear contact paper to protect them.

To Do

- Hand a photo to a child. See if the child can tell you what it is.
- Then ask the child to take the photo over to the real thing.
- This could be an activity with individual children, one at a time, or with a small group.

More Ideas

- Instead of photos, use pictures of exactly the same the objects in your room that you cut out of toy supply catalogs.
- For a more complex activity, cut out pictures from catalogs or magazines that are similar but not exactly the same. The picture might be of a door that does not look exactly like your door, a doll or ball that differs slightly from those in your room. Instead of simply "matching" the picture to the object, the child has to form classifications for objects.

Emerging Skill

This activity gives children practice in using symbols. Pictures are symbols for objects. They are learning that things can be represented by marks on paper. This exercise is great for promoting receptive vocabulary.

Chapter 6

Make a Joyful Noise

Music & Movement Development

Children actually sing before they talk. It's amazing how very young children can learn the sounds, the vocabulary, the grammar, and the intonation of languages—and music is a language. With babies, language development and music development are the same thing. They happen at the same time and in the same way. As babies are learning to form their mouths to produce desired sounds, they are also learning to make their voices go up and down to imitate the melodies of our language, our intonation patterns.

You may hear many endearing "baby songs" as children babble and chant, learning what they can do with their voices. They will repeat syllables, develop rhythms, and make melodic tones.

Focus on Music

Instead of playing records as background music, focus on music at specific times. A lot of stimulation already exists in a typical environment. Let's make it easier for infants to focus on our words and our meanings by not having a lot of extra sounds in the room. Use children's recordings, but also your own favorite music, such as a pop album you enjoy, some lively folk music to dance to, or a favorite passage in a Beethoven symphony. If you can play an instrument, do that as well.

Music Is a Social Experience

Music has important social aspects. Singing together is a beautiful and loving way human beings relate to each other. We feel a sense of belonging when we realize we all know the same songs.

Try singing a soothing song or chant to a child who is upset or is having trouble separating from the parent. Music is a language that communicates above words, and is a comforting way to deliver the message "I care" to someone who does not yet understand your words.

Enjoying music is also a cultural experience. Every culture has its own form of music, its own melodies that strike at the emotional core of its people. You might wish to collect lullabies from different cultures to use with your children. Even better, use melodies from the children's own cultures. Ask parents to share their favorite music with you. Perhaps they would loan you recordings, or even come in and teach you and the children some songs.

Using music with children provides them with cognitive benefits as well. Children learn about sequences—things happen in a certain order when you sing songs—and about repetition of patterns.

Chant, Dance, Clap

Let children make sounds using objects, and take the opportunity to enjoy music together. The more you sing, the more the children will sing! We don't know for sure why some people are musical and can sing relatively "on key" and other people can't carry a tune in a bucket. Is it a "gift," or is it the outcome of early exposure? Is it due to heredity or environment? If a child has any aptitude at all, early exposure to music, learning to play with it and enjoy it, can go a long way toward developing the "gift."

Parent Involvement Ideas

- Send a copy of the words to songs home so parents can learn them. If they are not songs parents would know the melody to, make tapes and let the parents take them home.
- Encourage parents who play any kind of musical instrument to share it with the children. They don't have to be accomplished players. The children will enjoy hearing the instrument.
- Invite parents to visit your group and sing any songs that they know from their own childhood. Perhaps their child can help and sing along with them. If possible, record this on a tape recorder, or write down the words and learn them.
- Consider developing a lending library of children's music cassettes that parents could take home to enjoy with their children.

Simple Steps

- Invite parents to share recorded music they enjoy, even if it is not children's music.

- A fun "parent event" might be to have a dance, children included. As well as teaching the parents the various movement games you enjoy with the children, you can play a variety of lively music and invite parents to carry a child and "move as the spirit moves them." This captures the basic joy of music. Combined with an easy pot luck or pizza supper, what could be more fun?

Hints for Doing Music with Toddlers

- Keep it short—under 10 minutes. Make participation voluntary.

- Let puppets participate.

- Be spontaneous. Sing or dance at the drop of a hat, whenever the opportunity seems to present itself.

- The melody is approximate. Young children cannot be expected to sing perfectly on pitch. However, if they are familiar with the song, their voices will go up and down at the right places.

- Combine music with movement. Look for songs that involve movements like walking, stopping, jumping.

- Sing a familiar rhyme and leave out a word. "Twinkle, twinkle, little ....." The children will join in.

- Repeat often. Children don't learn a song from hearing it once. And they very much enjoy singing familiar songs over and over again.

- Don't sing too fast. Young children need a slow pace and clear words.

- Find songs that are right for young children, not songs designed for an older age group. Good songs for toddlers have a small range from the lowest to the highest notes and are very simple with lots of repetition. "The Muffin Man" is a good example.

Play a Soft Musical Instrument

6 WEEKS +

Materials

musical instrument such as a flute, guitar, or soft chime or recording with this type of music

To Do

- Play the instrument out of direct view of the child. If the child seems to notice and enjoy it, keep playing.

Observations

- Does the child stop moving momentarily, as though to concentrate on the new sound?
- Does she move her head toward the source of the sound?

More Ideas

- Vary what you do with the instrument. Play fast and slow, high and low, different tones and tunes.

Emerging Skill

This gives the child something interesting to hear. She may stop an activity to listen and turn toward the sound.

Humming and Body Contact

6 WEEKS +

Materials

To Do

- When the child is fussy, hold her against your chest while you hum a soothing melody or chant.

Observations

- Does the child calm down while absorbing the vibrations of your voice?

More Ideas

- Combine humming with various types of rocking.
- Sing a familiar lullaby.
- Invite the father or mother to tape record a lullaby for their baby. Play this cassette near the child when the child is fussy.

Simple Steps

Emerging Skill

This is a calming activity as the child learns to respond to a comforting voice. It's also a social-emotional activity to have someone find just the right way to comfort.

Trade Funny Sounds

 4 MONTHS +

Materials

To Do

- Make a funny sound when the child is paying attention to you, such as a "raspberry" or kissing sound.
- Start with sounds you have heard the child make.

Observations

- See if the child tries to imitate you.
- See if the child will take turns, going back and forth.

More Ideas

- Imitate the child if she comes up with a fun sound on her own.
- Make the fun sounds with the child while you dance or bounce in rhythm to music.

Emerging Skill

The child gains practice in imitating non-speech and musical sounds and enjoys fun social interaction.

Wanna Dance?

 6 MONTHS +

Materials

recorded music

To Do

- Hold the child on your hip and dance around the room to lively music.

Observations

- Does the child delight in this activity?
- Does she hold up her arms and ask for more?

More Ideas

- Dance to many different types of music.
- Before you start, ask, "Wanna dance?"

Emerging Skill

The child experiences music as a great social activity while moving rhythmically.

Things That Make a Noise Collection

6 MONTHS +

Materials

lots of different objects that make a noise (the more the better), such as rubber squeak toys, a slide whistle, bells of all types, shaker toys, empty tin boxes, simple rhythm instruments, metal juice can lids

attractive box or container to put them in

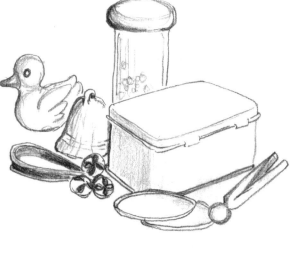

To Do

- All you really need to do is put the objects within reach of the child on the floor.
- The child will do an "object survey" that she does with all new objects, which includes banging them on the floor.
- You might say, "Look, I have all kinds of things in this box that make a noise...see?" and then demonstrate banging them lightly on the floor.

Observations

- Make note of what the child does with the objects.
- Does the child bang the objects spontaneously?
- Does she seem to be trying to find out what kind of sound they make?

Safety

- Make sure the objects are safe for children to handle—too large to choke on, no sharp edges, etc.

More Ideas

- The variations are endless, of course! You could add new things to the box every week.
- You could create noise "categories" and put all the bells in one box, all the shake-shake toys in another box, all the hollow toys that are fun to hit with a small stick in another box, etc.

Simple Steps

Emerging Skill

Young children are learning that they can "make things happen." They enjoy the cause and effect of making noises. This is also a language or a sensory activity.

Put Your Finger in the Air

8 MONTHS +

Materials

To Do

- Create a simple chant involving the child's name and simple instructions.
- Sing it and demonstrate at the same time, such as:

  Jason, Jason, put your finger in the air.
  Jason, Jason, put your finger in the air.

Observations

- Does the child imitate you?
- Can the child later follow your direction in the song without the demonstration?

More Ideas

- From day to day, vary the actions, and involve other children.

Emerging Skill

The child starts to follow simple directions with familiar words while having fun with music.

Na, Na, Na, Na, Na, Na

10 MONTHS +

Materials

To Do

- With the child right in front of you, watching you, chant the melody to "Ring Around the Rosie" (the most basic melody) repeating the syllable "Na" instead of the words.

Observations

- Does the child join you singing?
- Does she match any of the notes?
- Does her voice go up and down in a similar pattern?

More Ideas

- Try it with "Twinkle, Twinkle, Little Star."
- Chant different syllables.

Emerging Skill

The child can use her own "jargon" language to participate in singing.

Shake Your Body to Music

 10 MONTHS +

Materials

recorded music

To Do

- When the child is standing up holding onto something, or standing independently, play some lively music and start dancing.

Observations

- See if the child also starts to dance, bouncing and shaking arms and legs.
- Does she let go for a second?

More Ideas

- Give the child something interesting to shake while she is standing there bouncing to the music, such as a rattle or small tambourine.

Emerging Skill

The child is learning to move rhythmically, feeling the beat of the music. As the child bends and bounces in a standing position, she is practicing balance and coordination, enjoying music in a social situation.

Musical Fence

 10 MONTHS +

Materials

wide variety of objects that make interesting sounds when hit, and that could be hung on a fence, such as a toy xylophone, a metal triangle, hub caps, cookie sheets, a washboard, trash can lids, metal pipes, wind chimes, and large plastic buckets inverted to be drums
small wooden mallets or dowels to strike objects with

To Make

- Attach these items to the fence of your playground, all in one area.
- Put the mallets or dowels in a container attached to the fence, or attach them with string so they don't get misplaced.

To Do

- Encourage children to strike the different objects to see what sounds they make.

More Ideas

- Beat a rhythm on the objects and encourage the children to dance. Teach them how to do this for each other. Add new things as you think of them.

Emerging Skill

Children gain an awareness of how musical sounds are made and have fun playing with sounds.

Baby Band

12 MONTHS +

Materials

simple toys and objects that make interesting noises when shaken or hit together such as shake-shake toys, two spoons, coffee can drums, pots and wooden spoons, pot lids

To Do

- Give several children some noise-makers and play lively music. Also play one noisemaker yourself.

Observations

■ Do the children play along?

More Ideas

■ It is not really necessary to play music along with this experience.

Emerging Skill

Children like to make noises with objects, making their own music. This is also a cognitive, cause-and-effect activity.

Bounce, Bounce, Bounce

12 MONTHS +

Materials

record player or tape player
lively recorded music

To Do

■ Put the music on and hold hands with the standing child. Bounce up and down, bending your knees.

Observations

■ Does the child also bend knees to "bounce" up and down to the music?
■ Does the child do this automatically when lively music comes on, without you as a partner?

More Ideas

■ Try rocking from side to side, stiff legged. Does the child do this?

Emerging Skill

The child experiences rhythm with his body in a fun, social experience.

Sound Hide and Seek

18 MONTHS +

Materials

toy that makes a noise

To Do

■ Have another adult or an older child hide somewhere in the room and use the toy to make the noise.
■ Encourage the children to find the person by following the sound.

Observations

■ Are they able to follow the sound to locate the toy?

■ If not able at first, can they do it after someone shows them how?

More Ideas

■ Hide a musical wind-up toy somewhere in your room. The challenge is to find it before the music stops.

■ You could use a portable radio. It would not stop playing, so there would be no time limit.

Emerging Skill

Children figure out what direction the sound is coming from. They must use some of their new problem-solving skills to find the sound.

Hoop Ring Around the Rosie

 18 MONTHS +

Materials

hula hoop

To Do

■ Get children to hold hands, walk in a circle, and sing the familiar song, "Ring around the Rosie, Ring around the Rosie, Ashes ashes, All fall down."

■ Teach them to fall down together at the appropriate time.

■ When they know this routine, help each child hold onto the hoop with one hand, facing in the same direction, and then play the game.

Observations

■ Does the child hold on the whole time, or let go?

■ Is it difficult for children to go the same speed?

More Ideas

■ Use other recorded music, and just let the children hold the hoop and walk in a circle while the music plays.

■ See if they can hold the hoop high, over their heads, and low, following your instructions.

Emerging Skill

While moving to music, children are engaging in a social activity and learning a little more about what a circle is.

Holler Tubes

Materials

paper towel tubes

To Do

- Let the children sing or holler through the tubes as you play music.
- Or, try singing some of your favorite songs together as everybody sings into the tube.

Observations

- Collect other things that are fun to holler into or through, such as large buckets, longer gift wrap tubes, shorter toilet paper tubes, pieces of plastic pipe, or flexible dryer duct vent tubes.

Emerging Skill

Young children love experimenting with their voices. What fun to see how different they sound talking or singing into a tube!

Dancing Rings

Materials

any smooth large rings or small hoops that children can grip easily. You could also cut the middle out of plastic coffee can lids or margarine tub lids.
two or three colors of plastic surveyors tape, crepe paper, or ribbon
scissors

To Make

- Cut the tape or ribbons into lengths of about twelve inches (thirty centimeters) and tie five or six of these to each ring.

To Do

- Children love waving them around while they dance to lively music.

Observations

- Do they move the rings differently to different types of music?

Simple Steps

More Ideas

■ You can build vocabulary by giving children instructions, including location words, concerning what to do with their rings while you all dance together, such as "wave your rings up high over your head" (or behind you or in front of you).

Emerging Skill

Toddlers and two-year-olds are "instrumental" and like using objects. Dancing is a physical activity. Plus, they like doing things together, so this is a social activity.

What Made That Sound? 24 MONTHS +

Materials

three or four different rhythm instruments or different objects that make some type of sound
a visual barrier of some sort, such as a flannel board or large box

To Do

■ Show the children the objects and demonstrate the sound that each of them makes.
■ Then put them all behind the screen.
■ Make one of the objects make its noise. Then remove the screen.
■ Have a child guess which object made the sound by pointing to the object. Then let the child make the sound with the object to see if it is the same.

Observations

■ Do the children understand what you want them to do?
■ Does it help if you let them play with all of the instruments first?

More Ideas

■ This activity will be most successful with two-year-olds. The younger children will simply enjoy making the objects make their noises.
■ With more experienced children, do not demonstrate the sound of the object ahead of time.
■ You could vary this activity every day by simply using different objects. To make it more difficult, increase the number of objects to choose from.

Emerging Skill

This is an auditory discrimination exercise where children learn to distinguish different sounds, an important skill for language development and reading.

Materials

To Do

■ Sing to the tune of "Frere Jacques" (Where is Thumbkin?):

> *Where is Johnny (name of a child in your class)*
> *Where is Johnny....*
> *There he is, There he is,*
> *How are you this morning,*
> *Very well, I thank you,*
> *Now sit down, now sit down.*

■ At the "There he is" line, the child pops up. See if you can get him to sing, "Here I am, here I am!" and "Very well I thank you."
■ Repeat with different children's names.

Observations

■ Does the child understand the "rule" to wait until her name is heard and then pop up?
■ Do the children know the names of the others in the group?

More Ideas

■ This will be most successful with your older children who are more verbal, and with those children who have watched others perform it correctly. With younger children, simply keep singing.
■ A puppet could tap the designated child.

Emerging Skill

Children feel important and experience a strong sense of belonging when they hear their names in a song.

Two by Two 24 MONTHS +

Materials

lively recorded music to dance to

To Do

■ Pair children up and have them hold hands facing each other.
■ Play lively music and have them rock from side to side or jump up and down together.

Simple Steps

Observations

- Are they able to coordinate their rocking from side to side?
- Do they make eye contact and seem to enjoy the dance?

More Ideas

- Try it with three or more children holding hands in a circle. Can they rock from side to side in the same direction at the same time?

Emerging Skill

Children learn to move rhythmically. This is a great social activity as well as a movement activity.

Teddy Bear Ring Around the Rosie

24 MONTHS +

Materials

teddy bears and/or other stuffed animals or dolls, one per child

To Do

- When children know how to play "Ring Around the Rosie," have them hold the arms of stuffed animals or dolls between them in the circle and then play the game.

Observations

- Do the children have difficulty figuring out how to get a stuffed animal between each of them?
- After you have helped them with this several times, are they able to figure it out themselves?

More Ideas

- Pick one child at a time to be the "Rosie" and stand in the middle of the circle.

Emerging Skill

"Ring Around the Rosie" is actually one of the first "games with rules" that children can learn to play. There is only one rule—don't fall down until the end! This reinforces a listening skill. A sense of camaraderie develops when children do something like this together. They develop a feeling of being "one of the gang." Putting a stuffed animal between each child gives practice in a math concept (one-to-one correspondence) and children are creating a pattern.

Song Props

Materials

props that reflect the words of familiar songs, such as simple felt frog hand puppets for the "Five Little Frogs" song; paper headbands, crowns, hats; or stick puppets

To Do

■ When you sing the particular song, let the child hold up, move, or wear the prop.

Observations

■ Do the children prefer using the props to singing the songs without them?

More Ideas

■ Take out a particular prop and ask the children if they can guess which song you're going to sing.

Emerging Skill

Young children, especially toddlers, like using objects as they sing words. These objects are symbols.

New Old MacDonald

Materials

variety of rubber, plastic, or stuffed farm animals in a basket or other container

To Do

■ Sing "Old Mac Donald" with the children. They especially enjoy chiming in on "ee-ei-ee-ei-o."
■ When you sing the name of an animal, "...and on this farm he had a *cow*," let a child pick that animal out of the basket, put it in front of you, and then continue singing the song.
■ After all the animals are out of the basket, you could sing a new verse and let the children put the animals back one by one.

Simple Steps

This old cow she went to bed, Ee-ei-ee-ei-o.
This old cow laid down her head, Ee-ei-ee-ei-o.

More Ideas

- Let each child in turn pick the animal out of the basket to sing about next. Or, let each have an animal before the game starts, to add in turn.
- When the children are well acquainted with this game, change what is in the basket. Instead of the animals, put in an assortment of familiar objects for Old MacDonald to have on his farm, such as a truck, a drum, and a bell. Let the children make up the sound that goes with each object.

Emerging Skill

Children have a chance to demonstrate both receptive and productive language as they enjoy the social experience of singing a song together. They may also learn new vocabulary, and they practice math skills of sequencing and reverse sequencing.

Class Song File

24 MONTHS +

Materials

large plastic file box
index cards that fit in file box
clear contact paper or laminating paper

To Make

- For each song you sing with your children create a card with a picture or some sort of symbol that represents that song. Write the words on the back of the card.

To Do

- Look through the cards with one or more children.
- See if they can tell you what song each picture represents.
- Sing the songs with them as you look at the different cards.
- Leave the box where children can look through it independently.

Observations

- Do children ever pick out cards and sing the songs by themselves, without you prompting?

More Ideas

- Take one or two cards out and display them where you gather for an informal story time or small group gathering. The children can anticipate which song you will sing together.
- You could make a tape recording of you and the children singing all the songs you know. As they learn a new one, add it to the tape. They will enjoy listening to this and singing along with it. You could make copies for parents to play in the car.

Emerging Skill

Children interpret the symbol of the pictures to something they recognize that is meaningful to them. It can help them (and you) remember which songs you have sung together and the words to the songs.

Who's That Singing?

 24 MONTHS +

Materials

cassette tape recorder and cassette

To Make

- Ask people who are very familiar to the child to sing a song of their choice.
- Record their singing.
- Or invite each child in the group to sing in turn.

To Do

- Play the tape for the child and see if she can identify the singer. "Who is that?" "Do you think that is Daddy or Mary singing that song?"

Observations

- Can the child identify the singer?
- Does the child sing along?

More Ideas

- Ask the person to talk before singing, perhaps identifying the song.
- Find other familiar sounds to record and identify, such as a car horn, the garbage truck, a siren, and a dog barking.

Emerging Skill

This causes the child to listen carefully and realize that people's voices are different. It's a fun social activity as well.

Chapter 7

Getting in Touch With the World

Sensory Development

Children are born eager to gather information about the wonderful world that they have entered. Their five senses of touch, taste, smell, vision, and hearing are their information-gathering tools. They use these senses to gather physical knowledge about their world, learning about the properties of all objects around them. These sensory experiences are the essential activities that must take place so that cognitive development can also occur. Put simply, children must explore to know. A direct connection exists between sensory experiences and the development of creativity. The child has to learn about materials, handle them, smell them, and so on before learning to combine and manipulate these substances to "make things."

Everything the child encounters is brand new to his senses. Things that may seem ordinary or boring to us can be quite fascinating to a young child, such as moving shadows on a wall, a shaft of sunlight hitting the floor, the noisy garbage truck, the beep of a microwave, the ridges of corduroy, the smooth coolness and taste of gelatin, or the smell of a wet dog. We need to find ways to add interesting variety to the experiences with senses and practice noticing things from the child's fresh perspective.

Sensory Development

The Five Wonderful Senses

Seeing

For vision activities, think of interesting things for children to look at, such as patterns and colors, interesting movements, and shadows.

Hearing

How can you add variety to the sounds children hear? (In some environments, your goal may be the opposite, trying to reduce the number of sounds in the environment!) What ways can you invent for children to make interesting sounds?

Feeling

The world is full of interesting textures. Create a "smorgasbord" of textures for them to enjoy with their fingertips. Many touch activities are also fine motor activities, encouraging children to use their fingers to explore. Dribbling water, poking and rolling playdough, digging in sand, and similar activities are among the most fascinating for toddlers, and hold their attention for a long time. One of the driving forces for toddlers is experimenting with the principles of cause and effect—making things happen, in other words. These materials allow children to make lots of things happen! Having at least one sensory activity available to toddlers and two-year-olds during every playtime is a good idea. In addition to all the other benefits, these are usually activities that children can do with relative independence. They are good "alternative" activities while children are waiting for their turn at other special projects you have set up. Many sensory activities involved primarily with the sense of touch are also soothing, making them ideal for tense children.

Smelling

The richest source of smell activities is likely to be with food! While young children are not actually conscious of the process of smelling something, that does not prevent you from giving them a wide variety of interesting aromas to sample. If you are fortunate enough to be near the kitchen, see if older children can guess what's cooking. Maybe the cook will bring in a small sample for them to just smell.

Tasting

Let children taste small samples of a wide variety of different foods. Cut things up into very tiny portions and present them to children at times other than lunch or snack time, just to make them special. For example, cut up different fruits into thimble-sized pieces and present in a similar way.

Simple Steps

Sensory Table

Use a water table, sensory table, dish tubs, or baby bathtub. For variety, use a long, rectangular plastic window box.

Possible materials to explore:

- Water
- Snow
- Rice
- Sand
- Confetti
- Shaving cream

Accessories to add include:

- Plastic scoops
- Measuring cups
- Funnels
- Toy boats
- Measuring spoons
- Plastic bottles
- Muffin tins
- Plastic containers of all kinds
- Clear plastic plumbing tubing cut into various lengths (available at a hardware store)
- Little people and plastic animals and dinosaurs
- Toy vehicles
- A collection of things that float

Don't make everything available at once. Put out one sensory material and add one or two different accessories. You might let the children choose several things they want to use each day, and store the rest on a shelf close by.

Put smocks on children when the material is messy and be sure to roll up their sleeves. Stay close so you can curb inappropriate behaviors, such as eating, throwing, or splashing.

Playdough

What did people ever do with young children before playdough was invented? This staple of the early childhood classroom is endlessly fascinating. Yet even playdough can get boring if it is just the same old substance day after day. Here is a favorite playdough recipe to try, and a variety of simple activity variations to offer children over time.

Let children help you measure, stir, and knead this playdough. For variation, you can add cooking extracts such as lemon or peppermint for an appealing fragrance. (Be aware that younger children are more likely to eat the dough if you do this.)

Cooked Playdough

Materials
4 cups (1 L) flour
2 cups (500 ml) salt
4 tablespoons cream of tartar
4 cups (1 L) water
2 tablespoons oil
Food coloring or tempera paint

Combine all ingredients and cook over medium heat, stirring constantly until stiff. Let cool and knead. (Children will enjoy helping you knead it when it is still warm—this is very soothing.) Store in plastic bag in refrigerator. This is nice, springy dough, close in texture to purchased playdough.

Things to Do With Playdough

■ Give children rubber stamps to press and pound into their pancakes of playdough to make repeated patterns.

■ Create a collection of all sorts of odd things to poke into the dough. Very young children like to stand things up in their dough.

■ Give children small plastic animals to stand up in their dough.

■ Give children small wooden pounding bench hammers to pound their dough with. You could carve a pattern or glue on a raised pattern in one hammer so children see the mark repeated.

■ Give children small containers such as jar lids to smash the dough into and dig it out of.

■ Let children play with it while it is still warm, or warm it up for a few seconds in the microwave. This is especially soothing on a cold morning.

■ Make a collection of things that make interesting impressions when pressed into the playdough. Possibilities: strawberry baskets, sneaker soles, potato mashers, spirals from the spines of notebooks, shells, and buttons. Let the child press the object into the dough and pull it out again to see the indentation left behind. Can the child tell you later which object he used to make which impression?

- Roll out a large amount of playdough to cover a whole tabletop, or fill a large cookie sheet about one-half inch deep. Leave it out all day. Let children stick things in it and make imprints, as described above. They could "erase" their marks using a rolling pin or by pressing the mark flat, if they wish.

- Let children roll dough into snakes and then use child-safe scissors to cut off pieces. (Supervise closely.)

Other Types of Clay

Every now and then offer children different types of clay to play with, such as plasticene and regular earth clay that potters use. The latter is cool and natural and wonderful to use. Stay close by to make sure children don't eat this clay.

Children With Tactile Sensitivity

You will find that some children simply don't like messy activities. They don't like to stick their fingers in playdough or fingerpaint. Sometimes this is just a strong preference, other times a real sensitivity. Touch sensitivity can show up in many ways. Some children are sensitive to new clothes, tags, or threads. Children who are sensitive to touch are often sensitive in other areas as well, so we should be aware of the broader issue of sensory sensitivity. Such sensitivities are more prevalent in children who were premature at birth, because of neurological immaturity.

More than one sense can be affected. The smallest sound, or certain frequencies like sirens, may arouse children who have auditory sensitivity. They might have difficulty paying attention to one thing when there are other noises in the room. Some children who have olfactory sensitivity can't stand certain smells, such as those from particular foods. Many children who are visually sensitive can't stand bright illumination, so you need to dim the lights.

What to Do When Children Don't Like to Touch Messy Things

- Try to introduce a substance "out there" on a table. Let the child choose to touch it or not.

- Introduce familiar things first, like a dry cloth followed by a wet one.

- Put gooey play substances inside a plastic zip-closure bag for them to play with.

- Earth clay thinned with water can be more tolerable than thicker clay. Or try the opposite and offer the child clay that is nearly dry.

- Let the child try touching shaving cream. The white color, softness, and sweet smell can be less threatening than other gooey substances.

If the child is really bothered by messy substances, ask yourself if it is really necessary for his learning to play with these things. Try other experiences to teach the same concepts.

Rainbows

Materials

cut crystals designed to hang in windows

To Do

- Hang the crystals in a sunny window to produce beautiful rainbows.

Observations

- Does the child notice the beautiful colors?
- Does he try to play with the colors, touching them on a surface he can reach?

Safety

- Make sure the crystal is out of reach of children and remains firmly attached to the hanging device.

More Ideas

- Make the colors move by pushing the crystal.

Emerging Skill

The child has something interesting and beautiful to look at. Older children might start to learn some color vocabulary.

Chimes

Materials

numerous types of wind chimes

To Do

- ■ Hang all the chimes in a row either outside or inside.

Observations

- ■ Does the child seem to notice the music from the chimes?

More Ideas

- ■ You could lift the child so he can make the chimes sound.

Emerging Skill

The child becomes aware of different types and qualities of sounds. If the child hits the chimes, it is a cause-and-effect activity.

Crunch It! 6 WEEKS +

Materials

cellophane, tissue paper, or other paper that makes good crunching sounds

To Do

- ■ With a younger baby, crunch the paper near the child and see if he is attracted to the sound.
- ■ Let babies who are grasping have fun crunching the paper.

Observations

- ■ Does the child enjoy listening to or making the sound?
- ■ Does he repeat the action to make the sound?

Safety

- ■ Supervise so that the child does not eat small pieces that may tear off.

Emerging Skill

The child can listen to interesting sounds. This is a fun fine motor activity and also a cognitive cause-and-effect activity.

Baby Lotion Hand Massage

Materials

baby lotion

To Do

- After the children's hands are washed, give them a special, gentle, soothing hand massage using baby lotion.
- Talk about each of their fingers as you smooth on the lotion.
- Let the children smell the lotion as well.

More Ideas

- Invite a toddler or two-year-old to give you a hand massage with the baby lotion in return.

Emerging Skill

This is a very soothing activity, ideal for late in the afternoon when everyone is tired and cranky.

Air Stream

4 MONTHS +

Materials

plastic drinking straw

To Do

- Gently blow through the straw and aim the airflow onto the child's hand, arm, or foot (not face).

Observations

- How does the child respond?
- Does it tickle?
- Is this a pleasant sensation for the child?

Emerging Skill

The child experiences the feel of moving air.

Satin Feels Good

4 MONTHS +

Materials

piece of washable satin fabric

Simple Steps

To Do

■ Simply hand this to the child, or place it near him on the floor.

Observations

■ Does he stroke his hands over the fabric?
■ Does he put it on his cheek?
■ Does he seem to enjoy the texture?

More Ideas

■ Collect other soft fabrics such as fake fur, fleece, velour, and chenille. You could give these to children one at a time at first, and later present them all together. Do they have favorites?

Emerging Skill

The child experiences various textures, associating touch with the visual appearance of the fabric.

Dancing Lights

4 MONTHS +

Materials

flashlight

To Do

■ Darken the room and shine the flashlight. Make the light "dance" on various surfaces. (This can be a fun activity late in the day, or on dark, rainy days.)

Observations

■ Does the child look at the light?
■ Does he want to "catch" the light and go after it, trying to feel it?

More Ideas

■ Play music and have the light "dance" in time to the music. Try this with fast music and slow, melodic music.
■ Add a piece of colored cellophane to the end of the flashlight, attaching it with a rubber band or tape to make colored lights.
■ Have two or more lights dance at the same time and chase and catch each other.
■ Let older children hold small flashlights themselves and make the light move.

Emerging Skill

The children follow the visual patterns. This is a music activity when you do the variation.

Water Shake Bottles

Materials

plastic bottles
hot glue gun or super glue
materials to put inside of bottles such as pieces of colored yarn, plastic sequins, buttons, small pompoms, tiny plastic toys, or beads

To Make

■ Fill the bottles with water, and put some of the interesting materials inside.
■ Glue the top on securely.

To Do

■ Let the child push, roll, and shake the bottle to make the materials inside move in interesting ways.

Observations

■ Does the child notice the movement inside, or is he mainly interested in making the bottle move through space?
■ Does he try to make the movement continue by shaking the bottle when the materials settle?

Safety

■ Check frequently to make sure the bottle tops remain glued on securely and no leaks develop.

More Ideas

■ Fill the bottle half-full with colored water and add dish detergent. Let the child shake the bottle to make bubbles.

Emerging Skill

These bottles provide interesting visual effects. This is also a cognitive, cause-and-effect activity.

Floating Bubbles

Materials

bubble soap or about one tablespoon dish detergent in one quart water (experiment)
bubble wand or wire loop

To Do

■ Blow the bubbles where the child is able to see them.

Observations

■ Does the child notice the bubbles and follow them with his eyes?
■ Does he show delight?

Safety

■ Keep bubble solution away from babies so they don't swallow it or get it in their eyes.
Take care not to blow bubbles into children's faces so they would pop near their eyes.

More Ideas

■ Blow bubbles in front of a fan for an exciting amount of movement.
■ Blow bubbles on a breezy day outside.

Emerging Skill

The child has beautiful, slow-moving objects to follow with his eyes. This is also a good social activity that children (even babies) of different developmental levels can enjoy together. Older children will enjoy going after the bubbles or trying to catch them or stomp on them.

Squeak Toys

6 MONTHS +

Materials

collection of all different types of squeak toys (as many as you can find)
container to put them in

To Do

■ Bring the container of squeak toys out and say, "Look, there are all kinds of things in this box that squeak when you squeeze them."
■ Demonstrate with one or two toys, then step back.

Observations

■ What does the child do with the toys?
■ Does he dump them all at once, take out one at a time, take out some and ignore others?

- Does he seem interested in finding out what kind of squeak each toy makes, and how to make it?

Safety

- Check frequently to make sure that the toys are intact and that the squeaker part does not come out to cause a choking hazard.

More Ideas

- Do the same with other types of noise-making toys.
- Hide a squeak toy in your pocket. Make it squeak. See if the child knows where to look for it.

Emerging Skill

The child has fun with sound effects and also gets some fine motor practice.

Texture Trail 6 MONTHS +

Materials

variety of textured floor materials such as carpet samples, rubber door mat, jute door mat, outdoor carpeting, astroturf, plastic bubble wrap, bumpy vinyl, fleece
duct tape

To Make

- Line these up end to end to create a trail.
- Tape them in place around the edges.

To Do

- Place the child near the trail, or put him on the first section.

Observations

- Does the child seem to notice the textures?
- Does he crawl along, feeling the different textures? Does he seem to prefer some and avoid others?

More Ideas

- Instead of taping the textures down, arrange the floor materials in different ways from day to day.
- Create a texture trail outside with various natural materials.

Emerging Skill

The child experiences different, interesting textures. This may motivate some gross motor movement.

Simple Steps

Suction Cup Soap Holder

Materials

one or more soap holders with the many small suction cups on the bottom

To Do

- Let the child play with this any way he wishes.
- The many indentations are inviting to a child's fingers and the object can be grasped in different ways.

Observations

- Note what the child does with the toy.
- Does this vary as the child gets older?
- Does the child enjoy "ripping" it off a hard surface such as a hard floor or table top?

Safety

- After a child has chewed on one of these, place it in a mild bleach solution and allow to air dry before making it available to another child.

More Ideas

- Provide a plastic basket full of different, attractive chew toys. They come in a wide variety of shapes and all have interesting bumps and textures to explore with fingers as well as gums.

Emerging Skill

The child will use small motor skills to explore small spaces.

Water Play

Materials

pan of water and towel

To Do

- Place the pan of water on a table or protected floor.
- Put the child on your lap and sit where the child can comfortably reach the water.

Sensory Development

- With an older child, simply sit next to the child.
- Describe what the child is doing and experiencing.

Observations

- Does the child reach out to the water immediately?
- Does he enjoy the sensation?
- What does he do with it?

Safety

- Stay close so there is no danger of the child falling in face first.

More Ideas

- Use cold and warm water and talk about the differences.
- Add mild dish detergent to have bubble froth.
- Add a small wash cloth or sponge.
- Add various float toys.
- Offer containers for pouring.

Emerging Skill

Water is endlessly interesting and usually soothing to infants, toddlers, and two-year-olds, especially when they are deciding what happens with it.

Cellophane in Embroidery Hoop 8 MONTHS +

Materials

embroidery hoop
colored cellophane

To Make

- Stretch the cellophane inside the hoop.

To Do

- Let the child hold the hoop up to his face and look through it.

Observations

- Does he delight in making the world change colors?

Safety

- Replace the cellophane when it gets torn and don't allow shreds of cellophane to be in the environment because they could pose a choking hazard.

More Ideas

- Make hoops with several different colors of cellophane.

Simple Steps

Emerging Skill

The child creates interesting visual effects and may learn a little color vocabulary.

Report Covers

8 MONTHS +

Materials

transparent plastic (acetate) report covers (available at office supply in numerous bright colors)

To Do

- Simply let children handle these.

Observations

- What does the child do with them?
- Does he look through them?
- Does he put them over his head? If not, you might demonstrate once.

More Ideas

- Tape the transparent colored panels to a low window.

Emerging Skill

The child feels powerful when he makes the world change colors. You could supply the name of the color the child is looking through, developing receptive color vocabulary.

Bell Collection

8 MONTHS +

Materials

many different types of unbreakable bells
container

To Do

- Sit down on the floor with the box of bells and see who "shows up."
- Say, "Look at all of these bells. They make pretty sounds. Let's ring them."
- Take out one bell at a time and make it ring.
- Then hand it to a child who has the fine motor skills of grasping and releasing to try ringing it.
- Ring several bells in succession and talk about the difference in the sounds.

Sensory Development

Observations

- Are the children attracted to the sound of the bells?
- When you hand the bells to them, can they make the bells ring, or do they simply put them in their mouths?

Safety

- If you are not right there to supervise, children should only play with "baby toy bells," which are designed to be safe. Some bells like jingle bells are small enough to choke on and clappers on other bells can come loose.

Emerging Skill

The child experiments with making a variety of sounds. This is a cognitive activity because it involves figuring out how to make something work. Older children might even do a little classifying.

Drum Up Some Fun

8 MONTHS +

Materials

collection of drums and other substitutes that make a hollow drum noise when they are beat upon such as small waste baskets, metal pots, and hollow boxes

variety of "drum sticks" such as short wooden dowels, unsharpened pencil with large rubber eraser *glued on*, small baby sock stuffed with cotton balls and securely fastened on the end of a wooden dowel

To Do

- Arrange these objects around the sitting child, or seat the child on your lap with the objects within reach around you.
- Demonstrate hitting one of the objects with one of the drum sticks.
- Then hand the stick to the child.
- Hand the child different drum sticks after a time.

Observations

- Does the child follow your example and hit the object? The same object?
- Does he also try hitting some of the other objects?
- Is it fun for him?
- Is interest renewed when you give him a different drumstick?

More Ideas

- Go on a "sound walk" letting the child tap various objects with one of the drum sticks to hear the different sounds.

Emerging Skill

This activity enhances listening skills and is also a cognitive cause-and-effect activity and music game.

Simple Steps

Texture Nest

Materials

small wading pool or other round enclosure

textured materials to put inside, such as a large collection of small stuffed animals, a lot of "stocking balls" (see page 178), pieces of fleece, or a bunch of balls

To Make

- Put the textured material inside of the wading pool.

To Do

- Place the child inside the "nest" along with the textured materials.

Observations

- What does the child do?
- Does he seem to enjoy being in the middle of the textures?
- Does he try to throw the things out of the nest?

Emerging Skill

The child can experience and act on differently textured materials with his whole body.

Sticky Floor

Materials

contact paper
masking tape

To Make

- Place a large piece of contact paper on the floor, sticky side up.
- Remove the backing and put tape around the edges, taping it to the floor.
- Replace the backing when not in use.

To Do

- Remove the backing from the self-adhesive paper.
- Let the child crawl or walk over to it and touch it with fingertips and pat it.
- Say, "Sticky, sticky, sticky."

Sensory Development

Observations

- What is the child's reaction to the sticky surface?
- Is the child interested in touching it?
- Does he repeat the action?

Emerging Skill

The child experiences a different type of texture and can approach it on his own terms.

Goo Bag

 8 MONTHS +

Materials

sandwich-sized zip-closure bags
hair gel
duct tape

To Make

- Fill the bag with hair gel and zip close. Double bag this by slipping another bag over the top and closing it as well.
- Tape the top shut with duct tape.

To Do

- Simply hand it to the child, or place it close by.

Observations

- What does the child do with the bag? Does he pat it, pick it up, poke it, squeeze it?

Safety

- Discourage the child from biting it. Supervise.

More Ideas

- Put a dollop of tempera paint in with the goo. It will mix as the child squeezes the bag.
- Create other "goo" substances to put in such bags that might vary slightly in feel. Possibilities include shaving cream and a cooked cornstarch and water mixture.
- Put the bag in the refrigerator so you can hand the child a cool bag (nice on hot days).

Emerging Skill

The child experiences soft viscous textures without any mess, and gains fine motor practice squeezing the bag.

Tire Sensory Tub

The advantage of the tire is that it prevents tips and spills.

Materials

automobile tire

round rubber or plastic pan to fit exactly in the space in the middle of the tire (plastic pan designed for draining motor oil works well)

sensory materials such as water, large buttons, or cotton balls to put in the pan

large terrycloth sheet or shower curtain to put underneath to protect floor

To Make

- Clean the tire thoroughly.
- Place it on the floor, on top of the terrycloth sheet or shower curtain.
- Fit the round pan in the middle, and fill it with the sensory material.

To Do

- Sit down with the child at the edge of the tire.
- Simply be there for support as the child leans on the tire and reaches over to touch and play with the material in the pan.
- Talk about what the child is doing and feeling.

Observations

- Is the child cautious and timid in touching "messy" materials, or does he lunge right into it?
- Is he more interested in just watching other children?
- What does he do with the materials?

More Ideas

- Offer this outside as well as inside.

Emerging Skill

The child explores using the sense of touch and is encourged to be an independent player.

Sensory Development

Materials

several small plastic bowls
warm, lukewarm, and cold water

To Do

- Place cold water in one bowl, lukewarm water in another bowl, and warm water in the third bowl.
- Put them on a table.
- Place the child on your lap in front of the bowls and let him touch the water in the different bowls.
- Talk about how it feels. With older children, you might say, "Put your fingers in the cold water. Put your fingers in the warm water."

Observations

- Does the child seem to notice the difference in temperatures?

More Ideas

- Place warm and cold water inside plastic jars and screw the tops on securely, possibly taping around them. Hand both to the child to play with at the same time. These can be "reheated" and "recooled" by putting one in a refrigerator and the other under hot running water, then drying it.
- Talk about warm and cold water when you wash the child, or when he has other contact with water.

Emerging Skill

The child is learning descriptive vocabulary while using the sense of touch.

Materials

variety of different commercially made teething toys
plastic basket or other container

To Do

- When a child seems busy gumming or chewing on everything in sight, place the basket of teething toys next to him.

Observations

- Does he enjoy these toys?
- Does he try several, or stick to one?

Safety

■ When the child puts the toys down and is finished with them, dip them in bleach solution and allow them to air dry.

More Ideas

■ You could also collect other plastic or rubber objects that would be safe for a child to chew on. Puppy toys are fun!
■ Encourage a child who has bitten other children to bite the toys.

Emerging Skill

While gnawing objects to relieve teething pain, the child learns about different textures by mouthing them.

Stick-It-On Picture

 12 MONTHS +

Materials

contact paper
cardboard (about notebook-paper size)
tape
lightweight materials such as
fabric scraps, leaves, yarn,
"border" strips (optional)

To Make

■ Tape the contact paper to the cardboard, sticky side out.
■ Remove the backing.
■ Put on border strips, if desired.

To Do

■ Seat the child in front of the sticky paper where he can easily reach it.
■ Let him feel the stickiness.
■ Show him how to put a piece of lightweight material on it and make it stick. Have more available and gesture to it, saying, "You do it."

Observations

■ Does the child imitate your action?
■ Is he intrigued that it sticks and doesn't fall off?
■ Does he try to peel it off again?

Sensory Development

More Ideas

- Provide a variety of different substances for them to stick on when you offer the activity again.

Emerging Skill

The child learns about "sticky." This is also an excellent fine motor activity, motivating the child to use the thumb and forefinger, especially when it comes to peeling it off again.

Tape

Materials

any type of tape

To Do

- Cut a small piece of tape (about one inch or three centimeters long) and hand it to the child.
- Say, "Sticky!"

Observations

- What does the child do with the tape?
- Is he fascinated that it sticks?
- Does he stare at it intensely?
- Does he try to peel it off and stick it to other fingers or other surfaces?

Safety

- Stay close, to prevent the child from putting it in his mouth and swallowing it.

More Ideas

- Use different types of tape, or contact paper pieces.

Emerging Skill

The child gains fine motor practice while experiencing the sticky texture.

Smelly Socks

Materials

baby socks
fragrant substances such as cloves, dried oregano, cedar chips, dried orange
    peel, cotton balls sprayed with perfume or room freshener
needle and thread
basket or small container

Simple Steps

To Make

- Fill each sock with a different-smelling material.
- Sew the socks closed.
- Put these in a small container such as a basket.

To Do

- Present the container of socks to the child.
- Hold one sock at a time in front of the child's nose. You smell the socks too, demonstrating what to do.
- Put these away when you cannot be right there, because they are not to be chewed or sucked on.

Observations

- Does the child seem to notice the fragrance?
- Is this interesting to the child?

Emerging Skill

The child may become more conscious of his sense of smell.

Sticky Wall

 18 MONTHS +

Materials

contact paper
lightweight materials such as plastic lids, feathers, fabric scraps, and laminated pictures

To Make

- Attach a long piece of the contact paper to the wall at children's height, sticky side out.
- Remove the backing.

To Do

- Let the children feel the sticky surface with their fingertips.
- In a few days, place the light materials in a container, such as a plastic bucket, and put the container near this sticky section of the wall.
- Let them place the materials on the sticky surface and peel them off again, if they wish.

Emerging Skill

Children enjoy the ability to make something stick. They also gain some fine motor practice. This is a good activity for children who peel off pictures that you have put on the wall for decoration.

Sticky Lids With Pictures

Materials

contact paper
plastic yogurt container or potato chip can lids
pictures or photographs

To Do

- Attach the contact paper to the wall at child-height, sticky side out.
- Cut out photos of children in your group or pictures cut from magazines and glue them to the tops of the plastic lids.
- The child can stick them to the wall and rearrange them.

More Ideas

- You could use photos of the children's families.
- Juice can lids work too.
- Make this a "Who's Here Today" attendance board for the children in your class.
- For two-year-olds, you could make this a sorting game, using pictures that could be grouped into different categories, such as animals, vehicles, and food.

Emerging Skill

This is a great fine motor activity as the child peels off the lids. It is also a social and language activity when the child identifies people in the photos or names and groups objects in pictures.

Floating Islands

18 MONTHS +

Materials

water table or large dishpan
shaving cream
waterproof smocks

Simple Steps

To Do

- Put a few inches or centimeters of water in the water table or plastic dish tub.
- Then squeeze in mounds of shaving cream.
- Let the children enjoy playing with these floating islands.

Observations

- What does the child do with the islands?

Safety

- Stay close in case a child starts to eat the shaving cream. Make sure any toys you offer are too large to choke on.

More Ideas

- Offer a few other toys or objects and let children find out if they will stay on the islands or fall through. Possibilities: plastic berry baskets, rubber animals, plastic vehicles.
- Small boats could "sail" between the islands.

Emerging Skill

Besides being soothing and fun, this activity might spark some interesting dramatic play with miniature objects.

Bath Time for Dollie

 18 MONTHS +

Materials

pan of water
bar of soap
washcloth
towel
washable doll

To Do

- Say to the child, "This baby is dirty. She needs a bath. Let's wash her."
- Then just stay close and see if the child knows what to do.

Observations

■ Does the child actually try to wash the doll, or does he just play with the water?

■ How long does this keep his attention?

Emerging Skill

As the child uses water, he is involved in pretend play. This is also a social activity.

Sandbox Play

18 MONTHS +

Materials

clean, loose sand at least 6" (15 cm) deep
various accessories (see below), outside or inside

To Do

■ When playing with sand is a new experience, parallel play with the child to model appropriate things to do with sand.

■ Avoid directing the child, however, and let him experiment freely.

Observations

■ How does the child approach the sand?

■ Does he need encouragement to touch and dig?

■ Does he prefer to use tools like spoons or does he use his hands?

Safety

■ Stay close to stop children if they throw sand or start to eat it. Show them things to do instead that are more fun.

More Ideas

■ Filling and spilling—give them lots of different shapes of containers and funnels.

■ Pretend cooking—add toy cooking utensils, spoons, a few rocks. A hibachi outside is fun. Bring a stove from the dramatic play corner outside.

■ Miniature play—give the children small people, animals, and vehicles to play with.

■ Moisten the sand with a spray bottle to make it easier to mold and pack.

Emerging Skill

Children use their fine motor skills as they fill and spill sand. Imagination, use of symbols, and social interaction happen in dramatic play with cooking utensils or miniatures. Children can feel powerful creating mini-scenes and directing the action in miniature play.

Simple Steps

Materials

bar of soap in a soap
    dish
small scrub brush
wash cloth
towel
water in a small bucket
    or dish tub

To Do

- Invite the child to wash the object you put out. Probably not much demonstration is necessary. You could show the process once, if you feel it is necessary.
- Let the child take all the time he wants and allow as many repetitions as he wants.

Observations

- See if the child knows how to put the soap on the brush or wash cloth, wash the object, rinse it, and dry it.

More Ideas

- This activity can be endlessly interesting, simply by offering different objects to wash from day to day.

Emerging Skill

The child learns what it takes to make things clean. In the process, the child explores all sides of a three-dimensional object, perhaps gaining a greater awareness of space.

Sensory Development

Slippery Bumps

Materials

plastic bubble pack sheet
tape
petroleum jelly

To Do

- ▇ Tape the bubble pack sheet to the tabletop, bumpy side up.
- ▇ Put a glob of petroleum jelly in the middle.
- ▇ Invite children to spread the petroleum jelly all over the surface. Stay close and be ready to wash hands when they finish.

Observations

- ▇ How does the child react to the feel of the gooey substance?
- ▇ Is the child interested in covering the whole surface of the bubble sheet?
- ▇ Does the child examine his fingers while he does this?

Safety

- ▇ Intervene if a child tries to eat the petroleum jelly.

More Ideas

- ▇ Collect several different sizes of bubbles in the bubble sheets, and tape these side by side. Describe the difference in size as they touch them.
- ▇ Add a drop of food coloring to the glob of petroleum jelly.

Emerging Skill

The bumpy surface gives children lots of interesting shapes to explore and feels good to the fingertips.

Mystery Bag

Materials

cloth drawstring bag
assortment of interesting objects to put inside it

To Do

- ▇ Every day put something different inside the bag and place it on a low shelf as a free play choice.
- ▇ Sometimes you can put in familiar toys such as crayons and a small pad of paper, or some small cars.

- At other times place some "good junk" objects inside such as spools of thread in different colors, large (fist-sized) colorful paper clips, a bunch of napkin rings, and napkins.
- The child will be drawn to the bag because of the novelty of discovering what is inside. He can feel through the bag and try to guess what it is.
- Then as he plays with the contents, the two of you can talk about the objects.
- Let him put the objects back in the bag and the bag back on the shelf when he is finished so someone else might discover it.

Safety

- Make sure the objects are large enough so they cannot be swallowed or pose a choking danger.

Emerging Skill

The child will use his sense of touch to guess what the objects are, and then his sense of sight to confirm the guess. Younger toddlers will be interested in simply emptying the bag and filling it again, no matter what the objects are. They like to make things appear and disappear (a cognitive activity). Opportunities exist for vocabulary growth as children explore new objects.

Cold Tub

24 MONTHS +

Materials

snow
icicles
ice cubes
food coloring
mittens

To Do

- Give each child a pair of mittens to put on and talk about how mittens keep hands warm.
- Children will enjoy molding the snow and sticking the icicles in it like birthday candles.
- Let the children decide if they want to add food coloring and where.

Observations

- How does their play change with different accessories?

Safety

- Don't allow children to eat the snow, and keep an eye on the ice cubes.

More Ideas

- Add small toys like plastic animals and people.
- Spoons and pots and pans are also good.

Sensory Development

Emerging Skill

The children will see that snow and ice melt, and turn liquid. They will experience the coldness and will see how colors dilute and mix. Dramatic play occurs when you add accessories.

Washing Dishes

24 MONTHS +

Materials

two plastic dish tubs
warm water
plastic dishes
dish soap
dish rag
dish scrubber
dish drainer
smock or apron for child

To Do

- Put a few inches of warm water in each dish tub and add dish soap to one of them.
- Show the child the sequence of washing dishes: put the "dirty" dishes in the soapy water; wash one at a time, rinse, put in the dish drainer.
- Then invite the child to do it.

Observations

- Is the child able to follow this sequence?
- He may just need "free play" with the materials first for awhile.

Safety

- Make sure all dishes are unbreakable.

More Ideas

- Once this washing sequence is mastered, add drying the dishes with a dish towel and stacking them.

Emerging Skill

The child enjoys playing with warm water and suds and imitating adult behavior.

Simple Steps

Wash Off the Table

Materials

spray bottle with water inside
sponge

To Do

- Show the child how to work the spray bottle and aim it at the table top, then how to wipe the wet spot with a sponge.
- Let the child experiment with this as long as interest holds.

Observations

- How long does the child stay with the activity?

Safety

- Do not let children use bottles with real disinfecting solution in them. Keep these out of reach. Observe to be sure that the child does not suck on or eat the sponge.

More Ideas

- Let the child "clean" other surfaces.

Emerging Skill

The child gains fine motor practice squeezing the spray bottle, and a possible self-esteem boost doing "adult looking" things, while enjoying playing with water.

Wash the Floor

24 MONTHS +

Materials

small string mop (with a cut-off handle so it is child height)

To Do

- Simply keep this mop near the water table or where water is used in other activities.
- When there is a spill, invite the child to use the mop to wipe up the spill.

More Ideas

- You could also offer a sponge mop that has the handle shortened.

Emerging Skill

Children are using real tools to do real work, boosting their self-esteem.

Materials

chairs
buckets of soapy water
sponges
scrub brushes
waterproof smocks

To Do

- On a warm, sunny day with no wind, have a discussion with the children and notice where the chairs in your classroom are dirty.
- Ask them, "What do you think we can do to make them clean again? Shall we wash them?"
- Let the children help you carry the chairs outside.
- Then put smocks on children, give them buckets of soapy water (use mild soap) and let them go at it.
- Later let them rinse the chairs with clear water.
- Help them notice how the sun dries the chairs.

Observations

- Do the children talk to each other or themselves as they wash the chairs?
- Do you sense any dramatic play going on?

More Ideas

- Two-year-olds love to wash just about anything. If you have a safe place to park a car inside a fenced area, children will have fun washing it!

Emerging Skill

While children play with water, they are also engaging in dramatic play, imitating adults cleaning things. They might learn a little bit about what it takes to keep things clean. This activity will hold children's attention for a long time.

Washing Napkins

24 MONTHS +

Materials

cloth napkins
two dish tubs with a little water for washing and rinsing in each
miniature wash board (optional)
bar of soap
clothes drying rack or clothesline
towel

Simple Steps

To Do

- Show the child how to rub soap into the napkin and scrub it, rinse it, and then hang it to dry.
- Let the child experiment with this as long as he likes.

Observations

- Note how much of the sequence the child repeats, or if he plays randomly with the materials.

Safety

- Put a towel underneath the drying rack to absorb drips so the floor won't become slippery.

More Ideas

- Give the children different things to wash from time to time, such as doll clothes.

Emerging Skill

The child will learn a bit about what it takes to make things clean. He will also notice that clothes that are hung up dry better than if they are left in a pile on the table.

Things Buried in the Sand

24 MONTHS +

Materials

sand in sensory table or
    outdoors
small toys

To Do

- Ahead of time, bury the objects in the sand.
- Let the children "discover" them as they play.

Observations

- What is their reaction when they find something?
- Do they show the other children, play with the object, or rebury it?

More Ideas

- Leave a small part of the object sticking out with very young children. Can they tell what it is?
- Do this with any of the other substances listed for sensory tables, such as shaving cream or confetti.
- Give children sifters to help them find things.

Emerging Skill

This is a cognitive (object permanence) activity. Children learn that something still exists when they can't see it, and they have to create a mental image of it.

Make Mud

24 MONTHS +

Materials

three dish tubs
sand
water
spoons and small containers
water table or wading pool

To Do

- Put sand in one dish tub and water in the second. Leave the third empty.
- Place these inside the water table or wading pool on a low table.
- Say nothing, other than to invite the children to play here.
- Make the spoons and containers available.

Observations

- See if they discover on their own how to make mud.

Safety

- Stay close so you can prevent them from eating it or throwing it.

More Ideas

- Add other toys such as miniature vehicles, animals, and people when they have experience.

Emerging Skill

Children learn that things may change when they are combined. They learn that they can make things happen.

Simple Steps

Materials

any type of fruit or vegetable
knife

To Do

- ▨ Have children wash hands.
- ▨ Show them the fruit or vegetable.
- ▨ Let them touch the outside, smell it, hold it against their cheek, etc.
- ▨ Talk about the color and the texture. Then wonder out loud what they might find inside. Young children love containers of all types, and fruits are really containers.
- ▨ Talk about the pattern that emerges when you cut it open. What is in there? Are there any seeds?
- ▨ You might cut two or three oranges in different ways to see the different patterns. Finally, of course, let them taste the fruit.

Observations

- ▨ Do they try to taste this right away?
- ▨ Do they later notice patterns in the fruits and vegetables they have for lunch and snacks?

Safety

- ▨ Be sure to put the knife away, out of children's reach, when you are not right there.

More Ideas

- ▨ You can do this with a wide variety of fruits and vegetables, everything from beans to eggplants to bananas to kiwis. All have lovely surprises inside. Let the children use plastic knives to cut them up further as they investigate and eat.
- ▨ Make a scrapbook describing all the different fruits and vegetables you have explored in this way. See if children recognize them when they show up later in meals and snacks.

Emerging Skill

This is a sensory, cognitive, and fine motor experience. This is the best kind of "cooking project" for toddlers because there is no waiting involved.

Sensory Development

Materials

a lot of one kind of fruit or vegetable, such as apples, carrots, pumpkins, or lemons
knife

To Do

- First, let the child simply play with the collection.
- Help the children notice the individual differences. You can probably find four or five different varieties of apples. But even in something fairly standard, like lemons, children might be able to notice individual differences in the fruits you have available.
- After they have had lots of time to explore the outside of the fruit, let the children watch as you cut into it.
- Enjoy eating what you have there. Does it all taste the same?

Observations

- Do the children do any sorting or organizing of the fruits by size?
- How do they recognize "individuals"—by size, markings on the peel, stickers?

Safety

- First wash the table top and the fruits or vegetables, and have children wash their hands.
- Put the knife out of reach as soon as you finish using it.

Emerging Skill

This is a cognitive as well as a sensory experience, and children will notice small differences, perhaps starting to order and classify these objects.

Juices, Shakes, and Smoothies 24 MONTHS +

Materials

fruits, such as banana, strawberries, or oranges
sugar or honey
water
blender
knife or peeler

To Do

- Let the children help you make juices from the fruits. They can wash and peel the fruits, or cut them into chunks with plastic knives and help you put the pieces into a blender.

Simple Steps

- Add the water and as little sugar or honey as you can get by with.
- Let one child put the lid on the blender. Let another child push the button to start the blender.
- Then enjoy drinking the juice together. Comment on how different it looks when it's chopped up.

Observations

- Do they like the juice?

Safety

- Put the blender, out of reach immediately when you are finished.

More Ideas

- Add milk or ice cream to make shakes.
- Add chopped ice to make smoothies.

Emerging Skill

Many children have only seen juice that comes out of cans. This will broaden their understanding, while providing a rich experience for all the senses.

Peel Corn 24 MONTHS +

Materials

corn on the cob in the husk

To Do

- Let the children help you peel off the husks from the corn and strip off the silk. They won't get it perfect, but can enjoy the process.
- While they're at it, comment on what they see, hear, and feel. Some very interesting textures present themselves.
- Cook the corn, let it cool to just slightly warm, cut it into small chunks, and let the children enjoy the treat.

Observations

- Do they enjoy it even more, now that they have been part of the preparation process?

Emerging Skill

The child has a rich sensory experience while "helping" and doing real work.

Materials

bread dough (thawed frozen dough, or dough you have prepared ahead of time)
baking sheet
bowl
raw egg
food coloring
fork
clean paintbrushes
non-stick spray
oven

To Do

- Break the egg into a small bowl.
- Let the child pick a color of food coloring and squeeze a few drops onto the egg and mix it up with a fork. You can thin this with about a teaspoon of water.
- Have the child shape a hunk of bread dough any way he likes and place it on a sprayed baking sheet.
- Then have the child dip the paintbrush into the colored egg mixture and paint his "pretzel."
- Bake these at about 350°F for about fifteen minutes.

Observations

- Does the child notice how the pretzel changes in the oven?
- Does it seem to taste better when it's been painted?

Safety

- Don't let children get near the oven.

More Ideas

- Sprinkle with coarse salt.
- Paint cookies with a similar paint, but add a little powdered sugar.

Emerging Skill

The child is combining a sensory experience and an art experience and is likely to notice changes in the final product.

Simple Steps

Chapter 8

A Sense of Wonder

Nature Activities

Infants, toddlers, and two-year-olds are natural scientists, driven to investigate and experiment with everything they encounter. Children have an inborn drive to explore their world, but they learn attitudes about it from the people around them—whether something is "yucky" or interesting, for example. If the important adults in their lives love to be outside and look with awe at interesting animals and plants, children will learn the importance of respecting nature. Rather than teaching children specific facts about nature at this stage, we should be encouraging their natural curiosity.

Children should spend time outside every day, weather permitting. Infants can sleep in a shady area outside in buggies or cribs with mosquito netting over the top. The environment chapter (pages 229-240) gives some specific suggestions for creating a safe and interesting outdoor play space. Outdoor space is the richest sensory area, offering a wide variety of textures, temperatures, smells, and sights.

Of course, you can offer children experiences with nature indoors as well. For instance, you can bring in a large rock that is too heavy for children to pick up. They will enjoy examining the texture, and seeing the color change when they wash it. Tree stumps or a collection of leaves are other things to bring indoors. Put real flowers in the classroom from time to time and let children

Nature Activities

examine them, or provide pussywillows in the spring and icicles or snow in the winter. Change what you make available from week to week.

Many beautiful non-fiction children's books about nature are available. Although many are for older children, you could share the pictures and marvel at their beauty together. Help children notice and label the things they see. Tell them what they are looking at. Describe the patterns, textures, and colors. Model your own wonder and enthusiasm.

Nature Walks

- A simple nature walk around the neighborhood, or even just the playground, can yield rich experiences.
- Prepare children ahead of time. Talk about what you are going to do. Help them guess what they might see.

- Bring a container to collect things in. Let the children put in pretty stones, dry leaves, etc. Discourage them from picking flowers.

- Turn over rocks and logs, then put them back. Some amazing things may be living underneath, like worms, ants, and even little salamanders. Replace the cover carefully, explaining to children that it is the roof of the insects' or animals' house and they need it for protection.

- Take a photo of interesting things you see.

- Do something afterward that relates to this outdoor experience. You could peel off the backing of contact paper and let the children stick on the things you brought back, or they could sort things into different containers to put on a low shelf.

- Make simple felt board representations of your nature walk experience by drawing pictures of objects you saw and backing them with felt or velcro.
- Tell a story in "once upon a time" style about the walk that you just took. You could use the pictures described above to add as the sequence of the story unfolds.

Wildflower Window Panels

6 WEEKS +

Materials

clear contact paper
flowers

To Make

- Remove the backing from the contact paper and press the flowers onto it.
- Press the paper's sticky side directly onto a window. The light will shine through and the colors last a surprisingly long time.

To Do

- Place this on a low window where the children can see it.
- You might carry the child over to it and look at it together.

Observations

- Does the child enjoy looking at the colors and patterns?

More Ideas

- Colored leaves also make a beautiful panel.
- Try colored tissue paper and colored cellophane for variety.
- Older children can help you gather the flowers and leaves and press them onto the sticky paper.

Emerging Skill

The child sees something beautiful from nature, and it enhances your room decor.

Wind Sock

6 WEEKS +

Materials

manufactured or homemade decorative wind sock

To Make

- A homemade windsock can be fashioned from streamers of crepe paper or light, brightly colored fabric tied to a hoop and then suspended with fishing line.

- Hang the wind sock outside from a tree or a building overhang where it can move freely in the wind.

To Do

- Place the child where she can notice the windsock nearby.

Observations

- Does she move her head toward the flapping, fluttering noise of the windsock?
- Does she stare at the moving colors? Does she reach out toward it?

More Ideas

- Move the windsock(s) to different places from time to time.

Emerging Skill

Children will have something bright, beautiful, and interesting to see and hear.

Things to Do With a Tree

 24 MONTHS +

Materials

a tree

To Do

- Suggest to the children that you all go over and get to know a certain tree.
- First let children investigate the tree in their own ways.
- Describe what they do and others will imitate.
- Model behaviors yourself too. Feel the bark with your hands. Put your cheek up to the bark. Smell the tree and describe it. Pick up some things around it. Lie down on grass and look up into the tree.

Observations

- What do the children think of to do?

Safety

- Make sure children don't pick things up and put them in their mouths.

More Ideas

- On a warm day, read stories under a tree or have rest time under the tree. Talk about how nice the shade feels.
- Visit the same tree on a regular basis. Take pictures of it and help the children notice changes in the tree.
- Make an indoor display of the tree—photos, samples of the bark, leaves, seeds, etc.
- Play "Ring Around the Rosie" around the tree.

Simple Steps

Emerging Skill

Children will learn to love this tree and see all trees as special.

Tape Nature Bracelets

24 MONTHS +

Materials

masking tape

To Do

- ■ Make a bracelet for each child, sticky side out.
- ■ As you go on a nature walk with the children, or even just play on the playground, let children put dried flowers, leaves, seeds, etc. on the sticky side of the tape.

Observations

- ■ Do they "get into" this, actively looking for interesting things to stick to their bracelets?
- ■ Or are they more interested in playing with the tape?

Safety

- ■ Make sure children don't put items in their mouths.

More Ideas

- ■ Do this in different settings. Bracelets made in different environments will look different.
- ■ Undo the bracelet indoors and stick it on a piece of paper to take home.

Emerging Skill

Children will learn to notice the details in nature.

Find One Like This

24 MONTHS +

Materials

assortment of objects from nature that are abundant in the environment you will be in with children, such as a round stone, a pine cone, a dandelion, a fallen leaf, a seed pod

To Do

- Show the children the objects and talk about them.
- Name them and describe the textures and colors.
- Then give each child one of the objects and see if she can find another one like it and bring it back to you.
- Compare them and talk about them.

Observations

- Do the children know the meaning of the words "same" and "different?"
- Do they notice the slight variations in similar objects?

Safety

- Since many objects from nature can break off or tear and become a size children could choke on, supervise so that children don't put these things in their mouths.

More Ideas

- You could "plant" a variety of objects in the yard to make sure children will be successful in finding a match. You might assign an older child to go with a younger child in the search.

Emerging Skill

A basic same-and-different exercise, this could be classified as a cognitive experience. But children are also more likely to notice the variety of shapes and textures in nature, feeding the development of a sense of wonder.

Our Nature Walk Book

24 MONTHS +

Materials

camera and film
photo album with "magnetic" plastic pages

Simple Steps

To Do

- When you and the children go on a short nature walk or stroll in the neighborhood, take a picture when you leave the building; take pictures of interesting objects, people, and animals you see along the way; and take a final picture when you return to the building.
- Get the film developed quickly at a one-hour processor, if possible.
- Let the children help you put these photos in the photo album and decide what you should say about each picture in the caption you write.
- Read it to them at your story time and whenever they request it. Set it out within their reach so they can page through it by themselves.

Observations

- Can children put the pictures in order?
- Do they remember what they saw?

Safety

- Have enough adults to supervise children on your walks, or take just two at a time.

More Ideas

- If possible, take a walk with children in several different environments, such as a wooded area, a field, and a mowed grass area. Make a book for each. Then let them compare the pictures and notice the differences.

Emerging Skill

This will become a favorite book of theirs because they actually experienced everything in it. Seeing themselves in a book is good for their self-image, and looking at the pictures is also a prime pre-reading experience. The book may also help them remember more of the specifics from the walk. Seeing the sequence of events is a cognitive connection.

Nature Walk With a Sensory Focus 24 MONTHS +

Materials

To Do

- Tell the children you are going on a walk to see how many different things you can find to smell.
- As you walk along, demonstrate what you want them to do, because young children don't always know what it means to smell something. Sniff at flowers, tree bark, leaves, grasses, etc.

Observations

- Do the children catch on and try it?

Safety

■ Make sure they don't taste things.
■ Have enough adults to supervise children on your walks, or take just two at a time.

More Ideas

■ On different days, go on walks to see what you can see, feel, and hear.

Emerging Skill

Children might become more aware of their individual senses and the variety of experiences nature has to offer.

Ice Collages

24 MONTHS +

Materials

freezing cold weather (or a freezer)
disposable pie tins
water
items from nature
string, yarn, or wire to hang it with

To Do

■ Let children collect items from nature.
■ When inside, have the children place the nature items in the pie tins, then pour water over them.
■ Carry these outside, and, if possible, place them where children will be able to see them from indoors.
■ Place a loop of string in each so it hangs over the edge.
■ Let the children check them every hour or so and notice any changes.
■ When they have hardened, hang them from a tree or fence.

Observations

■ Do the children associate the frozen collage with the materials they collected?

More Ideas

■ Add a drop or two of food coloring.
■ In warm climates, put these in the freezer.
■ Let children see these melt again in your water table.

Simple Steps

Emerging Skill

Children will notice the shapes of the objects and may learn a little about how cold makes water turn into ice. (They will need many experiences with this to really comprehend the process.)

Gardening

24 MONTHS +

Materials

fenced-off garden plot or gardening container
small plants
small shovels
watering can or hose

To Do

- Gardening is not terribly satisfying to very young children because it takes so long to see results, but they do like the process.
- Let them help you dig.
- Notice any worms or bugs, but leave them there.
- Let the children help you water the plants.
- Every day notice the progress of the plants. Talk about what the young plants need to make them grow.

Observations

- What is their reaction when they see a worm or a bug?
- Do they notice changes from day to day?

Safety

- Make sure they do not eat anything they dig up, and do not expose them to fertilizers or manure.

Emerging Skill

Young children may not associate the growth and the final product with earlier efforts, but they have enjoyed doing something outside with you.

Materials

several colorful umbrellas
rain boots children can slip into, shoes and all

To Do

- On a day when it is raining lightly (not a storm), take one or two children at a time for a brief walk in the rain, even just around your playground.
- Let them hold the umbrellas and step in puddles.
- Notice how things look when they are wet.

Observations

- Can they figure out how to hold the umbrella to keep from getting wet?
- What do they like best?

Safety

- Go back inside at any hint of thunder, lightening, or strong wind.

More Ideas

- Take a photo or two.
- Leave a painting outside for the rain to work on.
- Go out again right after the rain. What do they see?

Emerging Skill

The children will enjoy being outside in different circumstances, enjoying the rain rather than hurrying through it.

Simple Steps

Chapter 9

Making Your Mark on the World

Creative Development

What is art for infants, toddlers, and two-year-olds? What can they do? What *should* they be doing? "Art" activities that are appropriate for children under three to do over and over again are painting; making things stick with paste and glue; smearing fingerpaint; making marks with sponges dipped in paint; and scribbling with crayons, pencils, markers, and chalk. All have endless variations to keep them interesting to children and adults.

Developing Creativity

What makes a person creative? What early experiences give someone the aptitude to express himself creatively? "Pre-creative" activities—the foundations of creativity—start in the first year. Art is certainly an important part of creativity, but the issue and concept of creativity is much broader.

Feeling valued

In order for a person to want to express himself creatively, he must first feel that someone out there thinks he is interesting and that his ideas have value. We communicate this to children in many ways. We try to understand and interpret all their various grunts, facial expressions, and gestures. We also "shine" on babies when they accomplish things. "Look at you!" we say, "Look what you did! You put all the couch pillows on top of each other." Even a teacher's appreciative gaze, interested look, smile, nod, or applause from across the room as a child looks back for approval communicate to the child that he is interesting and valued.

Combining things

Creativity is sometimes defined as the ability to combine materials in new, original ways. Just think for a minute about what young children do in a room full of safe objects when they are left to their own devices—endless combining! The child is on a compulsive quest to find out what fits in what, what kind of noise something makes when it is banged against the floor, what sort of object gets stuck where. This child is a creative scientist! To do this, the child must have access to objects (not toys that do everything for him) such as empty boxes, scarves, egg crates, plastic containers of all shapes and sizes, things to put into containers and dump out again, things that nest, things that fit together.

Exploring space and direction

Infants have to crawl in, out, and under things to gain a sense of directionality, down and up, inside of, underneath. Then, as toddlers, they enjoy making objects such as balls, wheel toys, and blocks go where they want them to. Later they learn to make *marks* go where they want them to on paper.

Making hands do what they want them to

First, babies just stare at these amazing objects that appear in space above them. Later, they realize that they are causing the movement they see in front of their eyes. Reaching and grabbing at objects and learning to let go comes next. Then they start aiming objects, seen in the compulsion of sticking things in holes. Eventually, the child learns to hold onto a crayon and exert downward pressure while moving it across a paper. Art activities of all types offer good fine motor practice.

Variety Is the Spice of Creativity

Many people think of art in terms of the final product—helping children make cute things to take home. While it is not appropriate to require that young children (or any age child) produce something to take home each day, you do want to give children frequent experiences using a wide variety of art materials, without any sort of final product in mind. *Instead of racking your brain thinking of cute things for children to make to take home, rack your brain thinking of interesting materials for children to use.*

Toddlers and two-year-olds use art materials to find out what they can do with the material. They love watching the color streak across the paper. They love watching glue dribble out of the bottle. They love watching their fingers stick together when paste gets on them. Gradually they learn how to control these substances.

Telling a child what to make or what to draw is futile and only frustrates both you and the child. Instead, protect clothes with smocks, aim the child toward the materials, and let him "go at it." It's about power! The child learns that he can make things happen. The very young child is often delighted to discover that he can make a mark!

Hints for Success With Art and Creative Activities

- Do activities with one individual or with a very small group of no more than four children. A large group can be over-whelming to both the children and the teacher. In a large group, children spend their time jostling for position and have more difficulty concentrating. If you do the activity with a small number, the children can relax and get more deeply involved in the process.

- Arrange it so that one adult can stay with or near the activity to supervise and prevent children from putting the art materials in their mouths. Even though non-toxic, the materials can be messy.

- Let the child discover the activity and choose to do it out of curiosity. On rare occasions when no one is spontaneously attracted to the activity, you may want to "invite" one or two children to participate, but allow them to refuse. Usually, any new material will attract interest. Other children will be drawn to it when they see their friends involved.

- Protect children's clothing with smocks and roll up sleeves.

- Don't rush them. It's more important that a child relax and enjoy the process, inventing variations and socializing with others rather than rushing through it so everyone can have a turn. Repeat the activity the next day if necessary so that all who want to can participate.

- Allow the children to repeat the activity. When a child finishes a painting, for instance, ask, "Do you want to paint again, or do you want to play somewhere else?" This avoids the "once over lightly" aspect of much art-work. If a child does three paintings in a row, his understanding will be much deeper than if he has to relinquish his space to someone else.

- Offer the activity again and again when you see that a process is interesting to children and holds their attention. If you feel the need, you can add variety by changing one small part of it—the color, width of brush, or texture of fingerpaint, for instance. You will know when the activity gets stale. The children won't choose to do it, will rush through it, or abuse the material.
- Allow them to vary the intended process. If the child thinks of something else to do with the materials that is not destructive, allow it.
- Have everything ready ahead of time. You don't want to leave the scene to get the paint, paper, or any other materials needed. There's no quicker way to spoil an activity than to leave children waiting.

What Do You Tell the Parents?

When parents think of art as something nice to hang on their wall or refrigerator, they can be perplexed when handed a half disintegrated piece of paper with brown paint all over it. Because of that, some teachers are tempted to lie to parents and pretend that the craft was created by the children when ninety percent of it was actually the teacher's work.

Instead, describe to parents what the child actually did in art play—how the activity fit into the child's overall development of creativity. This doesn't take any more time than all the preparation that craft-oriented teachers do, and it gives parents a true understanding and appreciation for the wonderful creative processes that young children practice on their own every day.

Scribble Spot

10 MONTHS +

Materials

butcher paper attached to the wall at child level
one or more hooks put in the wall securely above the reach of the children
3 or 4 pieces of string or yarn about 3' (1 m) long, to reach from the hook to the bottom of the butcher paper
fat crayons

To Make

- Tie each crayon to one end of a string (you can make a little notch groove in the crayon for the string).
- Tie the other end of the string to the hook, leaving it long enough so that the crayon will dangle just above the bottom of the paper.
- The advantage is that you can have crayons available all the time and children cannot take them to other places and scribble.

To Do

- Let two or three children stand side by side and scribble on the paper. Describe their actions.

Simple Steps

Observations

- Do they notice the other children and the marks they are making?
- Is there interaction between the children?
- Does one child seem to imitate the other?
- Do they make their marks overlap?

Safety

- Make sure the hooks are well-anchored in the wall. The string should not be long enough for children to accidentally get entangled in it.

More Ideas

- Change the color of the crayons each day.
- When the paper fills up with scribbles, put up a clean sheet, maybe of a different color.
- Talk about the colors as they use them.
- Let the children scribble inside a large box such as an appliance box.

Emerging Skill

Scribbling allows children to gain fine motor control as they gradually learn how to control the marks they put on the paper. When children scribble side by side, they are also engaged in a social activity.

Scribble of the Day

 10 MONTHS +

Materials

large piece of paper, such as butcher paper, taped to the wall or table top
something different to scribble with each day of the week, such as crayons, chalk, markers, large pencils, paint in roll-on deodorant bottles

To Do

- Attach the paper to the wall or table on Monday.
- Each day, let the children scribble on it using a different material.
- Take the scribbled-up paper off on Friday and start the next Monday with a clean sheet.

Observations

■ Do the children do different things with different materials?

More Ideas

■ Save the paper and use it to decorate your room, create borders for bulletin boards, cover storage boxes, etc.

■ Cut it up and use the back for note paper for your communications with parents.

Emerging Skill

Children get a sense of the passage of time as they see the paper fill up week after week. You can use words like "yesterday," "today," and "tomorrow" in context as you talk about the materials they use for their scribbles. This can also diffuse the impulse to scribble on walls, giving them a place where the activity is acceptable.

Stick Drawing 12 MONTHS +

Materials

dirt or moist sand, outside
small sticks

To Do

■ Encourage children to use the sticks to draw lines and patterns in the dirt. You might have to demonstrate.

Observations

■ If you lay appropriate sticks out near an undisturbed piece of earth, do children do this activity spontaneously?

Safety

■ Stay close so that the sticks are not used inappropriately.

More Ideas

■ Find things like stones and leaves that could be added to their designs.

■ Moisten the sand in a sensory table indoors and offer a variety of sticks and other implements to draw with.

■ Find other interesting things such as a large comb or a potato masher to make marks in the sand with.

Emerging Skill

Children discover that they can make a mark with natural materials. Later they might incorporate this into their dramatic play.

Simple Steps

Chalk on the Sidewalk

Materials

sidewalk
large, soft chalk
moist wipes

To Do

■ Let the children scribble on the sidewalk using the chalk.
■ Have moist wipes handy to clean hands when they are through.

Observations

■ Do they enjoy making a mark on the bumpiness of the sidewalk?
■ What is the size of the marks they make?

Safety

■ Stay close to make sure they do not put the chalk in their mouths.

More Ideas

■ Let them wash the scribbles off with water, or leave them until it rains and then notice what happened.

Emerging Skill

Children are likely to use large, swinging motions as they scribble, rather than the smaller motions used to scribble on paper in a more confined space.

Water Painting

Materials

small pails of water
large, regular house painting brushes

To Do

■ Simply let children dip the large brushes into the water and paint the sidewalk and building with the plain water.

Art and Creative Activities

Observations

■ Do they notice how the surfaces get darker when they are wet?

More Ideas

■ Children will also enjoy using regular easel brushes or smaller brushes.
■ Scrub brushes might be fun too, or try toothbrushes.
■ Let them paint on colored construction paper at the easel, using easel brushes and plain water. This is a good introduction to easel painting.

Emerging Skill

Children are learning how brushes work to hold liquids, how they drip, and how they should be held to avoid dripping. They will also see that some surfaces become darker when wet. They will observe how the sun makes water evaporate, and that the dark water marks disappear more quickly when they are in the sun than when they are in the shade.

Fingerpainting on Paper 18 MONTHS +

Materials

fingerpaint
fingerpaint paper or freezer paper
sponge
water

To Do

■ Put a smock on the child and make sure sleeves are well rolled up.
■ Moisten the paper with the sponge.
■ Put a blob of fingerpaint in the middle of the paper and encourage the child to smear it around.

Observations

■ Is the child hesitant to touch the gooey substance, or does he dive right in?
■ How does he experiment with different ways to smear the paint?

More Ideas

■ Give the child two or three different colors at once, initially placed far apart on the paper.
■ After the child has plenty of experience with fingerpainting, encourage him to use different parts of his hand to make different types of marks.
■ After many "pure" fingerpainting experiences, give the child other things to use to make marks, such as combs and sponges.

Emerging Skill

The child is learning many different ways to make a mark and discovering that he can change something. He may also be learning color words.

Fingerpaint Directly on Table Top

Materials

fingerpaint
smooth table top

To Do

- Put a smock on the child and seat him at the table.
- Put a blob of fingerpaint in front of him and let him smear it across the table top.

Observations

- How does he approach this?
- Does he wait to see what others do?
- Do you have to help him touch it?
- Does he enjoy the texture?

Emerging Skill

Children are likely to make larger, more sweeping motions without the confinement of the paper edges.

Lift Off a Print

18 MONTHS +

Materials

fingerpaint
any kind of paper

To Do

- Put a smock on the child.
- Let him fingerpaint directly on the table top.
- Wipe most of the paint off the child's hands and help him lay a piece of paper on top of the spot where he has been painting.
- Let him press the paper down firmly and then help him lift it off to reveal the print underneath.

Observations

- What is his reaction to the print on the paper?
- Does he relate it to the design on the table?

Emerging Skill

The child will see a duplication and reversal of the pattern on the table. Noticing a pattern is a cognitive skill as well. This allows a child to have something to take home from a free art process.

Art and Creative Activities

Materials

styrofoam or paper cups
fingerpaint or shaving cream
small cars, people, or animals

To Do

■ Put a smock on the child and let him fingerpaint with the paint or shaving cream on the table top.

■ Allow this to continue as long as it seems satisfying to the child.

■ Then hand him a cup, invert it, and show him how to push it along the table top to clean the paint off.

■ Allow the child to play with the negative space trails that appear, if he wishes.

■ Give the child small cars or animals to use on the "streets" being made.

Observations

■ Is this fun for the child?
■ How long does he continue with the cup before losing interest?
■ Does his interest increase if you add extra objects?

More Ideas

■ This can either be part of the clean-up process or an addition to the play process.

Emerging Skill

The child learns another way to make a mark, and this lengthens the process, creating a new type of involvement with the materials.

Salt Paint Squeeze Bottles 18 MONTHS +

Materials

plastic bottles with a squirt top, like a mustard bottle
flour
water
salt
tempera paint
stiff paper or cardboard

To Make

- Mix equal parts of flour, salt, and water to make a creamy consistency.
- Add paint. Provide several different colors.
- Pour into squeeze bottles.

To Do

- Young children love to squeeze the bottle and watch the paint come out.
- Let them dribble the paint onto the cardboard.
- Let them use several different colors and see the patterns emerge.
- Set it aside to dry.
- When dry, the pattern will be raised from the surface and sparkly from the salt.

Safety

- Supervise so that children don't suck on the bottles.

More Ideas

- Let children dribble the mixture onto plastic coffee can lids. Punch a small hole in the lids first. When they are dry, hang these to make a pretty mobile.

Emerging Skill

Children can have the fun of watching something dribble out of a bottle. Unlike glue, this substance is not expensive. The activity also provides good hand muscle strength exercise.

Stamp Printing

 18 MONTHS +

Materials

rubber stamps of various designs
paper
sponge cloth soaked in tempera paint
something to hold sponge

To Do

- Let the child pick a stamp.
- Show the child how to put the stamp on the sponge first, then pound up and down on the paper to create a repeated pattern.

More Ideas

■ Roll out playdough or plasticene clay into a thin pancake. Let the child pound the stamp on this surface and notice the imprints (no paint or ink necessary).

Emerging Skill

Multiplication! The child may notice a repeated pattern. Older children may begin to organize the pattern to make it go across the page or around the edge.

Lots of Ways to Paint

 20 MONTHS +

Materials

things to paint *with*, such as easel brushes, house painting brushes, sponge-tipped edge trim paint tools, small rollers, household sponges, dish brushes, toothbrushes

things to paint *on*, such as easel paper, junk mail, newspaper, cardboard boxes, wax paper, aluminum foil

paint, sometimes mixed thick, sometimes thin, sometimes with things mixed in (try cornstarch)

To Do

■ Over time, give children one thing from each category above to paint with.
■ The combinations and variations are unlimited.

Observations

■ See how a child uses materials differently at different stages.
■ Does a two-year-old use a sponge brush differently from the way he did at twenty months?

Emerging Skill

Each different combination provides a new experience, a new opportunity to make a mark in a different way. The child gains fine motor practice as he learns to control his hand and arm to make marks go in different directions and make shapes, sometimes covering the whole page.

Cold Cream Face Paint

 24 MONTHS +

Materials

cold cream
liquid tempera paint in various colors
small containers to put face paint colors in
small paintbrushes
mirror

Simple Steps

To Make

■ Mix a small amount of the paint into the cold cream to form several pastel colors.

To Do

■ Let the child use the brush to spread the paint on his hand, or look in the mirror and paint his face.

■ Don't worry about design. This can be wiped off with a tissue when the activity is finished.

Observations

■ Can the child do this looking in the mirror? If not, just let him paint his hand.

Safety

■ Watch to see that the child can handle the brush properly so that he won't poke his eye.

More Ideas

■ Let the children paint their parents' faces at a parent function.

Emerging Skill

This is an interesting sensory experience as the child feels the paint going on his own skin.

Ice Painting _____ 24 MONTHS +

Materials

ice cubes or icicles
fingerpaint paper or shelf paper
powdered tempera paint in a shaker jar

To Do

■ Put a smock on the child.

■ Seat the child at the table in front of a piece of paper good for fingerpainting.

■ Let the child pick a color and shake some of the powdered paint onto the paper.

■ Then let the child hold the ice and smear it across the paint, causing it to liquify and spread.

Observations

- Does the child mind holding the cold ice?
- Is he surprised when the powdered paint makes a big streak?

More Ideas

- Let the child use two colors at once and discover how they mix.
- Have mittens on hand for the child to wear.

Emerging Skill

While making a mark, the child also notices some of the properties of ice—that it is cold, that it melts and turns liquid.

Rain Painting 24 MONTHS +

Materials

large sheet of butcher paper
powdered tempera paint in shaker jar
a gentle rain

To Do

- Let the children help you shake the powdered paint onto the butcher paper.
- Let them hold the door open for you as you drag the paper outside.
- Place it where they can see it by looking out a window.
- From inside, help the children notice what the rain is doing to the paint.
- Later, bring the paper back inside.
- Let the children notice it and how it changes as it dries.

Emerging Skill

This might broaden children's observation skills and give you some interesting things to talk about.

Thing Printing 24 MONTHS +

Materials

objects with an interesting shape or design to use for printing, such as strawberry basket, potato masher, spray can top, cookie cutters
paper
sponge cloth soaked in tempera paint
something to hold a sponge or cloth, such as pie tin

To Do

- Give the child one of the objects listed above, or let the child choose one.
- Show the child how to put it on the paint—press onto saturated sponge first, then on the paper to make a print.
- Let the child decide how many prints to make on the paper.

Observations

■ Does the child catch on quickly and repeat the sequence independently?
■ Is the child interested in the pattern and overlaps created?

More Ideas

■ Offer two or more different colors of paint to use.
■ Let the child trade objects.
■ Encourage the child to use different sides of the same object and notice the different shape of the print.

Emerging Skill

The child may notice the shape of different sides of an object. The mark that remains on the paper becomes a symbol of the object used. Noticing these things can build cognitive skills.

Paste

24 MONTHS +

Materials

non-toxic school paste
old greeting cards, cut-up pictures, etc.
background paper

To Do

■ Give each child a small mound of paste on a piece of paper, or in something like a jar lid.
■ Show the child how to stick his finger in the paste, smear it on a small piece of paper, and then invert it for placement onto another piece of paper.
■ Then just let the child experiment.

Observations

■ Watch what the child does. Many children put the paste on the design and then are puzzled why it disappears when they invert it.
■ Often they are more fascinated at how their fingers stick together than what is happening with the paper. Just let them "mess around."

Safety

■ While many children will taste this, stay close so they don't consume huge amounts.

More Ideas

■ Over time, give them many different materials to "make stick."

■ Try a simple homemade flour and water paste.

Emerging Skill

Children are gaining "physical knowledge" of paste and how sticky things act. With many repetitions, they will gradually learn how to manage paste and use it methodically. Regard it as a "sensory" experience.

Glue

24 MONTHS +

Materials

white glue
cotton tipped swabs
jar lids
paper
things to stick on, such as scraps of paper, leaves, small sticks, yarn

To Do

■ Pour a small puddle of glue into the jar lids and give one to each child.

■ Let the child use the cotton-tipped swab to "paint" the glue onto the paper and then stick things on top.

■ Step back and let the children experiment, and don't mind if they paint their fingers instead of the paper.

Observations

■ Note what individual children do with the glue.

Safety

■ Stay close so the child doesn't poke the cotton swab in ears or nose.

More Ideas

■ Over time, with many repetitions, let the children experiment gluing a wide variety of materials.

Emerging Skill

As children handle different things to glue, they gain more knowledge of the objects and the process. Glue is more satisfying than paste for materials other than paper because it sticks better.

Chapter 10

Let's Pretend

Dramatic Play Development

Dramatic play, pretend, or make-believe is very important in early childhood, and starts to show up in children's play in the toddler years. This kind of play is enjoyable for children and also extremely valuable for their development. Be sure that children always have the option of pretend play during both indoor and outdoor playtimes.

Value of Dramatic Play

Emotional

Children often play out scenes with emotional weight, such as being put to bed or going to the doctor. They usually cast themselves in the most powerful roles. Instead of being the baby being tucked in, they are the powerful parent doing the tucking in and reassuring. Instead of being the child getting the injection, they are the doctor giving the shot. This helps children come to terms with their feelings in such situations. When a child does not have much power in real life, being powerful in pretend play has great appeal.

Children who have had much experience taking on different roles are better at *empathy*—putting themselves in the other person's shoes, imagining how someone else feels. They practice this skill when they engage in role-play.

Social

Dramatic play is best when two or more children are involved. Especially when an adult is playing along with them and facilitating, dramatic play develops social skills as children negotiate for roles, decide what the situation will be, and interact with each other. Friendship skills are also developed.

Language

Children begin to practice language skills when they play make-believe together. They use words to decide what they are playing, and talk to each other within their roles. Often one child or the other will pick up new vocabulary or expressions. They learn to use gestures and facial expressions to communicate. Also, when children have had a lot of experience playing out their own scenes and stories, they are better able to follow the story line, or plot, in a book.

Cognitive

Learning to use symbols is an important part of cognitive development. Children are constantly using symbols in their play. Toys are symbols of real objects; they "represent" something the child has seen. A toy telephone or steering wheel will prompt a child to a certain kind of play. Later the child learns to use more abstract objects or gestures as symbols for play. She might turn a paper plate into a steering wheel, or just move her hands in a steering motion. When children have had lots of experience creating and using their own symbols in play, like scraps of paper for money or gestures to represent drinking, they will be better able to use other people's symbols, like letters and numbers, later on.

The Development of Dramatic Play Skills

You will see the first shades of pretend play in the infant year when a ten- to twelve-month-old picks up a toy telephone and puts it to her ear. The child is demonstrating that she knows what the toy represents and what people do with it. Other types of play may look like dramatic play, but may simply be "object play" where the child gains physical knowledge of the objects. When a young toddler hauls dolls around the room, she may not be pretending to be the mommy. When a child stacks dishes, she may not be pretending to organize a kitchen, but simply be exploring shapes.

Imitation

Simple imitation represents the most basic form of dramatic play. Even this is quite remarkable when you think about it. A not-yet-talking, very small individual undertakes to act like an adult, identifying with the species! We see lots of imitation in young toddlers. A child will pretend to feed a baby doll, imitate an adult's gestures such as shaking a finger or putting hands on hips, pushing around a toy lawn mower, or pretending to stir a pot.

The "props" young children use in their play have to be very realistic in order to trigger the play. Young children do not plan ahead, think of a scenario that they want to play, and go about gathering the materials they need. Instead they see something, like a toy lawn mower, and say to themselves..."I know what that is and how it sounds..." and then proceed to use it. Unless an adult interacts with them while they are doing this, the play is not likely to be sustained very long. "Object play" is also involved; they just like using interesting objects.

Gradually, although usually not until the preschool years, the child learns to use more abstract things for play props. Anything cylindrical becomes a baby bottle. A block can be a telephone. A pie tin can be a steering wheel. However, a child can learn to do these things earlier with an adult play partner.

Taking on a role

Instead of just playing with the prop, the child now *pretends to be* someone else. You can notice this in gestures. A little girl sits down on a rocking chair with a doll, rocks the doll, and pats the doll's back. She is obviously pretending to be the "mommy," or the one who comforts.

You may hear some language when the child plays a role—at first just a word or two—"Go bed..." "Eat." As children gain experience with pretend play, they learn to change their voices when they are speaking from inside the role. The voice may go up or down as a way of signaling to the world that this is pretend play.

Interacting in a role

Two or more children are playing different roles and talking to each other or otherwise interacting from those roles. A "doctor" pretends to give a shot to a "mommy's baby." This is very sophisticated play for toddlers and usually doesn't happen until the child is almost three. A toddler is usually too egocentric to think of what someone else is doing and how her actions may influence the other individual. It is more common to see children "parallel playing" the same roles. Three "mommies" will be feeding or bathing three "babies."

The child's language abilities have a big influence on her ability to interact with other children in make-believe play. So much is dependent on making oneself understood. Dramatic play is a great motivator for the development of expressive language. Often it is in dramatic play that you hear the most expressive language from a child.

Playing With Children

You will need to do more to support dramatic play with toddlers and two-year-olds than is necessary with older children who are more experienced. Contrary to what one might think, this is not a spontaneous activity of early childhood. Children actually need to be "taught" to pretend play. Usually this is done so casually by parents and older siblings as well as other children in the neighborhood or childcare setting that we are unaware of the teaching/learning going on. Occasionally, though, you will find children who have no idea of what to do. You can bring them along.

Observe

See what is really going on in the play. Make note of the child's use of objects as well as the situation being played. If a child is deeply involved in play, don't intervene. However, if the play is "flat" and not going anywhere, join in as a fellow playmate.

Play a supporting character role

Let the child be the "star" of the play and have the dominant role. Let her be the mommy and you the sister, or the neighbor. Let her be the doctor who gives the shots, and you be the patient. Your presence, your actions, can add complexity to the play. You can make suggestions, "Will we need to get gas for the car?" but allow the child to decide the direction of the play. She's the "boss," in other words.

Change your voice

Demonstrate how to change your voice as you take on roles or talk for dolls or stuffed animals, "Oh, she's sad because she's on the floor behind the door and can't see what's going on."

Use objects for pretend

Have a tea party, model pretending to drink liquid from a cup or just use gestures, suggest you go for a ride in the car, help the children line up chairs and make "car noises," ask, "What could we use?" and show them how to improvise.

Simple Steps

Help them interact with others

If you see a child holding a doll, for instance, you might ask, "Are you the mommy of this baby? How is your baby feeling, *Mommy*?" Change your voice when you talk from within your role. Involve other children. "We are going on a pretend picnic. Who wants to come along?" "This is the doctor's office. I'm the nurse. Do any of you have sick children?"

Extend the play

At this age most pretend play is fleeting. They enter the kitchen, drink a cup of coffee, and are gone. Can you extend their play by suggesting they help wash the dishes, answer the telephone, or hold your baby?

Recreate recent experiences

Has the child been on a trip recently? A suitcase and chairs lined up like airplane seats may generate an interesting scene. Did the family go out to eat last night? What can you reproduce of a restaurant setting? This helps the child develop the ability to create scenarios.

If you ever have older children visit your group, this would be a good type of activity to ask them to do. Older children can greatly enrich the play.

Guided Dramatic Play

In guided dramatic play, the adult describes what is going on and the children act it out. One example might be the teacher narrating a scene such as going for a drive to the beach, unpacking the picnic basket and eating, digging in the sand, and going for a swim.

A delightful way to combine dramatic play and literacy is to encourage children to act out a simple and very familiar children's book or story. "The Three Billy Goats Gruff" or "Goldilocks and the Three Bears" are favorites for this. Two-year-olds can help think of and gather props. A second adult might help the players do their actions while the other adult reads or narrates the story.

Although this type of pretend play doesn't allow children to generate their own ideas very much, it coaches them in dramatic play skills such as learning to use objects and gestures for pretend, interacting with others, following a logical sequence, and sustaining the play for a greater length of time.

Boys and Girls

Both boys and girls love pretend play and in the early years you see less difference in their play than when they get older. But already they are becoming conscious of whether they are a boy or a girl and are more likely to imitate roles of their own gender.

First, be sure they are exposed to a wide variety of role models and images of adults engaged in all types of traditional and non-traditional roles. Make sure both boys and girls feel welcome in your housekeeping corner or other pretend play setting. Issue special invitations if necessary. Include props that are interesting to both genders. Little boys may not be as quick to pick up a doll to nurture, but often a stuffed animal will work quite well. A boy can rock and tuck in a teddy bear. Gender-neutral props like clip boards, brief cases, lunch boxes, and steering wheels generate good play.

Although boys are often the first to start playing roles of action heroes, girls are by no means left out. This type of play with toddlers and two-year-olds is usually an imitation of what they have seen other children doing or what they have seen on television. Intervene and redirect when the play gets wild or frightening to more timid members of the play group. The superhero can often be redirected to cook dinner and considerably broaden the role portrayed on television. If older children in a mixed-age group initiate superhero play, you could ask them to think of different roles when the young children are involved. Solicit their help as "play coaches."

Miniature Play

Another valuable type of pretend play is when children use miniature people, animals, vehicles, and props. This type of play makes young children feel very powerful. The block corner, the sensory table, or the sand area outside are ideal settings for this type of play, but the materials can be used independently as well.

Again, you can play along side the child, simply imitating what the child is doing with the materials. If you are invited or the child seems to welcome you, you can add to the play in similar ways to those described in the section on playing with children, page xxx. Just be sure to let the child be the lead player.

Provide both realistic and abstract props. Hats for the players to wear are always popular. Miniature furniture and vehicles that are fairly realistic can start the play in a certain direction. Add more "abstract" props like aluminum pie dishes, shoeboxes, spray can tops, fabric pieces, and pieces of PVC pipe and see how the children use them.

Simple Steps

To Encourage Play

Rather than offer specific activities, as is done for other development areas, we're listing suggestions for "play starters" since the action is up to the child. The adult's job is to provide stuff, space, and time. Observe and note what's going on and join in the play, as described above, if you think it could use some added depth.

Props

The basics for an early childhood program for toddlers and two-year-olds include dolls, dishes, and housekeeping equipment. Always have a doll bed (even if it's a cardboard box with blankets in it) and small blankets available.

Add interesting objects from time to time to encourage a new direction in play. For example:

- A steering wheel will encourage vehicle play.
- Hats of all types inspire roles.
- A picnic basket with "stuff" inside will be eagerly used.
- A doctor's kit needs little explanation.
- A suitcase may inspire a pretend visit to Grandma's.
- Put out a pile of large fabric remnants. Children will find all sorts of uses for them.
- A few large boxes will find many uses.
- Add flashlights on dark days.
- Stuffed animals are good "neutral" toys that can be babies as well.
- An old, discarded camera will at first be explored in object play and later may be incorporated into roles.
- Wallets, shopping bags, and purses may inspire a "shopping spree."
- Dress-up clothes are great, but cut them off so they don't drag on the floor. Shoes are especially interesting.
- Provide a mirror so they can enjoy the effect.

Reflect Children's Cultures

Find objects that will be familiar to children and make them feel at home and more ready to act out roles. Parents might help you collect things, and will probably feel complimented that you want their child to play in a familiar setting.

■ Blankets that reflect patterns of a culture.

■ Dolls that reflect ethnic features of children in the group.

■ Food boxes and cooking utensils can reflect the family's cuisine.

■ Shoes, hats, scarves, and doll clothes can reflect a child's home.

■ Create a "grandmother doll" when you know an elderly person lives with a family.

■ Decorative items like tablecloths and things that hang on the wall can be added.

Settings and Situations

For play to be meaningful, the setting or situation must be one that is familiar to your children. Involve the children in gathering props and deciding what you could use to create settings like this:

■ Various rooms of a house, such as a bedroom, living room, kitchen, bathroom, garage

■ A car or bus

■ Pediatrician's office

■ Grocery store

■ Shoe store

■ Camping equipment

■ "It's for you...," then hand the child a toy telephone

■ The baby is tired/hungry/cranky/dirty

■ Birthday party

■ Teddy bear party

Bring It Outside

Children engage in much dramatic play outside where they can be loud, expansive, and active. Encourage this by making props available. In nice weather, you might even occasionally bring the housekeeping corner furniture into the play yard. Outside, you can add water for children to cook and wash with more easily. Tricycles can be parked outside a pretend restaurant. Also add different props for outside, like pieces of hose and firefighter hats. Dolls and stuffed animals also love to go outside.

Chapter 11

Playing and Learning

How to Set Up a Positive Learning Environment

Infants, toddlers, and two-year-olds live a large portion of their lives in the indoor and outdoor space you set up for them. This environment should allow a wide range of physical activity and be attractive for children and adults alike. How you divide, organize, and equip your indoor and outdoor space influences the effectiveness of your program. It is also an outward reflection of your philosophy. It tells people what you value and how you feel about children.

◼ If you value children's play, the environment will provide ample, safe play space and materials.

◼ If you value warm interactions between children and caregivers, the environment will offer places that are comfortable and welcoming for adults and children to be together.

- If you value cleanliness and health, the environment will be easy to keep clean, safe, and organized.
- If you value close relationships with parents, the environment will be welcoming, comfortable, convenient, and organized to facilitate good written and face-to-face communication.

The people and the atmosphere you create in your interactions with children and their parents is the most important aspect of your program, but your *physical* environment is a critical tool for creating quality care for infants, toddlers, and two-year-olds. It can work with you or against you.

The Play Area

If children are not sleeping, eating, or being diapered, they should be in the play area. This is a place for free exploration and movement where a child can experiment with objects and practice emerging motor skills. For this reason, this space must be absolutely safe for babies.

You could almost list yourself as an essential piece of "equipment" because you are an important part of this space. Don't simply put children in the play area, as you would put a child in a playpen, and watch from the outside. When you are not diapering or feeding babies, talking to parents, or otherwise occupied, settle down on the floor in the play area and make yourself available to the children. You can actively play with a baby, or simply observe the scene close by. You are accessible if a baby needs or wants you and ready to intervene if needed.

When deciding what equipment to put in the play area, think about all the things that infants, toddlers, and two-year-olds enjoy doing—like rolling, crawling, going up stairs, pulling up, cruising, climbing, banging things together, throwing things, dumping containers, and poking things in holes. Consciously arrange your environment so children can practice these and other new and emerging skills in as many ways as possible.

Nooks and crannies

Create nooks and crannies for children to crawl into, but not so small that they get stuck. When young children (especially babies and toddlers) explore such spaces they are learning about their bodies in space, such as how big they are and where they fit. They also use these places as "peek-a-boo" centers, making the

world disappear and reappear when they crawl in and out. These crawl spaces can be very simple, such as a blanket thrown over a low, sturdy table or some cardboard boxes from the grocery store. Think about how you can arrange furniture, dividers, and equipment to give children a variety of spaces to explore.

Different levels

Crawling babies and new walkers also like to explore different levels and surfaces. Ramps, low platforms to climb up and down from, couch cushions placed on the floor, and plastic wading pools filled with various things like soft balls or small stuffed animals are all possibilities.

Adult furniture

Adults should be comfortable too. A loveseat, soft chair, or small couch makes a good place to settle down with a child to cuddle, enjoy a book, or play.

Baby traps

If your program has a wind-up swing, walker, infant seat, or bouncing chair, use it sparingly. Children cannot explore or use their muscles freely when they are confined in these devices, and will not learn from them how to roll over, creep, crawl, or pull up to a standing position. The only reason to have them in the environment is to keep children safe when the adult is otherwise occupied in the room. Even if babies seem content in a wind-up swing or other piece of equipment, they are not in the best possible place. A good rule of thumb is to ask yourself if the child really needs to be in one of these devices. Usually the answer is no.

Tips for Organizing the Play Area

You may want to dedicate one part of your play area for "tummy babies"—the not yet crawling or toddling infants. This is to protect them from older children who may accidentally step on them, fall over them, or poke and bother them.

■ You can use manufactured dividers, bolsters, or pillows to accomplish this. If you don't have such a divided area, be sure to stay close to a non-mobile baby.

- Use a body sling, infant seat, swing, or playpen sparingly. Tummy babies need to be on a clean surface on the floor using their muscles.
- Put a clean blanket on the floor for tummy babies to lie on, or place a clean sheet over an area rug and tuck it under the edges. This can be washed at the end of the day.
- In the "crawler-cruiser" area for the older infants, have a sturdy toy shelf for toys. It should be very stable, in case a child decides to pull up on it.
- Try to place toys in the same place every day so that children know where to find them. You could "label" places for toys with either photographs or a picture of each toy cut from old catalogs and placed on the shelf covered with clear contact paper. This creates a matching game for older toddlers. Of course, children will carry toys all over the place and will not necessarily be able to put them back in the right place. At least this will help keep *you* organized.
- Collect interesting containers. Infants, toddlers, and two-year-olds are often as fascinated by the container as by the toy itself. One way to add new life to your room is simply to change the containers that things are in. Plastic tote bins are great. Consider also plastic dish tubs, plastic baskets, trays, shoeboxes, shopping bags, shoe  bags, cardboard boxes, and laundry baskets. The containers become a learning/playing device in themselves as children enjoy emptying and filling them and carrying them around.
- Create "mini-environments" inside your shelves by covering pieces of cardboard that just fit inside the back wall spaces with various fabrics, pictures, or Plexiglas mirrors.
- Create a "soft area" where children can cuddle up. Provide pillows with washable cases, washable stuffed animals, perhaps a mattress covered with a clean contour sheet, and other soft things.
- Place photographs of children and families and interesting pictures cut from magazines at the *children's* eye level. These can be laminated or covered with clear contact paper. Do not use staples or thumb tacks. Some wall surfaces tolerate clear contact paper overlapping the picture, stuck directly on the wall.
- Store toys that are not currently in use. If you "rotate" toys, putting some away and bringing them out again after a couple months, they will seem totally new to the children. Do keep certain favorite toys available all the time though, especially if a child seems to particularly enjoy and look for a certain toy.

Expanding the Play Area for Active Toddlers and Two-Year-Olds

More distinct "areas" of your play environment can be developed as children grow. When toddlers see a large, open space they want to run, so it's a good idea to divide play space with low dividers such as toy shelves. Because toddlers are easily distracted by other children, they may play with greater concentration if they are out of the direct line of sight of their playmates.

Messy play

When not in use for food service, low tables can be used for messy activities such as art, playdough, and clay. Place the tables over a hard floor for easy clean up. Hang waterproof smocks nearby, for your own convenience. A sensory table could be here as well.

A climber

Because toddlers and two-year-olds are compulsive climbers, have available a stable climber designed for this age group, with a padded mat underneath it. Other good additions are a collapsible tunnel, riding toys, and a rocking boat. (See Chapter 4 for gross motor development and activities, on pages 85-108.)

Dramatic play

A simple dramatic play setting can be set apart from the rest of the play area, making it a special space. A room divider could provide one wall. A window made from a picture or travel poster and curtains is another idea. Enrich dramatic play with dolls, cooking utensils, a telephone, dress-up clothes, and a mirror. (See Chapter 10 for more dramatic play ideas, pages 221-228.)

Books

No program for children is complete without a good assortment of quality children's literature. While you may keep some books out of reach and bring them out only when you are able to supervise closely, you should make other books accessible to toddlers and two-year-olds. A low bookshelf, good lighting, and a cozy chair, as well as some stuffed animals to read to, make this area inviting

Toys and blocks

Sturdy low toy shelves can hold simple puzzles, large pegs and rubber peg-boards, shape boxes, pounding benches, stacking cups and rings, push toys, pull toys, toy vehicles, and of course, a wide assortment of homemade toys. A laundry basket could hold a large assortment of balls, which toddlers love. Large, lightweight blocks are best for this age group. Toddlers feel powerful when they lift something big. They love to knock down a tower of blocks, so use blocks made of cardboard or vinyl-covered foam. Wooden unit blocks can be introduced as children approach age three.

The Diapering Area

In order to reduce the spread of germs, change diapers only in a specially designated area of the room. Do not change diapers on the floor or in cribs. Never prepare or place food on the same counter where diapers are changed. The diapering area should be located so that the caregiver can easily see the rest of the room to supervise the other children.

Tips for Organizing the Diapering Area

- The most important thing is to keep everything within arm's reach. One hand of the caregiver must always be on the child on the changing table, so all necessary equipment must be handy.
- Store the diapers and extra changes of clothing in individual bins on shelves over the changing table, with the children's names on the bins.
- Keep disposable plastic gloves in their dispenser box on the counter top.
- One bin might store small plastic bags for soiled diapers.
- Keep paper to place under the child at the head of the changing table.
- The changing table should be situated right next to a sink for handwashing.
- To cut down on the spread of germs, use a separate sink for handwashing after diapering, if possible, and another sink for other uses in the classroom. If the room has only one sink, make sure that careful hygiene procedures are followed.
- Put up a poster describing proper handwashing techniques near the sink, as a reminder.
- A foot pedal-operated diaper pail should be out of the way, where children will not be tempted to use it to pull themselves up, or play with it in any way. Ideally it should be inside a cabinet. Empty the diaper pail at least twice a day.
- A diapering chart with all the children's names on it can be on the wall or a cabinet close by. The record keeping can be accomplished after the child has been returned to another area of the room.

The Feeding Area

Feed children in a separate area of the room. This is the area where you store and prepare food and formula, and keep records about children's food and liquid intake. Children should never be left unattended in highchairs or at feeding tables, and when they finish eating, they should either be returned to the play area or placed in a crib to nap, depending on the child's individual schedule. Take pains to keep this area very clean and organized.

Tips for Organizing the Feeding Area

- Create a separate place in a cupboard for each child's food.
- Have a marker pen and tape handy for labeling food jars and bottles of formula with the child's name.
- Always wash hands before preparing food. Wash children's hands before they eat.
- Never prepare or handle food on the same counter where children's diapers are changed.
- Keep handy a supply of clean bibs and paper towels and clean sponges for spills.
- A crockpot of warm water is great for heating bottles. Be sure this is out of the reach of the children.
- If you use highchairs, arrange them in a semi-circle, or face them so that children can see each other, making eating more social.
- Older infants, toddlers, and two-year-olds can sit on chairs at low tables for snacks and lunch. The chairs should be low enough so that the children can sit on them with their feet on the floor. The table should be no more than mid-chest height so they can see their food and touch things on the table top with relative comfort. Meal time is often messy, so place tables over flooring that is easy to clean.
- A low sink that toddlers and two-year-olds can reach is ideal, or provide steps so that children can wash their hands independently, but still be supervised.

The Sleeping Area

The section of the room where children nap should be divided off from the rest of the room and yet be easy to supervise. Most programs have toddlers and two-year-olds nap on cots that can be stacked, stored, and set up in the play area at designated naptimes.

Tips for Organizing the Sleeping Area

- This part of the room should be as calm and quiet as possible. Children who are awake and playing should not have access to this area. Always check your state licensing regulations before deciding how to organize this area (or any other area) of your program.

- Cribs must be placed at least twelve inches (thirty centimeters) apart to reduce the possible spread of air-born germs. At least one side of the crib should have enough space to allow for easy access by staff.
- Each crib must be clearly labeled with the child's name.
- A child should use the same crib every day and that crib should be in the same position each day, in order to give the child a sense of security and familiarity.
- If two children come regularly on different days, they may use the same crib with fresh sheets provided each day. In this case, put both children's names on the crib and indicate which days they attend.
- Crib blankets are often supplied by parents, providing children a familiar "piece of home." The blankets should be washed at least once a week.
- Change sheets weekly, or as needed if the child soiled the sheet in any way.
- Darken this area of the room when children are sleeping here. Draw blinds on any windows in this part of the room, and turn off the lights, if possible.
- Because children should be in cribs *only* when they are sleeping or falling asleep, you don't need to decorate the walls or provide crib toys.

The Parent Area

Of course, parents of enrolled children have access to your whole environment, but make sure parents feel comfortable and communication is easy.

Communicating with parents can be a challenge with several staff people working different shifts and busy parents coming and going at different hours. You might consider creating a special area near the entrance of your room. In this area there should also be a place or cubby labeled for each child's belongings. Many programs label each child's cubby with a photo of the child as well as the child's name.

Things you might have in the parent area:

- A bench or other comfortable place to sit down while removing children's outer clothing—a place to cuddle and say goodbye. This should be near the children's cubbies.
- A bulletin board with items of general interest for parents, such as notices of special events, interesting articles, photos you take of the children playing, descriptions of things children did or said, and announcements of births or news of the other families.
- Photos of the other families whose children are in the program, to encourage parents to get to know each other.
- A parent lending library specific to the needs of infants, toddlers, and two-year-olds. It might be here or in another place in the center.
- Center newsletters. Some teachers have their own newsletter specific to their room.
- A lost and found spot. Do encourage parents to label *everything* with the child's name. Have a fabric marking pen available for parents to use to label the child's clothing, and tape and a marking pen for other belongings.

Decorating the Environment

You can do a lot to personalize your space and give it warmth. While you want your environment to be attractive and appealing with interesting things to look at, be careful that you don't make it overstimulating. If too much is going on visually, children can find it hard to rest or concentrate. Keep this in mind as you search for the right balance.

- What you first put on the walls should reflect who is in the room. Use photographs of the children engaged in a variety of activities. Also display pictures of parents, siblings, and pets. Make posters from a good negative or slide if you have good shots of the children in action.
- Try to find pictures of children and adults that reflect a variety of ethnic groups, portrayed in a respectful manner.
- A photo display of the routines of your day will be of great interest to children, parents, and visitors alike.
- Consider protecting photos and other pictures with clear plexiglass shields.

Indoor Environment Safety Checklist

Safety is achieved through awareness. This checklist is a tool to monitor the indoor environment. Add to it things specific to your environment.

General safety

- Put safety plugs on all electrical outlets not in use.
- Keep electrical cords out of reach of children.
- Put safety latches on cabinet doors and drawers.
- Put safety covers on doorknobs so children cannot open doors.
- Place signs on doors warning people to use caution when opening and closing.
- Put safety coverings such as Plexiglas or wooden bars on low windows so children cannot run into them.
- Be sure children cannot crawl out open windows.
- Place screen in windows that might be open for ventilation in warm weather to keep out insects.
- Keep fans or air conditioners out of reach of children and have safety mesh over any open holes where children might stick their fingers.
- Store toxic materials such as cleaning supplies in areas completely inaccessible to children. If in the room, keep them in locked cabinets out of reach of children.
- Wind up and place out of reach of children any drapery or blinds cords.
- Be sure any plants in the room are non-toxic and are out of the reach of children.
- Be sure there are no gaps in furniture or dividers where a child could get his head caught.
- Keep and use sharp objects like scissors and knives in areas inaccessible to children.

Feeding area

- Be sure highchairs or feeding tables are stable and that trays fit securely.
- Do not leave children unattended in highchairs.
- Store all medications in a designated area inaccessible to children.
- Keep all medications in the original bottle with the pharmacy label and the child's name on the bottle.
- Store unopened baby food jars in an area inaccessible to children.
- Do not heat formula in a microwave. This can leave dangerous hot spots in the liquid.

Diapering area

- When a child is on the changing table, always keep one hand on the child.
- Store a foot-operated diaper pail with a cover where it is not accessible to children.
- Keep water temperature in faucets below 110° F.
- Check that open storage shelves are stable and not cluttered.
- If a toilet is in the room, be sure that children are never allowed to play near it, and it is only used under close adult supervision.

Sleeping area

- Use crib bumper pads only with the youngest babies. When the child can pull to a standing position, remove the pads so the child cannot climb on them to get out.
- Lock the side rails of cribs firmly in place and adjust mattresses to the proper height so that the child cannot climb out.
- Provide clean crib sheets weekly or whenever the child soils the sheet.
- Disinfect weekly any crib rails and surfaces that babies could reach with bleach solution.
- Put in place a system of regular, systematic supervision of the sleeping area.

Play area

- Keep toys in good repair. Make sure no broken toys are available to children.
- Check toys (especially homemade toys) for safety.
- Be sure toys do not have sharp edges.
- Keep small objects that children might swallow or choke on away from them. These include tops of pens and markers, staples, thumb tacks, safety pins, hair barrettes, rubber bands, and pieces of toys designed for older children (such as Lego pieces, small puzzle pieces, and small pegs).
- Be sure the furniture at the children's level has rounded corners and is free of any sharp edges or splinters.
- Be sure the furniture is stable and won't tip if children pull themselves up on it.

Adults

- Place staff and parent purses out of reach of children.
- Do not drink hot beverages around young children.
- Wear soft-soled shoes, such as sneakers or rubber-soled shoes.
- Allow only parents, trained staff, and supervised visitors in the room.

Things that are specific to your setting

_____

_____

_____

_____

_____

_____

_____

_____

_____

_____

The Outdoor Environment

Weather permitting, infants, toddlers, and two-year-olds should spend time outside every day. Sunlight and fresh air promote good health, and children love being outside. The following are hints for making this important part of your play environment safe and fun.

- Outdoor play space right outside your room door is best.
- Do a quick check before bringing children outside to make sure no debris or animal droppings are in the area.
- Make sure the fence and gates are secure with no gaps in them or under them where a child could squeeze in and get stuck.
- A lovely shade tree is ideal, but create shade if the area has no natural shade. Protect children with sunscreen.
- A separate area for non-mobile babies lets everyone play in peace and safety.
- A mailbox mounted on a fence could hold facial tissues and other supplies.
- Water to drink could be in a thermos or cooler with paper cups available for children who are thirsty.
- See how many surface textures there are—grass, sand, sidewalk, chain link—and add what you can, such as large, smooth rocks, blankets for babies, or a log.
- Can you create a small hill on your playground? Toddlers and two-year-olds love to run up and run (or roll) down it.
- Swings need space. A wooden border about the height of a railroad tie around the swing area may stop children from walking in front of the swings.
- Make sure your climbers are designed for children under three, meet safety standards, and have an adequate cushioning surface underneath. (Check your state child care licensing office for guidelines.)
- Pathways for riding toys are easy to install and can lead in interesting directions.
- Wind chimes, windsocks, and fabric streamers can be hung from trees and fences to give the wind a visible and audible presence.
- Use the fence as a play surface and hang things from it such as noisemakers and toys.
- If the temperature is mild and insects are not a problem, prop a door open and let children decide for themselves if they want to be indoor or outdoors, going in and out at will. (Naturally, be sure there is adequate staff in both places.)
- Toddlers and two-year-olds love to dig in sand. Store sand toys in a rubber waste can with a lid, right at the sand area.
- Bring your curriculum outdoors. Books, art activities, sensory play, and dramatic play are all great fun outside.
- A storage shed in the play yard for storing things that are used outside is very convenient.
- Good supervision is your most important safety factor. Maintain appropriate staff-child ratios and make sure all new staff and substitutes know never to leave children unsupervised on the playground in order to take a child inside.

Chapter 12

Teaching and Coaching

Behavior of Infants, Toddlers, and Two-Year-Olds in Groups

The care of infants, toddlers, and two-year-olds offers unique rewards and challenges to those providing it. One challenge is that while you are enjoying the wonder of development in each individual child in your care, you are also "orchestrating" a good experience for the group, trying to meet the needs of individual children and their parents.

Behaviors, positive or negative, are outward expressions of children's emotional states. Some inexperienced parents and caregivers can be disillusioned when confronted with an angry, howling, protesting, infant or a willful, aggressive toddler. Unfortunately, there is no "cookbook" for handling difficult behaviors, because there are no consistent ingredients for this "stew." Yet, just as a cook knows that certain processes and principles affect the outcome in making a good stew or bread, we know that certain processes affect children's behavior.

Teaching acceptable social behavior and coaching children toward positive social development may be the most important thing that you will do. It will have the greatest impact on a child's later success in school and in life. Remember that infants, toddlers, and two-year-olds really do want to have friends and get along, but they are just learning the necessary skills so they

Group Behavior

stumble and bumble! Like any other beginning skill, children will make mistakes as they try to figure out how to act. They need good models and good coaching from the adults who care about them.

A complicating factor is that children's emotions often trigger adults' emotions. Before reacting to a child's outburst, take a step back and figure out what is going on from a developmental point of view.

Crying

Listening to a baby cry is very distressing for adults. Instinct is at work here: we are "programmed" to try to stop the crying so the species will survive! When we are unable to stop a baby's crying, or when several of them are crying at once, we feel stress.

The youngest babies cry because of discomfort, which can be due to hunger, gastric pain, irritation from a wet diaper, illness, or other cause. Their crying is a physical manifestation that something is wrong. They are asking for someone to please fix it. When adults respond promptly with the appropriate comfort, the baby learns to trust that someone is out there to comfort and care for him.

Try to figure out *why* a baby is crying and respond appropriately. You will gradually learn to differentiate the cries of each infant in your care. Talk to the baby. Although it may seem silly, talking to the baby about his crying is, in itself, comforting. Go over to the baby and let him see your face. Say something like, "Oh Michael, I hear you crying. Something is making you uncomfortable. I wonder what it is. Let's see, you were just fed, so I don't think you are hungry. No, your diaper is not wet. Maybe you want to be in a different position. I will put you on your side and see if that helps."

Infants also seem to cry just to exercise their lungs. They may experience a fussy period at certain times of the day, often right before dinner (just as the stressed parent arrives home and has a million things to do). Some babies are quite regular in their "fussy" times, making them predictable. Some need to cry before they go to sleep, and others wake up with a cry. Talk to the parents about the different crying patterns of their baby. Also ask parents how their child is best comforted.

As infants develop, they learn to use crying as a cause-and-effect tool. They do this to make the "magic face" appear. Toward the middle of the first year, crying becomes a social "doorbell." Behind the cry of anger or frustration is the statement, "Someone get over here and help me get what I want!" In that sense, this type of crying reflects both cognitive development and language development.

Remember that crying is a baby's first form of communication. Acknowledging that babies have a right to cry is important. While we should respond to an infant's cries and try to figure out if we can alleviate the discomfort that is causing the cry, we must avoid the tendency to stop the crying at all costs. Renowned infant specialist Magda Gerber cautions that if we always stop an infant from crying, we communicate to him that having a full range of feelings is somehow wrong. Many people automatically feed a crying baby or put something like a pacifier in his mouth. This may be giving the young child an unhealthy message that oral pleasure is the way to alleviate stress and could have a connection to overeating to relieve emotional stress in adulthood. Your judgment is best in these situations: if you know what is causing the baby's distress, you should take action to relieve it.

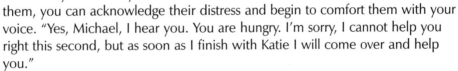

When older infants cry at separation, they may be experiencing grief, fear, and anger all at once. As you comfort the child, acknowledge what he is feeling. Instead of just saying, "You'll be fine," and trying to distract the child, say, "Yes, it's hard to be away from Mommy. I'm here to take good care of you and be with you until she comes back." (Even if the child doesn't exactly understand your words, the comforting message will be communicated.) If possible, let the child cling to you, and sit quietly rocking or holding him until he climbs out of your lap and seems ready to take in what the day has to offer. You may even see an empathetic response from another child who may bring over a blanket or otherwise try to offer comfort. Even when several children are crying at once and you are busy and cannot attend to them, you can acknowledge their distress and begin to comfort them with your voice. "Yes, Michael, I hear you. You are hungry. I'm sorry, I cannot help you right this second, but as soon as I finish with Katie I will come over and help you."

Remember that infants do not cry to bother adults. When you are appropriately responsive to the different reasons for crying, either by picking the baby up, feeding the baby, changing his diaper, moving him, putting him to bed, or otherwise comforting him, you teach him that he *matters*. Children learn that they can communicate and somebody out there cares—a very basic emotional message!

Tantrums

The emotional "melt-downs" that toddlers and two-year-olds are famous for usually come from frustration. Young children are so active and their world is so stimulating that they can, at times, feel overwhelmed. The toddler has a poor sense of time and may find it very hard to wait until later to do or have something. Nor does he have the language and cognitive skills to argue a point convincingly. It is natural that a child will fall apart occasionally; however, if the adult gives in to the child's tantrum, the child may use this method of getting his way on a regular basis.

The most useful response to a child's tantrum is empathy and understanding, stating what the child is feeling, but holding firm and not letting the child have his way. "I know, you wish we could stay and swing longer, but it is time to go home now. Yes, it's hard to stop doing something fun, but here we go..." It's not a time to lecture the child. Just be as calm as possible. Try to differentiate between a tantrum that occurs out of pure frustration and one that is "called up" for purposes of manipulation. If you feel that the child is having a tantrum just to get his way, simply say something like, "This will not work. Make yourself comfortable. When you are through, we'll be over here." After a few minutes, you might offer the child a glass of water as a graceful way out of the screaming.

Not all toddlers have tantrums. Sometimes the behavior is learned by watching other children. Tantrums usually decrease in frequency once the child learns to express emotions with words and figures out that tantrums get him nowhere.

Fear of Strangeness

We've all seen a toddler stop in his tracks and refuse to go near someone he doesn't know or try something new. Costumed characters, such as Santa Claus or clowns, can look pretty strange to the child. He may be startled. Like all of us, a toddler is able to face uncertain situations with greater confidence with someone supportive at his side. If the parent or caregiver is calm, reassuring, and displays a confident attitude toward the new situation, the toddler will respond with less anxiety. Don't force the child to experience something new or strange, like meeting a costumed character. Instead sit with the child at a distance and let him observe the scene and how the other children interact with it. When a child is hesitant to try a new activity, such as fingerpainting, also allow the child to watch other children and approach it on his own terms.

Possessiveness

Young children often act possessively when they begin to interact socially. They do not like to share things or people. They may try to push other children off your lap and protest when you pick up another baby. They want whatever another child has. They may even try to hoard toys, keeping them away from other children. They are learning about where they stand in relation to others. This egocentrism is appropriate, even healthy. Infants think that they are the most important thing in the universe. A child will eventually learn that others have feelings and rights, but this takes time. First, she must feel that she is respected. She needs experience working out conflicts. Sometimes being on the "short end of the stick" helps the child learn how others feel when they are hurt or frustrated.

When we see a child take a toy away from another child who was enjoying it, our natural tendency is to step in and restore justice. "Jennifer had this first, you can have it later..." has no meaning for the child. An infant does not know about "first" and "later." Some adults threaten, "If you're going to fight over that toy, I'll just have to put it away." While this may stop the struggle, absolutely nothing is learned here. If you pay attention, you will see that most of the time, children "win some and lose some." If you sense that a child is becoming a bully or a frequent victim, you might step in and distract one child with another toy, get something else going, or show them how to use the toy

together. Don't spend too much mental energy on this. Keep in mind that as children gain a sense of themselves, they also gradually develop cooperative and reciprocal behaviors.

Hurting Behaviors

You may choose not to intervene in all child-to-child conflicts, but you should never allow one child to hurt another child. Try to work out ways to prevent this type of behavior in the future.

Much hurting behavior starts out as simple exploration

The child is crawling along and encounters another child, full of interesting textures. Fingers go to shiny eyes. A cry comes out of this interesting object. Suddenly, the child believes he has discovered a cause-and-effect toy—push this "button" and out comes an interesting noise.

Teach a gentle touch

Yes, this is easier said than done with children whose fine motor skills are just developing and their touch is hard and thrusting. Remember that a child of this age also does a lot of imitation, so model what you want to happen. When you see a crawling baby grab the hair of another child she encounters in her path, move close and say, "Gentle." Open her fingers to release the hair. Then touch her hair gently and say, "Gentle, like this." Help her touch the other child's hair gently with an open hand, and then praise. "Yes, that's the way! Gentle."

Be there to supervise

If you are on the floor, you will see situations developing and can prevent them before they start. Strategies to prevent conflicts include:

- Separate older, curious, exploring children from non-mobile infants, unless you can be right there to moderate interactions.
- Avoid over-crowding. Divide your space and move objects to draw children toward them when children start bunching up in one area, or simply relocate children to a different area of your space.
- Keep your group small. Try to have at least two adults with a group of toddlers. One adult can focus on a few children while the other keeps an eye on the whole group, ready to move in and redirect when the situation calls for it.
- Start something new. Play some music and start to dance, sing a song, or start a chase game.
- Make sure the children have enough to do. Get duplicates of the most popular toys.
- Develop a clear stable routine.
- Take advantage of young children's impulsiveness. If you show a young child another interesting object, you can often divert her attention from the one she wants to take away from her friend.
- Use redirection, which means finding the closest possible acceptable activity to what the child is doing and inviting the child to do that instead. *"Oh, I see you want to throw things. Blocks aren't good to throw because they could hurt someone. Here are some beanbags you can throw." "Whoops, this shelf is not a good thing to climb on because it could tip over. Let's go over here to the climber and you can show me how you can climb."* Give a chronic hair-puller a doll with long hair she can tug on. The biter might find relief from biting her own special teething toy.
- Model empathy. Empathy is a learned skill. Stop hurting behaviors as soon as they happen, and let the aggressor see you show concern and empathy for the other child's pain. With permission from the injured child, invite the aggressor to help you provide comfort, such as getting a cold cloth to put on the bite. Just make sure that the more aggressive child does not have so much fun helping you "comfort" that her negative behavior is reinforced and gets repeated.
- Anticipate behavior. Catch it on the rise. You can sometimes feel the tension building and intervene before the hurting act starts. Separate, distract, redirect. Stay close to your known aggressors, and dissipate tension. Put yourself between children if you sense aggression building.
- Acknowledge feelings and develop a relationship with the child. The child has to like you before she will care if you are upset and work to gain your approval. Play with the child. Enjoy time with her when all is going well. When a child is engaging in a lot of hurting behaviors, focus strongly on meeting the child's emotional needs, making her feel noticed, valued, loved, secure. Acknowledge the child's feelings: *"I know you don't want to stop playing, but it's time to go inside." "Yes, you want that car, but Brandon has it now. Let's ask if you can play with it when he is through."*

Simple Steps

Biting

Biting is the most serious "hurting" behavior, both in the amount of pain it inflicts and in the intensity of reaction of caregivers and parents. Nothing upsets parents more. Nothing makes caregivers more frustrated. You may find it helpful to give parents a handout on biting, such as the sample on pages 150-151, at the time they enroll their children. If parents are aware that biting can happen when children interact with each other, they may feel less shock when it does. This also communicates that you will do your best to prevent biting behavior. If a child bites, the parents' often ask, "How could you let this happen? Where were you? Why aren't you protecting my baby?" Good supervision is a prime deterrent of biting; however, biting can happen so quickly that even if the adult is right there she can't always prevent it. Parents need to understand this.

Why Children Bite

Oral exploration

Although children bite at different ages, the prime time for biting seems to be between twelve and eighteen months, during the "oral" stage when they use their mouths to explore everything. Do children bite because they are teething? Perhaps, but this is not the major cause since there are many other things to chomp down on.

Frustration

Except for early "exploratory" biting, most bites occur when children are frustrated. If children don't have the words to express themselves, or their words are not effective in getting their message across, they are more likely to bite to make their point. Most bites happen when children are defending their toys or space, or when they are trying to get a particular object from someone else. If the children in your care seem to be biting a lot (yes, even one bite is too much), take a good look at your space. Does the arrangement of furniture tend to push children all into one area so they are constantly bumping into each other? Are there enough toys so they don't have to wait or compete for favored objects?

Jealousy

Sometimes jealousy is the motive for biting. The biter may feel that another child is getting too much of your attention. This sometimes happens when a new child is introduced to the group.

Strategies to Reduce Biting

■ **Keep a teether collection**—Keep a collection of clean, attractive teething toys. You can tell the child, "These things are for biting." Praise the child when she picks one and bites on it.

■ **Catch the child's frustration as it builds**—This is the most crucial and effective prevention strategy. Usually, not always, you can sense a child's frustration building. Step in quickly and help the child figure out an acceptable way to solve her problem—especially if this child is a frequent biter. This requires that you stay close and aware. "Wait!" is a word that might "buy" you a few seconds as you move across the room. It usually works better than "no."

■ **Stay right with the biter**—If you have a chronic biter, assign someone to be next to the biter at all times, without making the child aware that her biting is the reason she is getting such close attention. This extra attention may also give the child the emotional nourishment she needs to overcome some of her feelings of frustration. The adult can help the child develop some problem-solving skills, such as offering another child a substitute toy when the child has something the "biter" wants. If you can prevent a chronic biter from biting for even two weeks, she can begin to unlearn this behavior.

■ **Teach the child what to do instead of biting**—Acknowledge the child's feelings. *"You were angry when she took your toy, but it's not okay to bite people."* Then give alternative behavior. *"Next time, tell her, MINE!"*

■ **Use a personal teether**—This sometimes works for the chronic biter. Show the child a new teething toy. Say, "This is just for you. It will help you remember not to bite people." Tie it to the child's clothing with a short ribbon. Say, "When you want to bite, bite this." Let the child demonstrate how to bite the toy and praise her. When you sense the child is feeling tension that may cause her to bite, remind her to bite on the toy.

■ **Train the victims**—Try training the other children to protest loudly and shout "No!" when a biter approaches in a menacing way. This works best with older children who are more aware of danger and have better language skills. Teach children to move away from an aggressive child.

■ **Work on language development**—Again, teach children to say what they want. "I want that." "That's mine!"

What to Do When a Child Bites

- Intervene immediately. Control your temper and avoid scaring the biter.

- Attend to the injured child. Step between the two children, if possible, with your back to the biter so she doesn't feel she's getting more attention from you because of what she did. Comfort the injured child.

- Say to the biter in a firm, serious tone, "No biting people!" Show her the bite mark. "You hurt Lucy. Biting hurts. No biting people."

- Model empathy and kindness. Let the biter watch as you gently wash the bite, put ice on it, and comfort the injured child. You might try letting the biter help comfort the other child.

- Fill out an incident report. Notify your director or supervisor of the bite.

- Notify the parent. This is a hard call to make, but it is easier than surprising the parent with the information at the end of the day (even worse is not being there personally to tell the parent about what happened). Empathize with what the parent is feeling, but don't apologize, for that indicates that you did something wrong. Tell the parent what led up to the incident, and what you did about it. "I picked her up, put ice on it, and held her until she stopped crying." The parent will often ask which child did the biting. The best policy is not to give this information, since it serves no constructive purpose.

- Make notes in the biter's anecdotal record file. What were the details? Record what the child was doing at the time, who was around, what you felt led to the bite, the time of day. This information can be helpful if the child bites repeatedly. You might notice a pattern. Does the bite always come before lunch? Is it always the same child who is bitten? Is it because of jealousy? Try to analyze the situation. That may help you anticipate situations or develop strategies for intervention.

- Help the biter's re-entry to the social stream of the classroom. After a short time, involve the biter in something totally different from what she was doing at the time of the bite. Sensory activities, such as water play or playdough, are often good choices. Don't hold a grudge. A little one-on-one time can go a long way. Play with the biter and re-establish a good relationship. While the child has gotten the message that what she did upset you very much, you still like her. If the child feels rejected by you, the behavior may get worse.

- Tell the parent of the biter about the incident. Often the parent of the biter is as distressed as the parent of the injured child. The first response may be defensive. "What are you doing to cause my child to be so frustrated that she needs to bite? She has never bitten before." If the parent has already read a handout about biting, the incident may be less of a shock. Be sure you don't imply that the parent is to blame in any way, and stress that you do not want them to punish the child at home. Just tell what happened and how you handled it. Later, if the biting becomes chronic, you may need their help in problem solving and analyzing the situation.

Sometimes Children Bite*

Finding out that your child has bitten (or been bitten by) another child can be quite a shock. Although not all children will bite, this behavior can happen in the best of families and in the best of child care programs. It is a group phenomenon and can happen any time that young children are together, whether in child care, at a friend's house, or at a birthday party.

Why Children Bite

Young children are egocentric, and they should be! They haven't been on the planet very long. They take a while to figure out that they are not the center of the universe and often feel that everything happens for or because of them. They can get very impatient when others don't cooperate with their wishes. They want what they want, when they want it. They don't know how to wait. If they are not successful in getting a desired object, or if someone takes it away, they may resort to biting.

Biting behavior usually occurs before children have enough language skills to negotiate with others. They sometimes resort to biting when they are frustrated and do not have the words to express themselves.

Teething is rarely the cause of biting. There are too many other things to chomp down on. Since young children go through a very "oral" stage when everything goes in the mouth, and chewing something may relieve stress, we often offer teething toys to head off biting.

Children learn by imitation, and sometimes they bite because they see others doing it. That is why we may go for many months without a biting incident and suddenly there is a "rash" of biting. We intervene quickly so that biting does not look like a good thing to do.

What We Do to Prevent Biting

- We model kindness, gentleness, and empathy. By showing concern when a child is hurt in any way, children learn that we care. Young children will often imitate comforting behavior modeled by adults.
- We supervise children well when they are playing. If we notice tension building, we move in, change the pace, or redirect the children's interest.
- We talk a lot about feelings and work to build children's language skills. When children struggle over a toy, we help them find the words they need to work it out.
- We balance our day with stress-relieving activities such as active outdoor play, music, and sensory activities such as water play.

* This may be reproduced for classroom use.

What Happens if a Child Bites

- In spite of all our preventive efforts, sometimes a bite will still happen.
- We attend to the injured child, comforting him or her and administering appropriate first aid.
- We fill out an official incident report.
- We firmly tell the biter, "No biting people." We try to get the message across in a very serious way without scaring the child, which defeats the purpose because then the message gets lost. Depending on the age of the child, we may separate him or her from the other children for a short time.
- We notify the parent of the injured child by phone and tell the parent of the biter at pick-up time.
- It is our policy not to give out the name of the biter to the parents of the injured child. It serves no constructive purpose. It could easily be the injured child who is the biter another time.
- We make notes in the files of both the biter and the injured child in order to analyze what led up to the incident and help prevent a repeat occurrence.
- Depending on the age of the child, we may also do some training, encouraging the injured child to shout, "No biting!" Surprisingly, this often helps stop the behavior.
- If biting becomes a frequent behavior of a particular child, we may ask the parents to help us think of strategies to deal with it.

How Parents Can Help

In most cases, we will not ask you to do anything after a biting incident. Your patience, understanding, and support of the staff is probably the most constructive help you can offer. We will handle the incident at the time with the child. "Delayed discipline" is ineffective, even damaging, with young children. If biting seems to be developing into a "chronic" behavior, we may ask for your help to develop some problem-solving strategies. You may be able to help us understand why the child is biting and what we can do to help stop this behavior. We will keep you informed.

Be assured that we care very much about this issue and will do everything possible to prevent it from happening while your children is in our care.

Reproduced from *Simple Steps* by Karen Miller

Chapter 13

Meeting the Needs of Children

Curriculum Development

How Do You Plan a Curriculum for Infants?

To plan a good curriculum, you need a knowledge of child development and an understanding of what can be expected of children of a particular age as well as of specific children in your group. Many programs describe their curriculum as "developmentally appropriate." In its truest sense this means that each stage of development is valued and no effort is made to rush a child to the next step; instead, the focus is on enriching the current stage. When teachers plan experiences for children they ask themselves two questions:

■ Is the activity suitable for a child of this age? and

■ Is the activity right for this individual child?

Curriculum Development

Curriculum for infants must be highly individualized. In planning learning activities for infants, your main tasks are to:

- ■ Know each child well, so you are aware of what skills are emerging—where he is in his development.
- ■ Make available to children a variety of materials and play options with which to practice their skills.

Keep track of each child

Create a file for each child at the time of enrollment. Then keep track of the child's development and what learning activities you have presented.

Start out knowing as much as you can about the individual child. Think of yourself as an investigator gathering information. You have several ways to do this. Read the forms parents have filled out. Even more important, spend quality time talking to parents, letting them tell you what is special and unique about that little individual. Ask what the child especially likes to do. Even young babies have interests!

Next, know what is developmentally typical of children that age, and the sequence of acquired skills. A general discussion of skills in the sequence that they typically develop is presented at the beginning of many chapters in this book. Read other sources as well to deepen and broaden your knowledge. Although the sequence of skills mastered is fairly consistent from one child to another, each child is unique and will develop skills according to his own inner time table.

Observe each child. This is probably the most important piece of the information-gathering puzzle. Watch to see what the child does naturally, left to his own devices in the play area. How does he move? What does he choose to play with? What skills has the child already mastered? What does he seem to be working on? Make some notes for the child's file.

Use the information you gather to plan a child's individual learning program. Ask yourself, "How can I give this child many and varied opportunities to practice the skills he has already mastered?" Also be mindful of what comes next. Provide opportunities for the child to practice a new skill, *when it emerges on its own.* In other words, make an opportunity available without pressuring children to try it. You do not need to push or hurry them. Instead, value what they are already doing and let them move forward at their own pace. For example, you might realize that a child is ready to start walking by holding onto things ("cruising"). To allow this new motor skill to emerge, the child needs opportunities to crawl around to his heart's content, pull up to standing in different places, and hold on to plenty of safe things as he moves around the room. If you hold the child's arms to "make him walk" he will not advance any faster. He must find the balance and coordination in his own body.

Make materials available

You don't sit a baby down and say, "Now we're going to have a fine motor lesson." Children learn best from activities they *choose* to do on their own. Make

Simple Steps

the material available and invite a child to participate. Allow him to refuse. Entice, but do not force. Usually all that is needed is for a certain material or object to appear in the environment to draw the child's interest. Use "the novelty factor." If you present new materials that the child has not seen before, he will likely be attracted to them without adult prompting.

Observe

When you try a new activity with a child, proceed slowly and observe the child's reaction. Does he seem interested? Is he paying attention? If he looks away, try it again another time. Each activity offers you new possibilities for observation. Then make a note or two in the child's file.

Create an "envelope of language"

Talk to children about what they are doing and perceiving at the moment. Do this during all of your interactions with them, not just during planned activities. You are putting sound labels on the things they encounter and giving them a valuable language model. Every experience is a language experience.

Allow repeat performances

Don't hesitate to repeat an activity that a child has enjoyed. While it's true that children like new things, they also like the familiar. They will enjoy repeating familiar actions over and over again. In fact, they are *driven* to do this, perhaps inventing their own subtle variations. Children don't learn from one-time experiences, but rather from hundreds of varied repetitions they invent.

Accept different stages of development

You may have infants who represent several different developmental stages in your program. That is why each child's learning plan needs to be individualized. In addition, the babies will have different temperaments, attention spans, and interests. How do you make your learning environment right for all of them? It's not as difficult as it might seem. Remember that children will use the

same toys with different levels of complexity. Put your main efforts into creating an interesting, yet safe, play area for the children, with lots of different, simple objects for them to play with. Make yourself available to children as they explore. They will look to you for approval, and sometimes as a play partner. Observe their play and intervene when necessary to keep a child from hurting himself or another child. Many activities can be done with more than one child at a time.

Curriculum in routines

Caregivers often complain that they spend so much time on the physical care routines of infants that little time is left for "learning activities." You can take comfort in knowing that children learn a great deal while engaging in the physical care routines. Their minds don't turn off when you feed them, diaper them, wash their hands, etc. Language, cognitive, and motor development all occur while a child is being fed and diapered. The all-important emotional development of attaching to caregivers happens mainly while you are involved in the physical caring.

How Do You Plan a Curriculum for Toddlers and Two-Year-Olds?

Whereas curriculum for infants is totally individualized, you can begin to think of "the group" when you plan for toddlers and two-year-olds, although still keeping individuals in mind. How will you make the day lively and interesting for the children and the staff? When you find the right balance of new and familiar activities, children will stay interested and alert and the day can "hum." When children and teachers are bored by the same old thing, or when they are overwhelmed by too many complex things or projects, everyone gets frustrated.

Plan for specific times of the day

Start by making a list of times in the day that need to be "filled." Make a note of a simple activity or two that you will do during your morning greeting time. What special project or activity will you offer during the morning play time indoors? Plan for your outdoor time as well. Many projects are fun and easier to do outside.

Plan for individual children

Activities work well when they are aimed at the interests and abilities of specific children in your group. In your mind, you might even give each child one day of planning focus each week. In other words, all the activities you plan for Tuesday will be designed for Sarah. Almost always, other children will be drawn to the activities as well. So you ask yourself questions such as:

- What is she interested in?
- Where does she choose to play in non-teacher-directed play?
- Who does she like to play with?
- What toys does she choose?
- What are her language skills?
- How long can she sit still?
- What are her fine motor and gross motor skills?

If Sarah likes art and other fine motor activities, blocks, and music, then plan activities that she'll be able to do with success and enjoyment, with just a tiny challenge that may cause her to stretch a little. Maybe Wednesday is "Billy Day." Billy loves to play outdoors, sing songs, and play with trucks. So you put some special trucks in the sand area outside, add a steering wheel to your dramatic play corner, and sing Billy's favorite songs throughout the day.

This is an enjoyable planning approach because it allows you to focus on the abilities of one child at a time and observe his performance and development. The other children will enjoy the activities too. If Billy doesn't show up on Wednesday, that's okay, Sarah might enjoy the trucks just as much. Children each bring their own skills to any activity that is offered. Some will use materials in complex ways while others will use them more simply.

Balance the day

Create a balance of opportunities for active play and quiet play, group play and solitary play. Children can become overwhelmed if they are forced to be too active all day or, even worse, expected to sit still and be quiet for too long. Certain activities are energizing, others are calming or focusing. When you come in from an active play session outside, for instance, you may need to calm children down before you try to read them a story. In the morning when everyone is a little groggy, an energizing, gross motor activity may be in order.

- Examples of active play: running, swinging, riding outside, dancing to lively music, marching.
- Examples of quiet play: painting, playing with playdough, doing puzzles, looking at books.
- Examples of energizing activities: stretching and moving to music, peek-a-boo/hide and seek activities, singing and moving to simple songs.
- Examples of calming activities: whispering, playing with sand or water, squeezing playdough, breathing deeply, waving scarves.
- Examples of solitary activities: doing puzzles, coloring with crayons, painting at an easel.
- Examples of group play activities: dramatic play, scribbling side by side at a table, listening to stories in small groups.

Plan for the environment

Look at the major areas of your room and ask yourself, what is there for children to do here? What will draw them over here? Also ask yourself, what can I change in each area this week? Try adding a new prop or two to the dramatic play area; have fingerpainting instead of easel painting in the art area; put away the pots and pans and pouring things from the water table and bring out the boats instead; and add a sheet to the large blocks. Additions keep children interested, but by all means leave favorite items for children to enjoy.

Plan for variety

You don't want to plan only art activities, or only gross motor activities. Strive to find a balance during the day, and especially over a week's time, involving art, sensory, music, language, gross motor, and fine motor activities. Other activities, such as those aimed at developing self-esteem and multicultural awareness, may be planned from time to time but attitudes concerning these issues can be worked into any activity.

Keep track

As suggested for infants, keep a file for each child. On a regular basis, describe how the child responded to activities you offered. Make notes about the child's interests and growing abilities. Place an occasional photo of the child in the file.

Create a file for you

Keep track of your own curriculum development efforts in a file folder, journal, scrapbook, or card file. This can be enjoyable and educational. How did a planned activity go over? If it was a disaster, what do you think went wrong? What will you try next time? Which particular children enjoyed an activity? Which children opted not to participate?

The Challenge of Working With Children at Different Developmental Levels

Even in classrooms where all the children are close in age, a wide variation in children's developmental levels can exist. How do you make it interesting and challenging for the more advanced children and still keep it safe and also interesting for the less advanced children?

- Know what you can reasonably expect from individual children. Observe the energy level, fine motor skills, attention span, language skill, and other characteristics of each child in your group.
- Think of ways that all the children can engage in an activity at their own level.
- Keep most of your projects open-ended, without a "product" in mind. Just let children experiment with the materials at their own level.
- Make sure that you have the variety of toys necessary to challenge children at each level.

Hints for Successful Activities

- Introduce them with simplicity.
- Add complexity when interest starts to lag.
- Let the child determine the time frame. Allow for repetition.
- Allow for child-invented variation.
- Observe and note what the child does.
- Add language; be a broadcaster. You are putting language markers and labels on objects, concepts, and activities.

What About Themes?

Planning curriculum activities around "themes," or certain broad topics, is a popular curriculum approach for preschool children. Is it the right way to go with younger children? That depends. While planning around themes can broaden a child's understanding around a central concept, it can also loose their interest if the concept is too advanced (a special problem for children under three).

A major "danger" of planning around themes (for children of all ages) is that the theme can dominate the teacher's interest and divert attention away from the interests and needs of individual children. This is as true for children over three as for children under three. For curriculum to be right, you need to consider each child individually and match your activities to each child's needs, interests, and skills. Young children are less organized than older children. While they enjoy doing things together, it is difficult to gather them into a group and keep them there. Themes often tempt people to plan too many large group activities.

To be a good theme for children under three, the topic should be understandable and of interest to them, involving things that they can see, touch, and manipulate. Always ask yourself, How can I let children use their senses to understand this concept? Think of objects and collections of objects. To find a good theme topic, watch what children are interested in. What do they like to do over and over again? What do those with verbal skills talk about? What grabs their attention?

As a rule **do not plan art activities to reinforce a theme**. Do not tell children, for instance, to draw a picture of a dog, or color in an outline of a dog, when you do a theme on dogs. Children under three cannot do representational artwork, and coloring in an outline teaches them virtually nothing about the theme. What *do* you focus on with a theme? Try dramatic play and the props to go with it; picture books; pictures; real objects to examine; food, if appropriate; and music.

Examples of Good Themes for Toddlers and Two-Year-Olds

- Shoes
- Rooms of the House
- Dogs
- Push and Pull
- Things on Wheels
- Babies
- Boxes
- Things With Holes

Creating a Living Baby Book for Each Child

Ask each family to purchase a blank video cassette when they enroll. Once a month, videotape that child for several minutes, engaging in activities that are new for that child. This is a great way to note each child's development, and at the end of the child's time with you, the parents will have precious moments to share. If your program does not have a video camera, take a photograph of the child engaged in the new behavior once (or more) a month. Write at least one descriptive paragraph each month to go with the photo.

Chapter 14

Becoming Partners

Working With Parents

Develop a Partnership With Parents

Experienced caregivers often list relating to the parents as one of the most rewarding and one of the more difficult aspects of their work. Yet, these relationships can make all the difference in creating a good experience for children. Let parents know in many ways that you are privileged to work as a partner with them to nurture the healthy development of a very special little person!

Although working effectively with parents is important for all child care teachers, those who work with babies, toddlers, and two-year-olds may find these relationships more complex. Parents of these youngest children require much more direct, face-to-face communication. Babies can't talk, after all. The emotional issues can be intense, especially if this is the first time the parents have left the child in out-of-home care. Many

parents are surprised at how difficult separating from their babies can be. All kinds of unexpected feelings come out—grief, guilt, anxiety, even jealousy. All of these things affect how people act toward each other and require patience, empathy, and understanding on your part.

Establishing good communication with parents is an extremely important priority in your work. Most programs have forms to facilitate the day-to-day details of caring. But the real communication happens between two human beings. Do what you can to develop comfortable social rapport with parents. Make sure that no matter how busy you are, every parent gets a warm, upbeat greeting from you. Remember to smile. Most parents enjoy some joking and humor. One reason to have fairly frequent "events" such as picnics and evening pizza parties with parents is to give staff and parents a chance to relax and socialize with each other. This can make it easier to talk about more difficult issues later on.

Develop a warm, trusting relationship

When parents are interviewed about what they look for in child care, they start with the obvious. They look for a clean, safe place. Often they first check out programs recommended to them by friends, but in the end the deciding factor is their perception of the caregiver. They want someone who is competent to care for their child, and is loving and warm. They also require someone with whom they feel personally comfortable. "This is more than a business relationship. I'm trusting this individual with the most precious thing in my life. I need to feel comfortable talking to the person who is caring for my baby—like I can express concerns and feel that she understands and respects what I want for my child." Parents also often mention a matter of personal style. "I want someone who will care for my baby and respond to her the way I would if I were home with her."

Another interesting aspect of the relationship is that the parent sometimes needs to feel nurtured. "When I entered this center, I felt that they cared as much about *me* as they did about my baby." "My child care provider is my best friend. She understands me. I always feel welcome here."

Grief, guilt, fear, and jealousy

Although much has been written about the adjustment of babies to child care, very little attention has been given to how it affects the parents. Some mothers even report *visceral* distress such as cramps when they leave their baby in child-care for the first time. Many parents feel grief for the close, intimate time they had. And there is the simple grief of being separated, attesting to the strength of the parent-child bond.

Parents also feel guilty. They are surrounded by cultural "shoulds." There may be the grandparent who says, "How can you even think of leaving that precious baby with strangers? I never left my children." Many parents don't have a choice—they must return to the workforce. Some families can afford to have one parent stay at home with an infant, and often these parents feel guilty for *choosing* to go back to work rather than staying home full-time. The guilt is magnified if for some reason the baby is having a hard time and cries at separation, becomes ill, is cranky when they get home, etc.

Parents are also fearful. "What if something happens and I am not there?" "I know it's irrational, but I just worry about her all day, wondering if she is all right." You may feel like the parent doesn't trust you when she calls and calls, or checks every little detail on the report forms, or gets extremely upset at some perceived failing on your part that is really nothing. This might indicate that the parent is trying to overcompensate for her fear by double checking everything, almost compulsively.

Parents may feel jealous and fearful that they will lose their baby's love. When the day comes that the child reaches eagerly toward you in the morning, the parent may feel ambivalent. Even when the parent understands intellectually that for the child to develop a strong attachment to the caregiver is healthy, she can have a hard time accepting this emotionally. You must constantly reassure the parent that a baby can develop attachments to more than one person and that the parent will always be number one with the child. It's not all one-sided either. Some caregivers are secretly pleased when a child clings to her or seems to prefer the caregiver to the parents. The caregiver may even feel she loves the child more than the parent does and may resent the parent.

It's important to recognize and come to terms with these feelings because it is never in the child's best interest when the adults in her life are in competition with each other. The best way to support the child is to help the parent feel good about being a parent and to strengthen that parent-child bond.

Sharing milestones

When the child sits up or rolls over for the first time or takes that exciting first step while in your care, do you share the news with the parents as soon as they arrive? Parents differ on how they feel about this. Some parents admit that their greatest grief at leaving their babies in the care of someone else is that they are going to miss many of the "firsts," and that is very painful to them. Others say they want to know right away so they can play with their child as soon as they get home and share in the fun. This might be something you could ask parents about in the intake interview. What many caregivers do is to fudge a little. Instead of announcing the new achievement, they say to the parent something like, "You know, we've been watching her closely today. She's really trying to crawl. I bet if you play with her at home she might give it a try for you."

Some parents are intimidated

Caregivers are often surprised when they realize a parent feels intimidated by them. Parents may feel, justly or unjustly, that you are judging them in their roles as parents. This makes them feel tense. At the same time, they may be in awe of your ease with children. It's easy to see how this can happen. Even the most educated parents, successful and highly effective in their careers, can feel like helpless fools around a new baby or a strong-willed toddler. To them, the caregiver makes it look easy. They are embarrassed that they can't get their child out the door when they've just watched you bring a whole group in from the playground. You make it look so easy to feed one child while still engaging several others. And you keep track of everything, do lots of paperwork, and report on their child's activities at the end of the day—when they often can't remember to bring in needed supplies for just one child. Yes, the work you do really is impressive!

Some parents are quite open in expressing admiration. Others may compensate for their hidden feelings of inadequacy by seeming overly picky or demanding. They may be trying to prove to themselves that nobody *really* can provide as well for their child as they can. Other parents simply try to get in and out of the place as quickly as possible so you won't "discover" how inept they are. Of course, these are all just feelings and may not at all reflect the reality of their talent at caring for their child. The way to overcome such feelings and make people feel comfortable is to make them feel liked as individuals and respected as the experts on their particular child.

You as an expert

Sometimes parents abdicate their own roles and begin to regard the caregiver as the all-knowing expert. They expect you to know all the solutions to any problem that arises with their child. Caregivers are often secretly pleased when parents ask for advice and eagerly tell the parent what to do, but this may not be what is best for the parent.

The wise caregiver will instead develop a sense of partnership with the parents, becoming the kind of expert that facilitates expertise in others. This caregiver emphasizes that although she knows a lot about child development and has worked with many babies, the parent is the ultimate expert on that particular child. One caregiver stated it well: "I give my parents a lot of information in the form of articles from magazines, books, etc., and I also share some of my experiences. But I make *them* decide what to do for their own child. I want to build their own sense of competence and confidence as parents."

On the other hand

Sometimes caregivers wish parents *would* regard them as more of an expert. One caregiver reports: "The most difficult aspect of working with infants for me is wanting to be able to give advice to the parents, but feeling like I am overstepping a certain boundary, especially with new parents who seem to feel offended that you would question their methods or ideas."

This caregiver may be misinterpreting defensiveness on the part of the parents as lack of interest. Try a subtle approach. If you phrase things in an experimental way, rather than implying that your way is *the* solution, people may be more willing to try something. "How do you feel about...?" "I've noticed..." "Have you ever thought about...?" "You might try..." "Sometimes other parents have found this to be successful..." Again, it is useful to have articles or books to support your view. Finding something in print that says the same thing you are recommending can strengthen your point of view.

Hard to be a working parent

Parents may also feel overwhelmed. On top of all the emotions described above, things may not be all rosy at work, the budget may be tight because of the cost of child care, and new adjustments may be creating tension in the family. The parent in front of you might be sleep-deprived because the child was up several times during the night. All of these things affect the parent's behavior.

When a parent complains

Is the "customer" always right? No. But the customer is always respected. Make a sincere effort to go along with parents' wishes whenever you can figure out a way. Make the parent feel listened to and respected while still sticking to a policy or regulation if you cannot go along with their request. When problems and conflicts arise, seek first to understand and then to be understood.

Acknowledge the parent's concern—rephrase it so they know you understand. If you have made a mistake, admit it and tell what you will do to resolve it. Work together to find a mutually satisfactory solution.

Share the giggles

Make a note of the memorable things children say and do and share these with parents. Consciously look for them; they happen all the time. Put a photo on the parent board of a child doing something that made you smile. Write a note about something a child said and put it in the diaper bag or include it in your newsletter. Sharing these moments communicates how you really enjoy this age group and value each child.

Working with children is fun and rewarding

Although this chapter has focused on the problems, working with most parents is great, especially when you learn the best way to work around a distant or critical personality. One parent said, "Yes, I get a little pang when he chants her name and reaches out for her in the morning. Then I realize how lucky I am to find someone my son loves and feels comfortable with. I can go to work with peace of mind." Another parent expressed that she feels she has done her son a great favor by getting him a special adult friend.

Five Things Parents Find Most Irritating About Child Care

- ■ **The child is ill**. This is practically unanimous among parents interviewed. First of all, they feel unhappy and concerned that their little one is in discomfort. They may even be angry if they feel that the child became sick because of germs at the child care center. In addition to feeling bad because of their child's discomfort, they must face the complications that the illness will have for their schedules. Having to leave work and take time off can cause difficulties. They may lose precious vacation time, personal sick days, or even income depending on company policy. Some parents even risk losing their jobs if they are absent too many times because of an ill child. Feelings of frustration and anger intensify if the parents feel the caregiver has been sloppy in hygiene and especially if they feel that the program is not evenly enforcing the policy of excluding ill children. "It's bad enough to be called away from work on a busy day, but when I arrive to pick up my child and see green runny noses on all the other children and hear their coughs, I wonder why it's only me who was called." For these reasons, be super vigilant in maintaining hygiene standards, especially hand washing. Even though most illnesses are contagious before actual symptoms occur, you must be even-handed in enforcing your exclusion policy. Health policies need to be clearly communicated, verbally and in writing, when a new parent enrolls. Also mention them from time to time in a neutral setting such as your newsletter. Parents should be encouraged to line up alternative care for illness ahead of time to minimize their stress and inconvenience.

■ **The child gets hurt.** Parents are the most angry when their child is bitten by another child, but parents also are very angry when they find scratches or bruises from falls or other bumps and scrapes. "Where was the teacher?" is their unspoken question. That's an appropriate question. Caregivers must do the best they can to supervise children to prevent dangerous situations from developing, but, in all fairness, preventing minor skirmishes between children is not always possible. It's helpful to have procedures in place to both prevent and deal with these problems as they arise. You might also give parents a handout about biting when they enroll their child (see pages 248-249 for more discussion about biting).

■ **The staff turns over frequently.** Parents realize the importance of consistency in caregivers for their child. They feel the child's confusion and grief when yet another face appears. They also suffer themselves. They must learn to trust the new individual. They don't know if the new person knows all the special things about their baby. That is why it is important that you give the work a long-term commitment.

■ **Their child's belongings are lost.** "This is the fourth time I've had to replace his sweater," a parent complains. They have a point! You need to keep track of children's belongings. Keep a clothing marker in the parent area so they can label coats and other items.

■ **Their child does not receive preferential treatment.** One parent laughingly admitted: "I know it's irrational and not fair and impossible, but when I walk in and all the babies are crying, I want it to be *my* baby that the caregiver is holding!" You must do the best you can to be responsive to babies and to minimize their distress.

Five Things Caregivers Find Most Irritating About Parents

■ **When parents bring their child in sick.** Interesting, isn't it, that the same issue is at the top of both the parents' and the caregivers' lists of irritations? The frequently reported scenario is that the parent who absolutely feels he cannot miss more work doses the child with a fever reducing medicine an hour before leaving home and tells the caregiver the child is fine, or gets in an out as fast as possible before the caregiver can question the child's "dishrag" demeanor. Not long after, the child has diarrhea and a raging fever, and the parent cannot be reached by phone. You are left with a miserable baby all day, while other parents give disapproving looks or make comments. Sometimes the parent really doesn't know the child is sick, however, so you can't always assume the worst. If you think their action was intentional, however, you may need some back-up. Your director or supervisor should stand behind you in restating your policy for excluding sick children. Parents do need to be reachable at all times and should be encouraged to line up alternative care for when their child is ill. Frankly, it is part of a larger issue—encouraging businesses to develop family-friendly policies so that parents do not feel compelled to lie about their child's illness and can stay home with a sick child without being penalized.

- **When parents leave the child long hours, even when they are not working.** The mother drops her child off at 7 a.m. dressed in her business suit. She picks him up at 6 p.m. dressed in her tennis outfit. You may think that the day is too long for the child, or feel that he is lonely and misses the parent. Maybe you fear that the parent doesn't really care about the child. Maybe you wish you had fewer children at the end of the day, or that you, too, could be playing tennis. If you truly feel the child is undergoing stress from the long hours, more stress than he would experience at home, you might talk to your supervisor. Quite frankly, many parents do not have a choice. Their lives are really packed full, and the child would be in just as much stress hauled around doing errands. And, yes, the parent is paying for this service and has a right to care for the hours agreed upon. Finally, many parents say that they can be a better parent if they shake off the stress of the day with some exercise, or do errands without hauling around a cranky baby.

- **When parents lack respect for your profession.** "Gee I wish all I had to do was sit around in a rocking chair holding cute babies all day." Even said in jest, this remark has a bite. If you think parents regard your work as "just babysitting," you may feel irritated. The way to be treated like a professional is to act like a professional. Be neatly dressed (for working with babies!) and well-groomed. Communicate well and directly with parents. Be proud of your work and show it. One caregiver, when called a babysitter, said with humor to the parent, "I have been an early childhood professional for seven years now and I have never yet sat on a baby—in fact, I spend very little time sitting down, period!" Truly, most parents have great respect and admiration for your work. They may not show it for some of the reasons listed above.

- **When a parent is constantly short of supplies.** You are constantly running out of diapers or a clean change of clothes for little Johnny. Use daily reminders, such as a "Your Child Needs _____" form. If you don't see the parent at the end of the day, leave notes in obvious places, like taped to the front of the diaper bag. One caregiver writes a note on the last diaper that the child wears home, adding a touch of humor!

■ **When the parent rushes in and out and doesn't seem to care.** Sometimes you might feel like the parent doesn't really care about his child, that he just wants to "dump" the kid and run away. Although it may look like this on the surface, it is rarely the case. This parent may be having a terrible time with separation. What might be interpreted as running away from a child could really be running away from the pain of leaving the child. The parent may be rushed and harassed by other responsibilities. Very few parents don't care. A consistent friendly greeting on your part, with a touch of humor here and there as well as expressions of caring for their child, will get through eventually.

The Pre-Enrollment Conference

The director will have had meetings with the new family, going over all of the business details of enrolling their child. Although the parent will undoubtedly have met the child's teacher and visited the room already, some time should be set aside for parents and the caregiver to get to know each other better. This is your opportunity to "get off on the right foot" with parents and make them feel listened to and respected. It is also when you get your first clues about the wonderful little individual with whom you will spend the months ahead. Although this meeting can carry with it all the dubious pleasures of a blind date, if you *expect* a positive experience it is more likely to happen.

Put the parents at ease

It's best if this meeting can take place in a room away from the classroom, or when other children are not there so you will not be distracted with other responsibilities. Offer the parent a comfortable chair and a cup of tea or coffee, if possible. Tell them that you are glad that they made the decision to put their child in your care and that you are looking forward to working closely with them and their baby.

Let them talk first

Invite them to tell you a little about themselves. Read their enrollment form ahead of time. You might apologize for all the forms and paperwork, but point out that each has a specific function to help you take good care of their child. Most important, ask them to tell you about their child. What is special about her? Ask them to describe her personality. What does she like to do? Does she need to be held in a special way? How do they comfort her when she is fussy? Do they have any special hints for getting her to sleep? Also ask about any health-related issues the child might have. Ask the parents why they chose your child care program. What are they especially hoping for in the care of their child? Show them that you are genuinely interested in meeting their needs.

Describe what you do

The parents will be interested in hearing about how their baby's day will go. Show them the diapering area. Explain your special handwashing and hygiene procedures. Let them see how individual children's supplies are stored. Show them the feeding area and how food is stored and labeled for each child. Next go over their baby's typical schedule, needs, and requirements. Record this information. Introduce them to any record-keeping forms and their uses. Tell them how you notify parents when supplies are running low.

Talk about separation

Let them know you realize how hard it is to leave their baby, especially at first. Describe the routine in the morning and at pick-up time. Talk about how you will comfort their baby when they leave. Describe typical reactions. Offer to call them at work later in the morning to let them know how the baby is doing.

Introduce them to other staff

A picture of each staff member with a little write-up should be posted at the Parent Information Area in the room. If possible, introduce staff personally. This is especially important if different people will be there in the morning to greet the child because you work a later shift, or if you will not see them in the after-noon at pick-up time.

Make them feel welcome

Finally, make the parents feel like welcome friends. Invite them to spend time visiting in your room whenever they have time. Tell them to call when they are worried. Tell them no question is a silly question. Convey to the parent that your aim is to create a working partnership. "I know about child development and have worked with many babies; however, you are the expert on this partic-ular, unique human being. Between the two of us, we can have a wonderful partnership."

Scheduled Parent Conferences

Even with all of your daily interactions with parents, you should try to schedule regular conferences to sit down and talk with fewer distractions. Young children are changing so quickly, you need to keep in touch. Touch bases frequently early on. At the end of the first week, spend a little time purposely listening to the parents. How are they feeling? Welcome any questions. Ask them if they have any concerns. It's nice to present them with a photo of their child doing well in your care. Share some joy. This does not necessarily need to be a long, drawn-out conference and can even happen over the phone if that is what works best for the parent.

Generally it's a good idea to have a conference with the parents whenever a child enters a new phase of development, such as becoming a mobile baby and learning to crawl. Encourage them to describe what their child is doing at home. Likewise, you can share your observations of the child at the center. It's great if you have photos or videos of the child in action to share. Take the time to marvel together at the miracle of development. You can also take time to set some goals together. Discuss what you will do to help the child exercise new skills that might show up in the coming weeks and months.

Take the opportunity to make sure you are both on the same "wave length" and to resolve any small difficulties. The main reason for parent conferences is to take a little time to enjoy your shared involvement with this wonderful little human being.

Helping Children and Parents With Separation

It's hard to say goodbye. It's hard to enter a strange situation. As adults we feel this acutely when we must say goodbye to someone close to us who we will not see again for a long time. Everyone has felt the anxiety of entering a room full of unfamiliar people who are having a good time—the proverbial "cocktail party" scenario. Infants, toddlers, and two-year-olds feel this way when they enter your program. They don't *know* that they will ever see their parent again, and the whole place is full of noisy, curious people who stare at them.

Rehearsals help

Just like starting a new job is easier when you have had an orientation, a child and her parent will feel more comfortable with your program if they have some advance preparation. The way you make young children feel safe and confident is to make their experience "predictable." They have seen it before. They know what to expect. They know how to act.

A pre-enrollment visit is a good way to accomplish this with infants, toddlers, and two-year-olds. If a child has visited with the safety of her parent at her side, she will feel more comfortable later when the parent must leave. If either the child or the parent is having a hard time at the prospect of separation, a three-phase approach can be helpful. At first the parent spends the morning and does all the routines, such as diapering and feeding the child, as well as playing with the toys together. Next, the parent is still present, but the caregiver performs the routines and plays actively with the child while the parent is more of an observer. Finally, the parent stays a short while, leaves for a short interval—maybe five minutes—and returns. Gradually increase the intervals that the parent is gone.

No sneaking out

They may find it so distressing to see their child cry that some parents are tempted to tiptoe out of the room when their child is not looking. While empathizing with these difficult feelings, discourage this practice. It builds distrust and the child will find it even harder to relax and play for fear that the parent will disappear. Support the parent by helping them develop a predictable ritual when the parent must leave. The parent can certainly stay until she feels her child is comfortable. But she should be honest and give the child a kiss goodbye. We know, but the parent doesn't necessarily realize, that the child usually stops crying shortly after the parent pulls out of the driveway. Offer to call the parent at work to report how the child is, if the parent wishes. Also tell the parent what you do to help the child after she leaves. The parent should know that her child will not be left miserable and crying alone in a corner.

Sometimes the parent suffers more

Occasionally a parent will linger and watch as her child is happily engaged and involved with the other children, and seem to actually try to make the child sad and cry before she leaves. The parent may be reassuring herself that her baby really does love and miss her when she is not present. If a parent seems to want to linger, encourage her to do it at the end of the day at pick-up time rather than in the morning. It's also possible that this is just their little ritual to reassure each other. Perhaps you can help this parent/child pair create a more upbeat ritual for partings.

Develop rituals

Rituals are good! They are reassuring and they help people get through hard times. You might say, "I've noticed that you two have kind of a hard time parting in the morning. That's natural. Saying goodbye to someone you love is difficult. How about establishing a little ritual or routine to do each morning? Maybe after you get her coat off and talk to me about any messages you have, you could pick her up, give her a big hug, one twirl around, a kiss on the nose, and then hand her to me. I'll go to the window and you can wave at her again and we'll watch you get in the car." One caregiver of toddlers developed a ritual around books. She placed a basket of books on a cubby near the door. In the morning children were allowed to pick out a book for the parent to read to them at the end of the day when they return. The book was put in the child's cubby until that time. Then, at the end of the day, when the children knew that they would accompany the parent out the door, they could settle down with a book as a reuniting ritual. The act of picking the book out in the morning helped reassure the child that the parent would return and gave them both something to look forward to. (Of course, this means that the parent has to budget the bit of extra time at the end of the day.)

Respect a child's grief

When a child cries at the parent's parting, she needs a reassuring adult close by. Don't be too quick to distract the child because the child might get the message that having feelings is not allowed, that it's not okay to be sad or angry. First acknowledge what the child is feeling. "Yes, it's hard to say goodbye to Mommy in the morning, isn't it. Mommy misses you too when she is at work. But I am here to take good care of you." Other children are likely to notice and you can help them understand. "Cassey is crying because she is sad that her Mommy left. I am trying to make her feel better." You might hold or rock the child, but do so in a way that is easy for the child to get off your lap when she is ready. You might position yourself near other children who are playing so the child can see what is going on. The other children will naturally interact with you as well. Allow the child to leave your lap on her own terms. However, having some interesting materials "out there" in the environment can entice a child's interest and allow her to let go of the feeling of rage or fear. Be empathetic and support-ive. You could also settle down next to the child and "parallel play" with something interesting, helping the child feel comfortable. If you have to get on with things, allow the child to stay near you.

It doesn't last forever

Children almost always adjust after a while, and the day will come when the child moves eagerly into the room to discover the adventures of the day. Chapter one describes a number of activities that help the child make a comfortable transition from home to child care and learn to expand her world. Your environment should have pictures of the child's family where the child can see them easily. It's a tangible way of saying, "We know you still have a mommy and a daddy." These photos could be posted down low on a wall, put in a special photo album, even placed on a key ring that the child can carry around. Some children find it helpful to have an object belonging to the parent to keep during the day. One parent left an extra set of car keys, as if to reassure the child that

Simple Steps

she will not abandon her. An old purse or wallet belonging to the parent might work too.

Use transitional objects

Many toddlers and two-year-olds are comforted by bringing in a special "lovey" toy such as a stuffed animal or a blanket. They are literally carrying their security around with them. Sometimes these security toys can be a challenge to keep track of. Many programs encourage children to keep their special toy in their cubby until naptime, except when they "need" it during the day, such as right after separating from the parent. Children often miss the parent at naptime and these objects can be helpful in getting the child to relax. Sometimes a child cannot tolerate having another child touch her special toy. Although young children often fight over toys, sometimes they seem to understand about special toys like this and respect them.

When the Child Cries at Pick-up Time

It is not uncommon for a baby to cry at pick-up time, when she has really had quite a "good day" and has not spent the day crying. Now you have a situation that calls up emotions in everyone concerned! This behavior is most common with children new to your program. The poor parent sees her crying child and thinks, "Oh no, I've made a mistake. My child is not happy here." Or worse, she may fear that the child does not like *her* anymore and isn't happy to see her. Because we don't want the parent to think we have been mean to their child, or that the child is unhappy with us, our tendency is respond defensively and tell the parent that the child has been fine all day and hasn't cried much at all, reinforcing the poor parent's fears.

You can help by explaining that what might be happening is similar to what happens to Miss America. The contestant in the beauty contest holds herself together with poise, smiling constantly through all the competitions. When the crown is finally placed on her head, she often falls apart and cries. She's safe now. The prize is hers. Likewise with the baby in child care, she participates with the group all day and seems to be fine—and she is. When the parent shows up, she feels safe enough to let down and cry or be cranky. This phenomenon usually occurs when the child is new to the program and everyone is in an adjustment period. It is also more common after holidays or when the child has been away for a while. When the child adjusts to the new routine again, the behavior fades. Really, what it shows the parents is that they are indeed number one! Be sure to point out to parents that the child's face brightens in love and joy when they appear, which is just as likely. *Both expressions are a child's way of saying to the parent, "You are very important to me!"*

Many infants, especially as they approach toddlerhood, simply do not like transitions. Point out to the parent that this is the same child who cried in the morning because she did not want the parent to leave. Her crying could also be an indication that she is having so much fun that she doesn't want to stop what she is doing (common with toddlers). Once they get used to it, parents often say, "I'm really lucky. My child has such fun at her child care that she doesn't even want to come home in the evening."

The First Hour at Home

Many parents report that their child is often extra cranky or "naughty" when she first arrives home—not what the parent wants or needs after a long, stressful day at work. This is a common phenomenon. Here are a few things to suggest that might relieve the tension of that first hour at home:

- Suggest that the parent share a late afternoon snack with the child at pick-up time, such as a few slices of apple and a glass of juice or milk. Children are often hungry at the end of the day and both the parent and child might cope a little better with something in their stomachs. This might mean budgeting a little extra time.
- Urge parents to take their time. Relax. If the child senses that the parent is rushed, resistance is more likely. Teach the parents some of the same transition preparations that you use. "Two more times down the slide, then it's time to get your coat on." Again, this takes planning on the part of the parent, but may make the afternoon go more smoothly, and will probably save time in the long run.
- The child and the parent should both take time to say goodbye to the caregiver and the other children. This gives some "closure" to that segment of the child's day and also teaches basic courtesy.
- The caregiver should help by having all the child's things gathered in one place so time does not have to be spent searching—another tension builder.
- Encourage parents to develop some "reunion rituals" at home. They might share a snack, play music and dance while Mommy changes out of her business clothes, read a book, and otherwise "reconnect" before launching into meal preparation and other chores of the evening.

Final Thoughts

The hardest thing about writing a book is limiting it. An author can never include everything a reader could possibly use, so I urge you to take it from here. Use this book as a starting point and keep learning.

As you do the activities in this book, the children will inevitably come up with variations. Invent new toys and activities that appeal to the children you know. Continually add to your list of "tried and trues." Be open to the surprises.

Remember throughout that each child is a masterpiece, different and complete in himself or herself. Enjoy the process of helping all children reach their full potential, and take a moment every so often to marvel at the wonder of development in each child.

Sharing the Knowledge

Creating Workshops

A book packed with information and activities to do with children can seem overwhelming. As a result, many fine early childhood resources end up sitting on a library shelf. One good strategy to help translate the information in this book into practice in the classroom is to break it down into digestible chunks in workshops or mini-classes lasting anywhere from one to six hours. This allows an individual or a center to tailor the material to make it fit a particular situation. Examining a smaller topic with co-workers and/or with a trainer can lead to more in-depth understanding and appreciation.

I am speaking from a very personal perspective here, sharing some thoughts about in-service training. I have spent many years both as an in-house training director in childcare settings and as a visiting "expert" doing workshops, keynote addresses, on-site consulting, and seminars. Putting ideas into practice is not easy, and presenting new material in a limited "flash in the pan" way has definite challenges. Done well, good training can have a deep impact on quality. Done poorly, it's a waste of money and time.

When people attend a workshop, they hope to gain useful tools that will make their work with children more effective and a little easier. They hope to find answers to their problems, and they want to be able to apply what they learn immediately. Workshops can offer a break in routine and can build camaraderie among staff. Such training can lessen a caregiver's sense of isolation, providing opportunities for caregivers to connect with other professionals who can lend ongoing support. Training and workshops can help caregivers feel proud of their work, motivated to try new things, and encouraged to work with energy, enthusiasm, and a creative spirit.

Defining the Topic

First, define your topic. Decide how much of it to cover and how deeply to explore it. Using the materials in this book, one approach would be to do a workshop on one chapter at a time, perhaps starting with a topic you think the participants grasp fairly well and then later tackling newer or more difficult ideas. You might decide to organize workshops by developmental stage, such as that of a non-mobile infant or young toddler, and pull material from all of the chapters that pertain to this stage.

A mistake many beginning workshop presenters make is to try to cover the whole topic in a short amount of time. I have learned that this is impossible. It's better to give an overview, then choose where to focus your attention. Suggest areas to explore in greater depth through your handouts or follow-up assignments.

Tailoring Workshops for Different Skill Levels

Just as you would match curriculum activities with children's emerging skills, try to meet the adults in your workshop right on their "growing edge" so they are barely conscious of their learning. Strengthen a disposition that is already there. Get the heads nodding, and you have a room full of learners. I always start a presentation acknowledging what the participants already know. I tell people that not everything they hear me say will be brand new to them, and that I am sure they are already doing much of what I am proposing. This reinforces and strengthens their good practices. Sometimes hearing someone else describe something you already do gives you new words to explain your practices to parents, administrators, and others who might be interested. Of course, you always strive to give people new information or insights as well, building on the base they already have.

Rarely will all participants in a workshop have the same experience and skill level. How do you keep it relevant to all people in attendance? Know your audience. Observe them. Interview them. If you are using a presenter from outside your organization, give information to this visiting trainer. Who will be there? What are their experience levels? Where are their stumbling blocks? What do they do well? If you jump too far ahead of participants' understandings, they will be left feeling frustrated and confused, creating resistance.

On the other hand, some experienced staff might be bored if the material is too simple. Ask experienced participants who have good knowledge of the subject to be discussion leaders, to share some of their experiences, to show scrapbooks or photos, and to act as "resident experts." They might demonstrate certain techniques such as handwashing or reading to a small group. You could ask them ahead of time to act in this role or give them a role in the workshop follow-up. If you don't know who these people are ahead of time, you might pause at various points in your discussions and ask people to add personal experiences to what you are saying.

Over the years I have found that, ironically, the people with the highest knowledge and skill level will enjoy the workshops the most and really get into the activities and the discussions. You are emphasizing something they are good at, and that makes them feel positive about their work. (The unfortunate converse is that the people who need training the most often don't show up!)

Advance Preparation

Participants are more likely to gain from a workshop if they have thought about the topic ahead of time. You might ask participants ahead of time to observe their children in relation to the topic and to come with a question, activity, or observation to share.

As the presenter, decide in advance just what you want participants to get out of the workshop. Practice some positive imaging of your ability to communicate effectively and inspire enthusiasm for the topic.

Timing the Workshop

Timing is one of the more difficult aspects of planning a workshop. You must decide how much of the topic you can cover in the given amount of time, as well as how much time you would need to cover the topic thoroughly. Within the workshop, think about how long you will take on various aspects of the topic, how often to change the pace, and whether to prepare "fillers" in case a piece doesn't take as long as you expect. Give those in attendance an outline of the schedule, at least verbally, so they know what will be covered, how long they will have to sit, if and when they will have a break, and so on. The most important thing is to start and stop on time, respecting the people who are there. It helps to have a clock visible so you can keep track of time easily.

Setting the Tone

Some people attending your workshop may prefer to be somewhere else and are reluctant participants. Others may have a bit of a phobia for learning situations—anything that resembles "school"—so it is important to create a feeling of safety in the workshop. That means gaining their trust and letting them know that you will not put them on the spot or expect them to get the "right answer" to a question you might pose. You build trust by inviting them to question and, in fact, welcoming and praising their questions. A good question, after all, shows that they are interested and thinking.

Get them relaxed and in the mood to have fun. By all means, use humor, starting with a friendly smile on your face. You may wish to share a funny or cute story related to the topic to start things off, but you don't have to be a stand-up comedian. In one organization where in-service workshops were a regular monthly happening, everyone was expected to share a "giggle" or "goosebump" to start things off, something funny or touching that happened since the last workshop. This shows that even experienced and respected people make mistakes and have "stupid" things happen to them. Laughter bonds people.

Introducing the Subject

Be enthusiastic about the topic and about helping others to learn the material. Talk about experiences you have had or observed related to the topic, or tell everyone why you think the subject is important. Perhaps share what you have learned along the way. Define the part of the topic you plan to focus on. You don't have to present yourself as an all-knowing expert, but rather as a fellow explorer.

A good way to introduce a topic is to get people thinking about what they already know. This also allows you to build upon strengths. Depending on the topic, the size of the group, and the time you have, you could either break into small groups to make lists or come up with questions, or work as a large group, listing words or ideas that participants come up with. Ask the group questions such as, "What do toddlers like to do using the large muscles of their bodies?" "How do you notice progress in language development in infants?" If the participants come up with a whole outline, that's wonderful! Then you are addressing their needs and concerns. Reinforce what they are already doing and elaborate the next steps. If the group does not come up with an outline, you can refer to a chart of the workshop as you progress. This process empowers people and shows that you respect what they bring to the training. Who knows—you might even gain a new insight or two!

Techniques and Their Uses

Many techniques are available to the workshop presenter. It is important to change the pace and format of the information you present in a given workshop. Few people can sit still and listen to someone talk for several hours with full attention. When you use various media and techniques, you are accommodating various learning styles. Try to build layers, presenting the same information in several different ways. Ask yourself how a given topic is best learned—by reading and discussion, by observation, or by active participation. The answer is likely to be a combination of techniques.

Get-Acquainted Games

Time spent helping workshop participants become acquainted with each other can be useful if they are going to continue to work together, or if you want them to interact a lot during the time of the workshop to generate ideas and discussions.

One way to develop rapport in longer workshops is to have people pair off, preferably with someone they don't know well, and find three things they have in common other than being at the workshop and the type of work they do. Then have them introduce each other to the group and describe what they have in common.

Be careful that these activities don't take more time than planned, especially if they don't serve your goal. You might decide that nametags that include place and type of employment are sufficient for short sessions.

Observation of a Young Child

A delightful way to "capture" your audience, especially if you are learning about various developmental stages, is through direct observation of a child. Be prepared with several simple activities or objects to engage the child in such a way that his emerging skills are well demonstrated. If the parent is present, most babies can be trusted to demonstrate skills. The novelty of a new object will attract the attention of the child. Before the baby is present, you might ask the group to predict what the child will do. Give a running commentary as the child interacts with the people or materials, and discuss what everyone observed afterwards. Even better, have several children of the same age appear, one at a time, and notice the differences. You are not making qualitative comparisons, but rather appreciating the uniqueness of each child. You could also use children representing different developmental stages (not together, but in sequence). You might have some of the same materials available and observe the different ways children use them as they mature.

Videotapes

The strength of videotape is in showing action and interactions in the child's natural setting. "Homemade" videotapes can be excellent training tools; however, unless you have access to editing tools, they can be a bit haphazard. You could make your own "ages and stages" videotape by picking one child and taping that child for five minutes a month from early infancy through toddlerhood. Plan to catch the child's emerging skills in motor, language, cognitive, and social development. It's even better if you can do this with several different children. The problem, of course, is that this takes several years to accomplish. You could also take the video camera into several different groups of children representing different stages and offer activities and materials that allow them to demonstrate their skill level.

Videotape is also an excellent way to capture staff behaviors that you want to demonstrate to new workers, such as diapering and handwashing procedures, how to feed a baby, helping a child and parent with separation difficulties, or playing properly with a child.

More and more quality commercial videotapes are available that highlight various aspects of child development and child care. You probably don't want to have people sit through an entire videotape in a workshop setting, but rather to show short clips that illustrate a point you are making. Such videotapes could also be shown a week or two after the workshop.

Slide Presentations

Slides are my favorite type of training tool. They can be arranged to suit the topic and the time available. "A picture is worth a thousand words" is really true, and slides can be an excellent visual representation of your words. It is easy to talk over slides—they can give you your outline. People generally enjoy glimpses of different programs, and you can constantly add to your collection. Be careful not to lose track of time when the room is dark during a slide presentation. Also, resist the temptation to let the slides be your whole program.

Photo Boards

You can arrange photos on poster board and write captions underneath. I have used these effectively in curriculum workshops, grouping photos of art activities, sensory play and motor play, and so on. Make them available for people to see during a period of free time, when the adults are also actively involved trying out various materials and activities. These photo boards could be displayed near the entrance of your workshop. They give participants something to look at beforehand and during breaks. The disadvantage, of course, is that photos are small and cannot be seen by the whole group at once.

Overhead Projectors

I have never used an overhead projector or opaque projector in my presentations, mainly because of lack of availability. Although I am sure they could be employed effectively to illustrate points, I have rarely seen them used well. Most often presenters make transparencies of their handout or of various graphs or charts, and then project them so that the audience can easily follow along. Presenters often leave the transparency up after they have finished talking about it, and the large projected screen may draw people's attention away from focusing on the presenter.

Small Group Discussions

One way to ensure that everyone has an opportunity to discuss the topic from a personal perspective is to break a large group into smaller groups during segments of the workshop. Some people are much more comfortable voicing an opinion or sharing an experience with a small group. Small group discussions can also acknowledge that everyone has something to contribute and allow participants to learn from each other. This is especially good for problem-solving situations.

Sometimes, however, participants resent listening to "peers" when they really want to hear the opinions and perspectives of the workshop leader. Small group discussions can also be more work because they require the participant to be actively involved. Some people may be reluctant to expose themselves—what they know and don't know, what they think, and what their attitudes are on a given subject.

Role Playing

Role playing is an excellent way to rehearse difficult situations in a safe environment. For instance, two people taking on the roles of "difficult parent" and "teacher" can help come up with phrases that are firm and professional as well as supportive, friendly, and respectful. A participant who role plays the "difficult parent" might gain insight into what the parent feels in a certain situation.

One effective way to structure role play is to think of situations, writing up the parent's situation and perspective on one piece of paper and the staff person's on another. Do not let the two "players" see each other's papers. Let them act out their roles, then discuss the interaction.

Simple Steps

One disadvantage of the role-play technique is that performing in front of a group can make some people feel very uncomfortable and afraid that their "wrong answers" might be exposed to the group. People can also get so caught up in the acting that the main message is lost, so be sure to be supportive and summarize the points learned afterwards.

Demonstration

Certain topics such as music, storytelling, and using puppets are best demonstrated by the workshop leader, with the participants playing the parts that the children ordinarily would.

Active Play

It's great fun—and a whole lot of work—to set up actual activities and materials (such as art and sensory materials) for people to experiment with during "free play time." They might have a chance to experience the different recipes for fingerpaint or playdough, much as a child would, and as a result might better understand what a child feels when making choices in an overstimulating environment.

Make It, Take It

"Make It and Take It" workshops are enormously popular. You provide the materials, directions, and the time to create homemade toys. The participants make them at the workshop, then take them home. Be sure to discuss the learning purpose of the toys; how to present, use, and vary them; and the overall sequence of development they highlight.

Lecture

Standing up and lecturing to a group of people is an efficient way to give out a lot of information in a short amount of time. Some people, however, have trouble absorbing and remembering information learned in a lecture. A good lecturer is part storyteller and effectively uses voice, gestures, and facial expressions to maintain the interest and attention of the audience. Most workshops have at least a little bit of lecture in which the leader presents information verbally. An effective presentation might include lecturing to introduce and summarize a topic; reinforcing the information with discussion, visuals, and other techniques; and then following up with a good handout.

Question and Answers

In shorter, tightly structured workshops, participants appreciate an opportunity to ask questions. Schedule the question period toward the end of the presentation because you might cover the information in your content. If appropriate, you could invite questions after each section of a presentation to make sure people are following you.

Even if I have an answer to a question, I like to throw it out to the group and have the audience answer it. "Have any of you ever experienced this problem?" "What advice would you have for this person?" I can then affirm or expand upon the answer, if appropriate. And, in truth, I often learn something.

Sometimes there will be no questions. This can mean either that you covered the material so well that everyone is absolutely clear, or they are tired and can't wait to get out of there. Have some "fillers" ready, or anticipate some questions to help them get started.

Handouts

A good handout enhances any workshop, especially if it relieves the participant of the necessity of taking elaborate notes, and allows more concentrated attention. The handout can also go beyond the precise content of the presentation, giving people new things to think about. People always appreciate the outline of the content, plus exact references to useful resources so they can continue exploring the topic. Do keep copyright laws in mind and get specific permission from the publisher before photocopying or reproducing materials directly from any source. Be sure to reference where ideas came from, even if not copied directly.

Coming to "Ah-ha!"

It is a delightful experience when you sense that people are "getting it" in a presentation. You can see the "light bulbs" go on over their heads. There is usually a sense of excitement and eagerness to apply new understandings. You hear people say things like, "I can't wait to get back to my kids and try this."

In order to reach this point, you must get people past the "Yes-buts." Some people resist change, perhaps because of defensiveness. If they have always done something a certain way and you suggest another approach, they might feel threatened or criticized. They might understand the principles of what you are saying and agree with you, but fear a lack of support from their administration. Get the administration on your side. Encourage people to voice their hesitations, because others in the group might have helpful advice.

Ultimately, they must comprehend the reasons to change. You must convince them that the change you are proposing is better for children's development, and makes the job easier to do.

Concluding the Workshop

Give the workshop a good conclusion, summarizing the things you wanted the participants to get out of it. Help them think about how they will communicate the topic of the workshop to parents or other audiences in discussions, displays, photos, newsletters, etc.

Give assignments that include suggestions, such as, "Do the same activity with three different ages, adding complexity" or "Develop a card file of successful activities with notes about which children enjoyed an activity, and what to do differently next time." You could ask people to write down several points to go away with.

I always tell people that no workshop could ever give them all the information they could use on any topic, and I encourage them to keep exploring the topic on their own. My main goal in almost any workshop is to get people excited about the topic and eager to learn more.

Try to have some sort of "inspirational close," a finishing touch to go away with such as a quote or short story, and encourage people to keep in touch.

Now What?

The most important part of a workshop is what happens afterwards. Often the administration or professional organization brings in someone to do training and then thinks they've done the job. The real test is turning principles learned in a workshop into reality. As a trainer or visiting workshop presenter, you can suggest some follow-up activities.

How can you know if the participants learned something from the workshop? It's important to realize that each person will take away different things. A portfolio approach can be very individualized and satisfying. The trainee can document what he learned in numerous ways such as with photos, videos, or journals. I like to ask people, "How did you personalize this? What did you use? Were there any surprises?" You could encourage someone, as a personal growth experience, to reproduce the workshop at a staff or parent meeting, or at a local early childhood professional conference. One useful question for them to ask is a "positive imaging" one: How would we look/act if we were carrying out the principles of the workshop? The whole idea is to get participants to see themselves as on-going learners who also have much to bring to a situation.

Value of Adult Learning

One final thought—I have gotten as much pleasure watching adult growth and development as enabling child development. When people have good training they feel supported and valued. Everyone, but especially those who work with children, should keep on growing and stretching. It gives vitality to the program and to their lives. Human development goes on and on.

A Sample Workshop on Fine Motor Development

Time required:

1 hr. 15 minutes

Pre-workshop assignment:

Observe the hand activity of the children in your group.

Photo board:

Post on the wall of the workshop room a collage of close-up photographs showing hands of infants, toddlers, and two-year-olds doing all kinds of things—tight fist, open infant hand, reaching, swatting, pulling glasses off adult, raking motion pick-up, picking up small object with thumb and forefinger, poking fingers in holes, fitting pieces together, reaching for something inside jar, squeezing play-dough, fingerpainting, and pasting.

Warm-up exercise:

■ 2 minutes:

Welcome and thank participants for coming. Tell a story about a child using hands, or some observation you have made about fine motor development, and why it is an important topic to learn more about.

■ 5 minutes:

Divide into partners and give each other hand massages. Provide hand lotion. While this is going on, talk about what our hands mean to us, and how they are a young child's instruments of exploration and learning. Have people think about what it would be like if they lost the sense of touch in their fingertips.

Small group exercise:

■ 5 minutes:

Break into small groups and list the sequence of fine motor development from birth through age three.

■ 3 minutes:

A recorder for each group reports on the list they came up with. The leader compiles all on a master list in sequence, and fills in any gaps. The point of this is to show what participants already know. It is visible and logical. To support this, we simply need to devise interesting ways for children to practice emerging skills. Discuss what an emerging skill is and how to spot it and reinforce it in children.

Simple Steps

Handout:

■ Pass out the handout. Outline the sequence of fine motor development and after each "milestone" list several sample activities teachers can present to reinforce the skill. Leave space for people to add additional notes and ideas. Include directions for the homemade toy and the assignments.

Slide presentation:

■ **20 minutes:**
Show slides of children engaged in fine motor activities and tactile play. As you show the slides, talk about the other learning/development areas the activities reinforce, such as cognitive, social, and creative.

Young children:

■ **20 minutes:**
One at a time, for 5 minutes each, present three children, ages 7 months, 14 months, and 2½ years with the same collection of small toys or interesting objects, such as small boxes with lids, table blocks, and some clothespins inside a plastic jar with a screw-top lid. Simply observe what the child does with the toys. The parent could also talk about other things that she or he has noticed the child doing with one or both hands. Spend a few minutes summarizing what you observed together.

Make and take:

■ **15 minutes:**
Have materials on hand for each participant to make one fine motor toy to take home, such as a poke box. As this goes on, talk informally with people to answer any questions they might have about fine motor development in general, and listen to their experiences.

Conclusion:

■ **5 minutes:**
Wrap up and summarize main points you want them to go away with. Relate a story about a child's busy little hands and encourage people to admire the hands of the children in their care.

Assignments:

■ Give the children in your care a hand massage using baby lotion.
■ Observe how the different children in your group use the new homemade toy.
■ Try at least one new fine motor activity in the next week and report on it, verbally or in writing, explaining the activity to parents.
■ Develop your own photo collage of close-ups of children's hands for a parent bulletin board.

Index

Index

Simple Steps

Simple Steps

U ~ V

W

X ~ Y ~ Z

Recommended Title

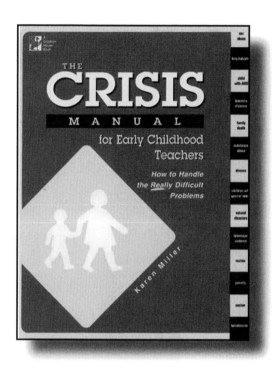

The Crisis Manual for Early Childhood Teachers
How to Handle the Really Difficult Problems

Karen Miller

An essential resource book you can turn to when faced with a really difficult issue in the classroom. Learn effective strategies that address the most challenging problems you may encounter as a teacher, such as: death of a family member, domestic violence, substance abuse, child sexual abuse, homelessness, natural disasters, community violence, and children with HIV/AIDS. 384 pages. 1995.

ISBN 0-87659-176-4 / Gryphon House 13748 / Paperback